BEATING THE ODDS

BEATING THE ODDS

Raising Academically Successful African American Males

Freeman A. Hrabowski III
Kenneth I. Maton
Geoffrey L. Greif

OXFORD UNIVERSITY PRESS

New York   Oxford   1998

Oxford University Press

Oxford   New York
Athens Auckland Bangkok Bogotá Bombay Buenos Aires
Calcutta   Cape Town   Dar es Salaam
Delhi   Florence   Hong Kong   Istanbul   Karachi
Kuala Lumpur   Madras   Madrid   Melbourne
Mexico City   Nairobi   Paris   Singapore
Taipei   Tokyo   Toronto   Warsaw

and associated companies in
Berlin Ibadan

Copyright © 1998 by Oxford University Press, Inc.

Published by Oxford University Press, Inc.,
198 Madison Avenue, New York, New York 10016

Oxford is a registered trademark of Oxford University Press

Library of Congress Cataloging–in–Publication Data

Hrabowski, Freeman A.
Beating the odds : Raising academically successful African American
males / Freeman A. Hrabowski, Kenneth I. Maton, Geoffrey L. Greif
p. cm.
Includes bibliographical references and index.
ISBN-13: 978-0-19-510219-2

1. Afro-American young men—Education. 2. Education—Parent participation—United States. 3. Afro-American young men—Family relationships.
4. Mathematics—Study and teaching—United States. 5. Science—Study
and teaching—United States. 6. Academic achievement—United States.
I. Maton, Kenneth I. II. Greif, Geoffrey L. III. Title.
LC2731.H73 1998
649'. 15796'073—dc21   97-462

15 14 13 12
Printed in the United States of America
on acid-free paper

Contents

Preface

Well, I guess I beat the odds. My parents didn't even read or write. They were sharecroppers. My mother would try to instill in me the importance of school, even though she couldn't help me with my homework. But I beat the odds.

Parent of young Black male

In our work, we often hear African American parents expressing the hope and desire that their children will achieve at the highest levels academically. What we also hear from these parents, though, is that one rarely sees in the media examples of young Black males who are achieving academically, being rewarded for those achievements, and feeling good about being smart. Even among advantaged African American families, we find that young males are heavily influenced by the popular culture that discourages pride in high academic achievement, demands that young Black males present a hard veneer to the world, and provides numerous opportunities for these young males to become involved in a world of crime and drugs. In fact, the idea for this book originated from our concern about the frightening status of young African American males and the need to find effective, family-based, educational solutions to enhance their futures. The book examines what families are doing to raise academically successful African American males.

Moreover, race now is a hot topic—one of those topics we have difficulty discussing and which quickly leads to tension and feelings of discomfort. Unfortunately, most of the discussion on race focuses on the problems minorities are experiencing; these groups, particularly African Americans and Hispanics, are too often seen as a burden to society because of what they cost taxpayers, rather than as groups that add to the economy and the social and cultural fabric of our society.

We are fortunate in finding one source for our answers in our own backyard, the Meyerhoff Scholars Program, created in 1988 at the University of Maryland Baltimore County (UMBC) for talented African American college males interested in research careers in science and engineering. As a result of the success and ever-increasing visibility of the Meyerhoff Program, growing numbers of parents of young Black boys ask us the question, "What can I do to make sure that my son one day becomes a Meyerhoff Scholar?" Clearly, what they are really asking is, "How do I make sure my son succeeds in school?"

So often, Black parents of young boys become anxious around the time their sons are in the third grade because it is about then that their academic performance begins to decline. In fact, Stevenson, Chen, and Uttal point out that differences in academic achievement among Black, White, and Hispanic children appear early in the elementary-school years and persist throughout the elementary-and-secondary school years. Their findings show that ethnic background is linked to poor academic performance. They state that,

> Although some evidence indicates improvement in minority children's performance during the past 15 years, the results of other studies suggest that ethnic differences are still large. For example, in a recent report of the performance of 28,000 elementary school students in Montgomery County, Maryland, the percentage of Hispanic and Black children who fell behind their White peers in mathematics increased markedly between the first and sixth grades. At the second grade, more than 15% of the Black and Hispanic children and approximately 5% of the White children were performing below grade level. By sixth grade, the performance of 20% of the White children, while the performance of over 40% of the Hispanic and 50% of the Black children, was below grade level.[1]

Many people are shocked to learn that African Americans constitute fewer than 3 percent of American scientists. While the nation suffers from a general shortage of African American scientists and health care professionals, the decreasing number of Black males enrolling and succeeding in college makes this shortage especially alarming. The Meyerhoff Program, with substantial support from Baltimore philanthropists Robert and Jane Meyerhoff, was established because of the disproportionately low numbers of African American males in college and the national shortage of African Americans earning Ph.Ds in science and engineering. The Meyerhoff Program represents one of many university programs across the country focusing on minorities in science and engineering. But, according to *Science*, "unlike many of the well-intentioned programs launched in the past 20 years, this relatively new one works."[2] In fact, without special efforts to identify talented African American males, and then to encourage them to complete the application process, the program would become predominantly female very quickly.

While in general many minority students do not wish to be viewed as smart in school, it is especially the case among many African American males that they do not want to be viewed as "nerds" or as too excited about academic achievement. And in many cases, males tend to be less mature than their female counterparts. In addition, our experience has shown that in coed groups, the African American women will tend to respond to questions and speak up about academic and other matters much more readily than the African American men. Even during the interview process with students, we find that young women are more apt to show their enthusiasm for science and often are more engaged in the dialogue than their male counterparts. (In contrast, researchers have noted that among Whites, girls are less apt to express themselves as openly in coed groups.)

Nevertheless, the challenge is that we have far too few African American women and men entering and succeeding in science careers. The general academic performance of large numbers of African American children is a major issue in American society. This book on African American males represents the first step in our exploration of the relationship between parenting and academic achievement among African American children. The next step will involve focusing on the families of young African American females.

The first group of Meyerhoff Scholars enrolled in the fall of 1989 and included nineteen young men competitively selected from across Maryland, the vast majority of whom had math SAT scores ranging between 600 and 800 (800 is the highest possible score on the math and verbal tests, with 1600 being the highest possible combined score) and high school grade point averages ranging from B+ to A. We decided to select very high-achieving African American males because so few, even among that group, have gone on to earn Ph.Ds in the sciences or engineering. The program was expanded to include women in 1990, and by the late 1990s, the program has reached a steady-state enrollment of approximately two hundred students from across the nation, including equal numbers of men and women. The program has already graduated over a hundred students, almost all of whom are succeeding in graduate and professional programs in the sciences and medicine.

These students not only are high achievers academically but also, in many cases, have excelled in a variety of other areas. They have performed in the arts, from playing classical piano to writing poetry and painting. They have won national competitions, from science fairs and debates to intercollegiate chess tournaments and computer-science prizes. And they have competed successfully in athletics, including playing intercollegiate basketball and track and earning black belts in the martial arts. It is important to acknowledge their success beyond the classroom because parents and children need to know that young Black males do not have to be seen as "nerds" or "uncool" simply because they earn As. In fact, we need to identify for young Black boys older Black male students who can be role models.

This book is unusual because rarely do we hear about large groups of high-achieving young African American males. In fact, when we ask audiences—Black and White, adults and children—what Black boy on television is known for his brains and intelligence, the response is usually Urkel, on the television show *Family Matters*. This character, unfortunately, is the perfect example of a "nerd," a child whom almost no one would want to be like, someone to be ridiculed and not to be taken seriously. More typically, everywhere we turn, we see examples of young Black boys in trouble with the law and in their schools. Anyone who walks into the central offices of many schools throughout the nation will often find young Black males sitting there, waiting for discipline as a result of fighting. It so often seems like a regular part of school activities that young Black and other minority boys are in trouble more than anyone else, and school data bear out these perceptions. Black students are almost twice as likely to be suspended from school; they are 50 percent more likely to experience corporal punishment; and the majority of children suspended are Black.[3] When Black boys are brought together for any sort of special programs, at least one will usually ask, "What did we do wrong this time?" because the only time they think of themselves getting together collectively in school, other than in sports, is in some negative context.

The tendency sometimes is to place all the responsibility on schools without looking at what goes on in homes and what students bring to school as a result. We know how important school officials and teachers are, but because teachers and others in the schools are influenced by students' initial performance and attitude, it is critical that we look at what parents can do to raise their children's initial level of performance. This book looks at what families do together to produce successful African American male students—from reading and talking to their children and exposing them to educational toys to the various ways in which parents instill in their sons a sense of the importance of academic achievement and ambition.

Most people would agree that growing up in America in the latter part of the twentieth century is a far more complex challenge to young people than ever before. To fend off the attraction of the negative peer culture, families try a variety of approaches to save their sons. The problem is that parents are often never really sure what approach will work, because parenting is clearly not a science and there are no set rules that will be effective for every family or even for every child in one family.

What we do know is that the more attention we, as parents, give our sons, the higher our expectations of them, the more consistency in our approach to parenting, the greater our determination to work steadily with them, the greater the variety of educational and cultural experience we provide, the more likely they are to succeed. The combination of loving, pushing, listening, disciplining when necessary, and never giving up can be particularly effective.

Large numbers of parents at one time or another become discouraged, however, when their sons do not live up to their expectations. So often, parents expect their children to think and act as they do, or certainly to do as well in school, not realizing that their children are growing up in a time very different from when they themselves grew up. Having the opportunity to hear from other parents can provide insights that help parents to direct their sons' attention and energy in constructive ways. It is important that parents talk with each other about the best approaches to interacting with their sons regarding, for example, punishments, rewards, and ways to motivate their children. It is important also for parents to come to understand and appreciate the differences between themselves and their sons.

In our book, we focus on how parents can help their sons succeed. In those cases when children succeed, we typically find that they have a close relationship with one or both parents, or with other adults with whom they can talk about their feelings, concerns, and victories. They also typically spend considerable time talking with their parents or mentors about what it means to be a young Black male in American society and how society tends to view them. It also helps when young males can observe African American adults who are successful in society and who exhibit those values and behavior we consider important to success: hard work, determination, interest in helping others, punctuality, accountability for one's actions, and responsibility for one's family.

Much of the previous literature on African American families has focused on their deficiencies and weaknesses. Our book complements the growing body of literature that looks at the strengths of these families. We believe that much can be gained by focusing on what produces success. This book should speak directly to a variety of African American families because the material here provides excellent examples of successful parents and young males from diverse backgrounds. In fact, many of these stories show us what is possible and give us hope for our children.

Acknowledgments

This book represents the collaborative efforts of three authors, including a university president and professors of psychology and social work, respectively. All three authors have focused much of their research on various issues related to the status of minorities in American society. Two of the three authors are fathers of sons (the third has daughters), and as we worked on this book, we all talked about points of similarity and difference in our own backgrounds and in our approaches to rearing our children.

Freeman A. Hrabowski

For me, as a Black child growing up in the 1950s and 1960s in Birmingham, Alabama, no one was more critical to my development than my parents and family. Both my father and mother made me feel that I was the most special part of their lives and that my future would be bright for two reasons: first, I would be well prepared academically because of my hard work and their efforts to give me as many opportunities as a Black child in the fifties could have; second, because of these opportunities, I would be expected to "give back" to others. My parents taught me by example the importance of work, faith, family, and being the best. Actually, like many of my Black peers, my parents told my brother and me that we had to work twice as hard. I also am extremely grateful to the many others in Birmingham who loved, praised, and raised me as if I were their own, including family members, neighbors, teachers, friends of the family, and my pastor and church members.

Regarding the preparation of this book, it has been an enormously gratifying and enjoyable experience collaborating with my coauthors, from whom I have learned a great deal. I wish to thank Mr. and Mrs. Robert Meyerhoff, without whose generosity, both financial and personal, there would not be a Meyerhoff Program and, consequently, this book would not have been written. I also want to thank the young men in the Meyerhoff Scholars Program and their families for allowing us to inquire in depth about their relationships and experiences as the young men were growing up. I am grateful, too, to the staff of the Meyerhoff Program, including especially Earnestine Baker, director, and Lamont Toliver, assistant director, who were extremely supportive throughout our research. Of course, I could never talk about the program without mentioning the outstanding young women Meyerhoff Scholars, who give endless support to their Meyerhoff brothers and to me. I also wish to thank my associate Doug Pear for his keen interest in the Meyerhoff Program and his tireless efforts to support the authors through his valuable editorial comments on many drafts. Most important, he helped us to express more precisely what we wanted to convey. My colleagues among the faculty and staff at the University of Maryland Baltimore County deserve much of the credit for the success of the Meyerhoff Program because they have taken ownership of it and have responded so positively to the issue of educating African Americans in science and engineering. I especially appreciate the support of my family, particularly my wife, Jackie, for her unconditional love, encouragement, and confidence in me; my son, Eric, for teaching me more and more about young African American males; and the other three women in my home, Ola (my cousin), Maggie (my mother) and Luezear (my mother-in-law), for their wisdom.

Finally, we dedicate this book to the outstanding young men in the Meyerhoff Scholars Program, their parents, and the millions of other African American parents throughout the nation who are working every day to prepare their sons for manhood.

Kenneth I. Maton

I was deeply moved the first time I walked into a meeting room full of Meyerhoff students, more than seven years ago. Forty or so young African American males were engaged in discussion and dialogue; they were poised, articulate, intellectual, and energetic. This image is the predominant picture I now carry in my mind when I think about young Black males. As someone who cares deeply about racial relationships, conditions facing African Americans in our country, and the barriers to progress, I have found the Meyerhoff students and their parents a source of great hope and inspiration.

An additional source of inspiration has been my two sons, Nathan, nine, and Tyler, two and a half. I thank them for being who they are. I have read together with Nathan many passages in this book over the past two years, and together we have appreciated and learned from them. I also want to acknowledge my wife, Mary Kay, who has enthusiastically supported all my research work with the Meyerhoff students, even during those long weekends when she was in charge of the boys for extended periods while I worked on the book. Finally, I want to thank my parents, Edith Lang, Oscar Lang, and Norman Maton, for their wisdom in educating and raising me. I see a lot of myself in the Meyerhoff students, and even more so many aspects of my parents in the parents we interviewed. In particular, I appreciate the (Jewish) heritage that was passed on to me about the importance of education; its benefits can never be taken away, no matter how hostile the environment. I only hope I pass on this message half as effectively to my own sons.

A team of graduate and undergraduate students has contributed importantly to the fruition of this book. We fully appreciate the commitment and insights provided by Chris Burke, Pam Caudill, Tracey Collins, Lara Frumkin, Troy Green, Monica Greene, Heather Heisler, Tricia Monmancy, and Stacey Robotham.

Geoffrey L. Greif

Raising two daughters (one in college and one in high school) has often left me in awe of the challenges that teenagers face as they try to wend their way through the school system and the social scene of the 1990s. Because my family is part of the "majority" culture, transitions from one environment to the next are easier for them than might otherwise be the case. For example, they will not stand out at most colleges because of their skin color. Their own concerns about fitting in will revolve around academics and personality, characteristics that are more in their control than their physical appearance. In turn, they will enter a work environment that will be more accustomed to accommodating to them, even as females. Growing up is, to a large extent, about finding comfort within oneself, about establishing an identity that allows growth and development. The crux of this book is about identity, about families' and sons' struggles to reach their potential. My daughters will be able to move from one situation to the next with greater ease than the African American males who are the focus of this book. In raising them, I have to teach them to appreciate that—it is part of their identity—just as the parents who we interviewed have to teach their sons about the obstacles that await them.

Becoming familiar with the Meyerhoff Scholars Program, its staff, the students, and their parents has been an extraordinarily rewarding process for me. I greatly appreciate the generosity of my coauthors in including me in this project. I wish to thank my wife, Maureen, and my daughters, Jennifer and Alissa, for helping me understand the dynamics of parenthood and the importance of teamwork.

1

Successful African American Males and Their Families

I urge every parent and adult to conduct a personal audit to determine whether we are contributing to the crisis our children face or to the solutions they urgently need. Our children don't need or expect us to be perfect. They do need and expect us to be honest, to admit and correct our mistakes, and to share our struggles about the meanings and responsibilities of faith, parenthood, citizenship and life.

Marian Wright Edelman, *Guide My Feet*

Almost everything we read and hear about young Black males focuses on the problems of crime, violence, drugs, teenage pregnancy, and poor academic achievement. Although many Americans have heard the calamitous statistics on the plight of young African American males, few can pinpoint a single reason for the downward-spiraling trends. Some attribute the problems to the general deterioration of urban communities, problems complicated by drugs (especially the increased use of crack cocaine) and increased crime over the past decades. Some blame racism. Others point their fingers at these young men and suggest that they lack responsibility or that they possess a victim mentality. Sociologist William Julius Wilson focuses on structural problems in the economy that prevent meaningful participation by these young men—the steady decline, for example, in manufacturing jobs in a service- and technology-oriented employment market.[1] Still others believe that without access to the marketplace, with the long, hard road to success closed to them, these young men seek out immediate gratification. No doubt all of these factors contribute to the current status of young Black males.

Millions of Americans daily see the faces of these young men on television and in newspapers, and to many these faces look angry or hopeless, communicating danger and intimidation. It is rare, though, that we see or hear about the hard work of millions of African American families and the aspirations that these parents hold for their sons. Yet the overwhelming majority want desperately to see their sons succeed, and many spend considerable time focusing on the future of their children.

Too often, the only activities Americans associate with young Black male role models are sports and entertainment. Think of the generation of young Black males in the year 2010, who grew up in the 1980s and 1990s having as their primary role models the basketball player Michael Jordan, the singer Michael Jackson, the track athlete Michael Johnson, and the boxer Mike Tyson. When we ask young males what they want to be when they grow up, the immediate response is often "a professional athlete or entertainer." If these are the only images they associate with success and glamour, what can we expect them to value or become? What can we expect them to do with their lives? We know, but they seem not to know, that these careers are almost always beyond their reach.

It is difficult for the vast majority of Americans to understand that growing up young, Black, and male in our society often means hearing that it is not "cool" to be smart and seeing kids ridiculed and penalized by their peers for trying to achieve academically.[2] (In fact, in one recent study of adolescents, researchers found that African Americans suffered in school performance because of the lack of peer support for academic achievement, despite being positively influenced by authoritative parenting.)[3] And it means living between worlds. In one world, the neighborhood, fighting sometimes becomes a necessity for survival. A young man must show a tough exterior in order to be respected and allowed to grow up. But in the other world, the school, being tough pits a young man against authority figures. Sitting in class, asking questions, and taking instruction are expected behaviors with which many young Black males often have difficulty.

Contrary to popular thinking, the threats associated with such problems as violence and drugs are not limited to the underclass; even the sons of the Black middle class face these tensions every day. Marita Golden, herself the mother of a young Black male, is the author of a book on the challenges of raising young Black males in this society. Through the conversations and anecdotes she recounts, we come to understand that even professional Black parents are concerned that their sons, too, are in danger of violence and crime in the Black community. In her own life, Golden says she "dream[s] . . . of my son slaying the statistics that threaten to ensnare and cripple him, statistics that I know are a commentary on the odds for my son, who isn't dead or in jail."[4]

In one of the interviews for her book, Golden talks to Ella Ross, an accounting technician, whose son Terrance, an honor student and track star, was convicted of first-degree murder in his senior year in high school. As we learn about this mother's love for and dedication to her son, we cannot help but wonder how such an inspiring success story could end in such tragedy. And yet we see every day the killings that involve not only the "bad" boys, those who appear at high risk, but also those boys we consider to be doing extremely well.

We also learn from Golden's own son, Michael, the challenges parents face when their boys do not do well in school. Many questions arise: What type of school is effective? Is my son being helped in the classroom? Does he have a learning disability? Do the teachers understand my son and try to relate to him in a way that will reach him rather than push him away?

Significance of this Book

The significance of this book is its assertion, to the surprise of many, that thousands of young Black males are succeeding. What most Americans sadly fail to see are the vast majority of Black males going to work everyday to support their families, and the large number of young Black males who somehow beat the odds by avoiding the temptations awaiting them on their way to school, who go to class, learn, and come home to study.

This book deliberately looks at young Black males who are achieving at the highest level of academic success in our country. These are students who not only are graduating from high school, but also are entering college with strong academic backgrounds, succeeding in science and engineering, and have as their goal earning either Ph.Ds in these fields or medical degrees.

Why is it important to examine such a group? First, because although some would suggest that this group of high achievers, who in half the cases have college-educated parents, would succeed anyway, the data show that this simply is not the case. In fact, the chances are extremely slim that they will succeed, especially in science or engineering. In 1995, for example, we find that while 73.4 percent of Black males twenty-five years old and over had completed four or more years of high school (in contrast to 83.0 percent of White males), only 13.6

percent had completed four or more years of college (contrasted with 27.2 percent of White males).[5] Moreover, while 19,298 White males earned bachelor's degrees in the sciences in 1994, only 1,063 African American males did. And even more alarming, in contrast to the 7,573 White U.S. citizens who earned Ph.Ds in the sciences in 1995, only 207 African Americans received Ph.Ds in science.[6]

Second, we find that although the 1995 average combined SAT score of Black high-school students whose parents lack a high-school diploma is 655, the average combined score of Black students in families where the highest level of parental education is a graduate degree is still only 844 (191 points below the national average score of 1035 for Whites in the same category).[7] Similarly, African American children whose family income is below $10,000 have SAT scores of 675, compared to only 849 for those with family incomes of at least $70,000 (which, again, is significantly below the national average score of Whites with family incomes of at least $70,000—1008).[8] L. Scott Miller, in his book on minority educational advancement, points out that "as a nation Americans must be concerned with improving the educational prospects not only of those living in poverty and those whose parents have little education but also of those who are middle-class minority students."[9]

Third, by focusing on the highest-achieving young African American males and their parents, we can identify attitudes, habits, behaviors, perspectives, and strategies that may shed light on what we as a society need to do, and what parents in their own homes will need to do, to reverse current downward trends involving Black male behavior and academic performance. Fourth, if we are to provide young Black males with role models other than sports figures and entertainers, who better to focus attention on than the highest academic achievers among this group?

One of the major premises of the book is that the family environment is crucial to the success of these young males. The source of strength most frequently mentioned is the mother, and when asked why they succeed, many young men suggest that if they did not, "my mother would kill me!" In fact, we learn that even in two-parent homes, the mother assumes primary responsibility for rearing and educating the child, particularly when the child is young.

We found that fathers too are important in raising children. In those families where fathers are present, fathers are identified as extremely important as the children become older. And for many of those students in this sample whose fathers resided in the home, the father played an important role in terms of encouraging sons to do their best, establishing rules for behavior in the home, setting high expectations for academic achievement (interestingly, in some cases the sons thought the expectations were too high), developing consistent and strong communication, emphasizing preparation for life, and serving as strong, positive, male role models.

A major purpose of this book is to identify strategies that parents, educators, and other professionals may wish to consider as they work with young males in general and seek to understand more about the success of young African American males. We choose, then, to focus on the strengths of these families and to learn from them what others can do to accomplish educational goals so important not just for these youth, but also for the nation.

The book takes on special significance in the light of discussions taking place nationally about the future of affirmative action. In fact, we have been talking with parents and students at the very point when affirmative action is increasingly under attack nationally. The 1995 vote by the University of California Board of Regents, for example, to eliminate race and affirmative action as factors in admissions decisions, despite the fact that many people look to California for the richness of its diversity, may become a national trend. Although systemwide the University of California's freshman class at the time of the Regents' vote was 36 percent White, 31 percent Asian, and 16 percent Hispanic, only 4 percent were African American (the same percentage as Filipino Americans). Projections predict that the impact of the Regents' ruling will reduce the number of Blacks by half.

Within urban public schools, discussion and debate have focused on various approaches to the education of African Americans and other minorities, including the potential of all-male classrooms or schools to enhance educational performance. A number of cities have implemented or are considering implementing various gender- and ethnicity-based approaches. These include the development of Black male academies aimed at promoting "the positive academic and holistic development" of the young African American male.[10]

Two important challenges facing America are to ensure that African American children gain the skills they will need to succeed, and to understand the repercussions of not equipping these children with such skills. We know that if we do not educate them, they are very likely to occupy the ranks of the unemployed or become involved in illegal activity, resulting in prison or early death. If they are underemployed, unemployed, or incarcerated, they will be increasingly dependent on the nation's system of health care and other social services.

The history of African Americans has been devastatingly influenced by slavery, segregation, racism, and educational and economic deprivation. But history would also tell us that fifty years ago, many hard-working Black families—the grandparents of the Meyerhoff Scholars, many of whom were uneducated—were making sure that their children developed values, habits, and attitudes that led to success. Nonetheless, we know that racism and discrimination still exist in our society, often in subtler forms, and that life for many African American families and their sons is very complicated. An important challenge we face as Americans is understanding the impact of our history on these problems and looking at appropriate roles for families, parents, children, and society in improving the status of African American males. The challenge facing Black parents is to help their sons believe truly that in spite of racism and societal barriers, their success will depend largely on their own efforts.

There is a thin line between helping a child understand that he may at times be the victim of discrimination, on the one hand, and teaching him what he must do in spite of racism in our society, on the other. How do parents prevent young males from having a "victim mentality" and help them to understand that despite factors beyond their control—racism, discrimination, low expectations by some in society—they can control their own destiny, and thus beat the odds? Henry Louis Gates Jr. and Cornel West place particular emphasis on the leadership role of professional Blacks and on the responsibility the Black community must take itself in addressing this critical issue:

> It is only by confronting the twin realities of White racism, on the one hand, and our own failures to seize initiative and break the cycle of poverty, on the other, that we, the remnants of the Talented Tenth, will be able to assume a renewed leadership role for, and within, the Black community.[11]

How great is the task? A number of studies have documented the current position of African American males in a variety of areas, from health care and education to socioeconomic status. What these studies show is that this group of Americans is doing more poorly than any other in our society. Majors, Billson and Mancini note that,

> the statistics show a clear disadvantage to being born Black and male in America: Black males have higher rates than White males of mental disorders, unemployment, poverty, injuries, accidents, infant mortality, morbidity, AIDS, homicide and suicide, drug and alcohol abuse, imprisonment, and criminality; they have poorer incomes, life expectancy, access to health care, and education.[12]

Health & Mental Health

Everyday throughout this county, we read about Black males killed by other Black males. A study by the National Institutes of Health reports that in the period 1990–92, the death rate from homicide among African American males ages fifteen to forty-four was seven times that for White men in the same age group.[13] But this is just part of the picture. We know that the incidence of morbidity is higher for African American males than for any other group in our society, for almost all diseases. The death rate, for example, of African American males from stroke is four times that of their White counterparts, and the death rate from asthma for children under fourteen is twice that of Whites. African American men also have the highest rate of prostate cancer. In fact, Black males live almost ten years less than White males (64.7 vs. 73).[14]

We also know that there is a strong correlation between socioeconomic factors and the status of people's health. These factors, including unemployment, substance abuse, low academic achievement, teen pregnancy, sexually transmitted diseases, crime (including homicide), and imprisonment, are all interdependent and represent major costs to society. [15]

Even though African Americans experience a substantially higher incidence of health problems than other Americans, their representation in the health professions is extraordinarily low. The latest data reveal that 1.3 percent of all doctorates in the biological sciences went to African Americans, and that, in total, they represent only 3.7 percent of physicians, although Blacks comprise over 10 percent of the national workforce.[16]

Regarding mental health, national data indicate that Black males are more than twice as likely to be admitted to mental hospitals than either White males or Black females.[17] The data also show that even elementary-school Black boys exhibit more psychological symptoms and have more behavioral problems than Black girls. By the time these boys become teenagers, they seem even more vulnerable than their female counterparts and have a variety of problems in all aspects of their lives, from the home to school to their neighborhoods—including behavior and learning disorders in school, emotional disturbances, and inpatient and outpatient psychiatric treatment. Gibbs, in her discussion of the health and mental health of young Black males, asserts that,

> Since studies also suggest that Black male children, as compared to females, are given less nurturance by their parents, treated more harshly by their teachers, discriminated against more by employers, and treated less favorably by nearly every other institution in American society, it is reasonable

to infer that their lowered self-esteem is the inevitable outcome of their persistent differential and demeaning treatment.[18]

Education

A substantial proportion of Black males are significantly behind their White counterparts in math and writing proficiency or drop out before graduating from high school.[19] Reasons students often give for leaving school include not liking school, receiving poor grades, being suspended or expelled, and deciding to work.[20] Majors, Billson, and Mancini point out that young Black males " leave school for discipline problems twice as often as Black females . . . [and] are suspended three times more often than Whites in elementary school and twice as often in high school. At both levels, Black boys have the highest suspension and dropout rates." [21] But what kind of job, if any, can a high-school dropout find? Although for some of these children school provides a temporary relief from problems of the neighborhood and even home, urban youth invariably encounter problems in school because of the street skills they have developed to survive in the "'hood," such as fighting, being "cool," or engaging in illegal activities involving drugs or guns. By junior high school, many are working below grade level or barely passing; consequently, they see school as a place where they fail. The environment becomes even more frustrating because of problems between these students, their peers, and teachers and administrators—problems often related to behavior.

Considering these problems, it is not surprising that these children receive significantly fewer As and significantly more Ds and Fs in all subjects. We see that Black students are more often tracked into lower-ability groups involving general education and vocational education and, in contrast, very few Black students are placed in gifted classes. In fact, White children are twice as likely to be placed in these classes as Black children. And the percentage of Black students (3.4 percent) placed in the category of educable mentally retarded is more than double that of all students (1.4 percent) and more than ten times that of Asian students (0.3 percent).[22] We also know that males, in general, are more likely than females to be overrepresented in the educable mentally retarded and learning-disabled children and underrepresented in gifted and talented programs. Ford and Harris report that Blacks, Hispanics, and Native Americans are underrepresented in as many as 70 percent of the gifted programs in the nation, and overrepresented in almost half of all special-education programs. Moreover, they report that although minorities represented 43 percent of the school population studied by High and Udall, only 11 percent had been assigned to gifted programs.[23]

We find that the academic achievement level of African American children, whether they are in urban settings or in much more integrated settings, is lower than those of their White and Asian counterparts for a variety of reasons. As a result of the disproportionate representation in lower-level classes, African American males receive far less education than their White counterparts. In light of their inadequate education, it is not surprising to see that African American students earn lower SAT scores and are less well prepared for college.

We also find many Black children are in urban settings where school systems receive far less funding per student than their suburban counterparts. The difference in funding, for example, between the city of Baltimore and Montgomery County, one of the wealthiest counties in Maryland, is almost $2,000 per student.[24] As expected, many of the nation's largest cities (for example, Atlanta, Boston, Chicago, Dallas, Detroit, and Los Angeles) enroll large numbers of minority students— between 70 percent and 90 percent, or more, of the students in some of the nation's largest cities come from minority groups, and, unfortunately, the lower level of funding means fewer resources devoted to education. Not surprisingly, these children do not do well on standardized tests, and they perform poorly in class[25].

Regarding the attitudes and expectations of school officials, we know that teachers, administrators, and school staff, through their words, actions, and body language, have an enormous impact on the behavior and achievement of students. Clearly, the placement of students in special tracks is tied to the attitudes and expectations of school officials in addition to the performance of students on tests. A student's academic performance is influenced by teachers' and administrators' perceptions of that student's ability and the expectations they convey. Weinstein and colleagues, in their study of expectations and change in high school, eloquently state this point:

> One important factor that places certain groups of children at risk is the operation of differential and very low academic expectations for what they can accomplish. Minorities and children from lower socio-economic classes are largely over-represented as the target of low expectations. The dynamics of teacher expectations and how they can become self-fulfilling prophecies have been well illustrated within classrooms (toward individual children and between reading groups) and between classrooms (in the tracking system of high schools). Studies of effective schools have also pointed to the expecta-

tions of principals and teachers as powerful influences on student performance.[26]

Expectations and attitudes of teachers and administrators toward children, in general, seem to be based on a number of interdependent factors: race and ethnicity, socioeconomic status, initial test performance, achievement, and even physical appearance. With regard to race or ethnicity, African Americans receive less attention in integrated classrooms. In addition, students from lower socioeconomic backgrounds are more likely to be perceived more negatively than students from higher socioeconomic backgrounds. Such perceptions can contribute to negative performance by students.[27] There are many ways in which a teacher's behavior affects students who perform at lower levels. For example, a teacher can inhibit a student by placing more emphasis on his failures than on his successes, by demanding less, or by failing to give nonverbal support.

Teachers and administrators develop perceptions about future achievement based on beginning performance and test scores. When young African Americans sense the negative attitudes and expectations, they often respond in negative ways, and young Black males, in particular, turn to their peers for approval in nonacademic ways. They become "cool" and adopt the movement, speech, and dress of men successful in the streets—drug dealers, pimps, and others. Many young Black males come to reject any behavior associated with being smart in school.[28] In this way, and as we discussed earlier, two worlds are maintained, each with different values. One critical question is, how can we reverse this disturbing trend of Black children not wanting to achieve in school, not wanting to be seen as smart? Marian Wright Edelman has eloquently articulated the issue:

> If our children of any color think that being smart and studying hard is acting White rather than acting Black or Brown and don't know about the many great Black and Brown as well as White achievers who overcame every obstacle to succeed, then we are a part of the problem rather than a part of the solution to racial stereotyping.[29]

We focus in this book on students who have fought against the odds of being placed in low-level classes (and, in some cases, of remaining in low-level classes), of performing poorly in school, of becoming too "cool" and dropping out of high school, and of going to prison or being killed. What makes this sample so special is not only that these students have avoided failure, but also that they are among a very small percentage of young African American males who excel in math and science in high school, who go on to college with the intention of becoming leading scientists and physicians, who have the necessary skills to succeed in math and science at the college level, and who actually earn outstanding grades in these fields.

Economic Status

In addition to grades and test scores, college enrollment is also related to the financial status of families. In 1995, 53 percent of African American college students were from families with total household incomes below $30,000; in contrast, only 19 percent of White students were. In addition, more than a third (34 percent) of African American college students were from families with household incomes below $20,000, compared to only 8 percent of the White students. And at the upper end, 21 percent of Black students came from families with household incomes above $50,000 in contrast to over half of the White students (52% percent).[30] We know that students from families with higher incomes are more likely to be enrolled in college than those from lower-income homes. We find that many Black college students are from lower-income families, and many do not persist because of financial problems.

In addition, it is very clear that financial status is strongly associated with academic achievement. Students from high-income groups are almost twice as likely to be enrolled in college as those from low-income families. Family income also appears to be strongly related to persistence in college. It has been estimated that an unmarried eighteen- to twenty-four-year-old from the lowest income quartile had about a 4 percent chance of completing four years of college by the age of 24, while students from the highest income group had a 76 percent chance.[31]

The Social Science Research Literature

Not only do we tend to see negative stereotypes of Black males in the media, we rarely learn from the media about any strengths of African American families. To counteract this unfortunate situation, a number of social scientists in recent years have looked at the current status of African American families, including their role in preparing their children to be successful. Noted sociologist Andrew Billingsley argues that "African American families are both weak and strong, but their strengths are by far more powerful and contain the seeds of their survival and rejuvenation."[32] Billingsley defines the African American family as

> an intimate association of persons of African descent who are related to one another by a variety of means, including blood, marriage, formal adoption, informal adoption or by appropriation; sustained by a history of common residence in America; and deeply embedded in a network of social structure both internal to and external to itself.[33]

His assertions that the most important function of the African American family is to teach their children how to succeed in a predominantly White society and that "parents [are] more likely to caution their sons (rather than their daughters) about racial barriers"[34] are clearly borne out among the Meyerhoff families.

What we observed among Meyerhoff parents, and what Billingsley found, are a strong commitment to education, an emphasis on self-help, the importance of a supportive learning environment in the home and in school, strong spiritual beliefs, supportive families, and a tradition of service to others. Most important, Billingsley emphasizes the significant role of social support among African Americans working together for the common good, and we also have seen this to be true for families in the study. It is encouraging that we found both two-parent and one-parent families, with varying levels of education, that were successful in raising high-achieving young males.

According to Signithia Fordham, rearing African American males can be more complicated than rearing females. One reason she suggests is that

> parents of males are compelled to take into consideration not only the racialized nature of America as a nation but also the patriarchal principles that exist in both the larger society and the imagined Black community. African American parents are thus compelled to teach their sons to embrace a twofold contradictory formula: to concurrently accept subordination and the attendant humiliation (for survival in the larger society) and preserve gender domination (for survival in the Black community).[35]

Fordham found that the families of high-achieving male students in an urban school were primarily stable, with two parents or guardians, while the majority of underachieving males were being reared chiefly by their mothers, with little or no support from the fathers. Most of the high-achieving males looked to their mothers or other female relatives as the closest and most influential adult figures in their lives. Interestingly, many of the parents of high-achieving students were ambivalent about the value of education and did not necessarily insist they go to college. The parents placed heavy emphasis on the sons' behavior and values; it was more important that they become respectful and honest than extraordinarily successful. As might be expected, for the parents of both high-achieving and underachieving males, no issue was of greater concern than their sons' safety. Parents used a variety of approaches to shape behavior, including corporal punishment; some sons felt their parents were unduly strict.

Fordham also discusses underachieving children who receive the family support typically considered necessary for success, including a stable home with caring and involved parents. She found that in some cases, parents may have indulged their children excessively and made few, if any, demands on them. On the other hand, in those cases where single mothers were successful in helping the sons achieve, the mothers were able to combine both mother and father roles, especially regarding discipline. In contrast, mothers of the underachieving males tended to become childlike in their interactions with their sons as they reached puberty, and "the mothers appear to have adopted a relationship style that closely approximates that which they have with adult males who are objects of their love and affection."[36]

Transmitting parental values is a significant issue on which Margaret Beale Spencer focuses.[37] She hypothesizes that effective parenting is associated with socioeconomic status. The results of her research (involving almost four hundred children ages three to nine) show that the more economic resources available to the family and the higher the educational levels of family members across generations, the higher the children's achievement and the fewer reports of behavioral problems among the children. Of course, these results are not surprising given the greater number of problems related to poverty.

Spencer finds also that both middle- and lower-income parents consider church attendance important, although middle-income parents rate it as even more important than do lower-income parents.[38] As might be expected, two-parent middle-income families are able to use a variety of resources in working through child-rearing issues, including, for example, a spouse's help, access to medical personnel, and literature. Both groups consider certain personal values important to transmit to their children, including kindness, racial pride, moral values, and education.

Spencer concludes that the stress associated with poverty and related problems understandably leads to more behavioral problems and undermines a child's full development, and that the problem is often exacerbated in single-parent families because single parenthood tends to be associated with lower socio-economic status.[39] Not surprisingly, when families have less money, they focus fewer resources in general on child-rearing. Nevertheless, as we see with some of the Meyerhoff parents, we can find numerous examples of low-income single-parent families that have been successful in raising young Black males. Kweisi Mfume speaks eloquently about the historical role of single mothers:

> I am in awe of my mother's ability to understand what a boy needed to become a man. Yet most people fail to celebrate the virtues of many black mothers who over the years have functioned—even thrived—in the dual roles of mother and father. Self-sacrifice is a valuable commodity in any human being, and I find it astonishing that so many black women who possessed so little materially were able to give so generously. They have provided generations of black boys with the crucial range of skills essential for survival.[40]

The question is, what can we learn from these parents that can be helpful to other parents? Consistent with what we see with Meyerhoff parents, Reginald Clark asserts that parents tend to develop relationships with their children similar to how they remember their own parents acting. In this way, parenting becomes an intergenerational process, with approaches to parenting and values about family handed down from grandparents to parents to children. As might be expected, parents of high-achieving children appear to be healthier mentally than other parents, and children in these families view their parents as appropriate authority figures to be obeyed. This often carries over to the school environment and takes the form of respect for rules, authority, and hard work, leading to high achievement.[41] Much of the research has focused on lower-income families and low achievement. We are just beginning to learn about students who achieve at the highest levels. In fact, our research adds to the existing body of work by concentrating on groups about whom we know very little, especially middle- and working-class Black families with academically high-achieving sons.

Methodology & Observations

The students in the Meyerhoff Scholars Program provided us with the opportunity to undertake this study. In order to find the answers to our questions, we took a variety of approaches. We contacted the fathers and mothers of these male students and asked them to take part in group interviews, the groups ranging in size from four to ten participants. The interviews (the fathers were interviewed by an African American male and the mothers by an African American female) took place between fall 1994 and spring, 1996.[42] We decided to separate mothers and fathers during our interviews because the experience of the program has shown us that when male and female students meet, and when mothers and fathers meet, the tendency is for many of the males in each group to be far less active in the discussions than the females. To emphasize the role of gender, we looked carefully at the relationships between mothers and sons, and between fathers and sons, from the perspectives of all three groups.

The parents also completed a questionnaire asking for specific information about their parenting practices.[43] We interviewed by telephone other interested parents who could not attend the sessions. This approach enabled us to get a sample of twenty-nine fathers and thirty-eight mothers. Among the fathers, twenty-two were living with the son and their son's biological mother; two fathers were raising their sons alone; two were raising the sons with the help of a stepmother; and three were living apart from their sons. Among the mothers, twenty-three lived with the son and the son's biological father; eight had lived with or remarried after being a single parent for a number of years; and seven were single parents for the greatest part or all of their sons' lives.

Each sample of parents has certain limitations. Because we spoke with only those parents who agreed to be interviewed, we may have a group of parents who, by definition, are more highly involved with their sons than is typical. At the same time, those who declined our invitation to be interviewed may have had other realistic demands on their time, so we hesitate to leap to any conclusions. While we included married fathers and mothers as well as single mothers and fathers who are raising their children, we tried to oversample for single mothers, a group that we recognize is disproportionately involved in raising children today, because we believed their impressions were particularly important. As a result, 40 percent of our sample of mothers spent some portion of their sons' childhood raising them alone.

At the same time we were talking with parents, we were conducting group interviews with forty-seven sons. Special care was taken to interview children raised in a variety of family, educational, geographical, and economic situations. Over 50 percent of the sons had spent some of their childhood with a single parent, usually the mother, although not always. (One in three Black children in the United States is living in the home with both parents.[44]) We were careful not to coerce the want to be interviewed. Thus, as with the parents' samples, we are limited by hearing from those who wished to be interviewed.

Editing their comments was necessary to make them more easily readable. In addition, we took great care to conceal the identities of the families involved without changing the nature of their stories. In addition to what we learned from the interviews and the questionnaires in this study, we had already gathered an enormous amount of information in connection with prior research through questionnaires administered routinely to the Meyerhoff students between 1989 and 1995.[45]

In many instances, the home environment among the families we studied has changed over the years: at some points, there may have been two parents in the home; at other points, only one parent; and at other times, grandparents or other relatives may have lived in the home and played a significant child-rearing role. In contrast, approximately 80 percent of the parents discussed in this book grew up in families headed by two parents in the 1940s and 1950s, which was typical of that time. The vast majority of the parents in our study were raised in the South or mid-Atlantic region. Also, the vast majority of the parents we interviewed reported that their own parents were not college-educated and had worked in a variety of jobs ranging from sharecropper to chef. The parents' parents were professionals in only a few instances. Because over half of the parents in our sample were college-educated, they held a variety of professional positions, as might be expected, including large numbers serving as teachers and a small number of professionals in science or technical areas.

Although the sons we studied came from all over the United States, the majority hailed from Maryland, a state with pockets of both great wealth and considerable poverty. All of the parents we interviewed in person were currently living in Maryland, as were many of the parents we interviewed over the telephone. Maryland has urban, suburban, and rural areas, including its Eastern Shore and western region. It was a border state during the Civil War, with large plantations near the southern portion of Chesapeake Bay. It is the home of Baltimore, which used to be one of the ten largest cities in the United States but has declined in population during the past generation. Baltimore's population is approximately 60 percent African American, while Maryland's is roughly three-quarters White.[46] The state also borders on Washington, D.C., a city with a population that is predominantly Black. When parents and children talk about going "into the city," it is a reference to these two urban areas, which have a strong influence on the state. Our sample, then, is drawn from a state with a rich history of social problems and social programs. In this sense, it is the perfect microcosm in which to study the issues that constitute the core of this book.

We often hear stereotypes about African American mothers and sons. People say, for example, that these mothers "raise their daughters, but love their sons." But we rarely hear the voices of the mothers themselves. In our interviews with mothers, it becomes clear that there is no single parenting style for African American mothers, and their approaches to raising their sons depend on such factors as family background and circumstances, the neighborhoods they live in, and the schools their children attend.

The stereotype of African American mothers notwithstanding, perhaps no parenting role is less well understood than that of the African American father. This is the case largely because we hear much more about the mother's role in society. Furthermore, in recent years African American fathers have been increasingly rare in their families' homes. Their views are especially important to us.

Our questions to mothers and fathers focused on (1) their assessment of the approach their own parents took in raising them; (2) the importance of education in their family of origin; (3) differences in the roles and expectations of mothers and fathers, and of boys and girls in their upbringing; (4) what they learned from those approaches that they, in turn, used in raising their own sons; (5) what the parents thought they had done, themselves, to help their sons achieve academic success; (6) how they raised their sons as African Americans; and (7) their approaches to discipline and communication with their sons. The critical theme throughout the interviews with parents was the level and nature of their involvement in their children's lives and schooling.

The questions to sons focused on their relationships with their parents and their relationships with their peers and others in school and the community. Critical issues included (1) important topics of conversation between the sons and their parents; (2) who had the greatest influence on their academic success; (3) what their parents did specifically to encourage them academically; (4) the types of discipline their parents used; (5) how the students view their academic achievement and their ability in math and science; and (6) the approach that their parents used in helping them understand what it means to be African American and male.

In listening to the voices of the fathers, mothers, and young men, we sense a keen awareness of the challenges that young Black males face in our society, and a strong determination to overcome the daunting odds against success. We look at factors that contribute to the problems, including unemployment, stress, pressures of multiple jobs (resulting in less time for child-rearing), crime, racism, inadequate schools, and adverse peer pressure, among others. We also examine factors that explain the success of the young Meyerhoff Scholars in this sample, including emotional support from their families and communities, parents' advocacy role, the emphasis on education in the home, the role of religion in the students' lives, and early attention to intellectual development before the school years.

We also look at the experiences of parents in connecting with schools on behalf of their sons. One recurring theme in these interactions is that parents tended to be assertive and, at times, forceful when the schools have appeared to have low expectations of their sons, when their sons seemed to be the victims of some type of discrimination in school, or when the children had problems at school.

As we examine the pre-college setting of the students, we focus considerable attention on their relationships with their student peers. The critical questions we raise are how their peers reacted to the students' academic achievement, how often and in what contexts they were accused of being "nerds" or of "acting White," and what strategies the students used to handle peer pressure. We also look at the role of friends, neighbors, and extended family in providing support to these students.

We make a number of observations based on our work. First, although we expected the group interview sessions with parents to last an hour, the parents became so involved that these sessions consistently lasted between two and three hours each. Second, we learned about specific parenting practices and strategies that were most effective at different stages of the sons' lives. Parents appreciated hearing about different approaches taken by other parents in addressing problems that arose during the years they were raising their sons. Some were surprised to learn that parents of other high-achieving males had also had difficulties with their children and with the larger society. Third, parents spent a great deal of time both trying to understand the strengths and weaknesses of their sons and trying different approaches to give them support. It is very clear that many of these parents have developed parenting styles in reaction to the child-rearing practices used by their own parents. Although the tendency in most cases is for the parents of these high-achieving males to build on the approaches used by their own parents, we find some cases in which parents placed considerable emphasis on education because their own parents did not do so. Fourth, these parents also have developed parenting styles that, of necessity, have differed by child. A parenting approach that works with one son in the family may not be effective with another one in the same family. In addition, children at various ages require different kinds of interaction with their parents. We are aware that parenting is a dynamic process that changes in response to the needs of the child and the ability of the parents to fulfill those needs.

Finally, in our investigation, we uncover six key parenting strategies that appear especially effective: (1) demonstrating love through involvement in the children's education, providing support and encouragement, and fostering a belief in self; (2) establishing an environment that sets limits on behavior and provides discipline when appropriate; (3) establishing high expectations for academic and other success; (4) developing open and strong communication with the children; (5) establishing positive identification as a male and as an African American; and (6) taking advantage of available community resources. We conclude a number of the chapters with a discussion of these six parenting practices.

The Next Chapters

This first chapter sets the context for the book; the next five focus on the information we gained. What is very clear from chapters 2 and 3 on fathers and mothers, respectively, is how consistent their parenting approaches are with what Marian Wright Edelman says about the importance of parents putting children first in their lives and the significance of "attention, time, love, discipline . . . and the teaching of values " in raising children.[47]

Chapter 2 focuses on the fathers. Here we begin to learn of the complex tapestry that is woven of three generations of African American life—the fathers' generation, their parents', and their sons'. We see in many cases that the fathers play a significant role in the lives of these successful young men and that the fabric of the family reflects strategies for dealing not only with academic vicissitudes but also with the challenges and threats posed by society.

In chapter 3, we hear the voices of the mothers. As significant as many fathers are, the mothers, in most cases, play an even more central role. From their early upbringing to their parenting experiences, we learn of the incredible investment they have made in their sons' lives and how they have attempted to help their sons achieve academically.

In the next two chapters, the sons move to the forefront. Chapter 4 concentrates on the successes the sons have achieved, and the obstacles they have overcome as they moved through childhood and through school. Most important, we learn from them why they believe they have succeeded when so many of their peers have not. We compare distinct groups of sons, including those raised by single parents and those raised by two parents, both college-educated and non-college-educated. We also explore the commonalities in the parenting they received. We pay particular attention to the types of support they benefited from at home and in school.

Chapter 5 examines how the sons were able to achieve at such a high level in math and science. We hear alternately from sons and parents about influences in the home, encouragement from teachers, community resources, and peers. We learn that the die is not always cast early in a child's life—not all the sons were "early bloomers" or initially showed an aptitude for math and science.

In the second section of Chapter 5, we describe the positive impact of a university-based program in sustaining academic achievement. We believe it is not sufficient for parents and educators simply to "deliver" a well-prepared African American male to a university's doorstep. Many students may not be able to sustain their academic achievements in math and science when away from a nurturing home and school environment. Rather, the college or university must be committed to providing a setting where the students will continue to be mentored and supported.

In the concluding chapter, we restate our key findings and offer specific suggestions for parents, educators, and policy makers. Our comments are based on the interviews we conducted not only with the family members but also with the more than two hundred students and their families who have been associated with the Meyerhoff Scholars Program since the late 1980s.

The vast majority of our sample comes from working- and middle-class families with varying levels of education. These families provide excellent examples of successful parenting that can be useful to a wide variety of Black parents, as well as to educators and others interested in the academic performance of Black males. At the same time, we believe that our findings can be helpful to all parents, regardless of their situation, because, to different extents, the families we studied have overcome remarkable obstacles. As their stories prove, high achievement does not come without hard work and perseverance. We also hope this information will encourage schools, from elementary schools to university settings, to continue their efforts to understand and educate all their students so that they can reach their full potential, thus empowering them to beat the odds.

2

Father-Son Relationships:
The Father's Voice

I grew up on a farm in Mississippi [just after World War II], and my parents were very religious, very hardworking. I think education was the thing that was stressed most. "You want to get away from the farm, you don't want to do this hard work, son, you'd better get an education," they told me. So education was always foremost. The thing I learned was you have to work hard, and you have to be focused. Those are the things I have tried to pass on to my son. You have to know what you want, you have to work for it, nothing is free. Unless you are willing to pay the price, you're not going to make it.

To understand how this high-achieving group of African American college-age men are succeeding, we interviewed the fathers who raised them. Most of these men were the biological fathers and were living with the sons' mothers. In a few cases, the father was a stepfather or a single father who had raised his son alone. Through our information gathering, we often felt we were weaving together threads that would result in a magnificent tapestry of family culture, history, and life. Part of that construction meant learning from these fathers about their own early experiences and how those experiences influenced how they raised, and are still raising, their sons. Their explanations provide an essential perspective as we progress in the next two chapters toward our interviews with the young men.

Here we focus on the fathers' stories. We asked them about their upbringing. How important was education to their parents? Did the fathers receive special messages about being Black and about being male? How did the fathers' mothers and fathers work as a team? We also ask how they raised their sons and how they help them to succeed when so many young African American males do not. Through this process, we assume an intergenerational perspective.

We gained a view of life in the African American family that, in some cases, has its roots in the beginning of the twentieth century (as with the father whose quote begins this chapter) and takes form in the United States of the 1940s and 1950s, when opportunities for Blacks were greatly limited. Although all the fathers talk about their families' influence, they also describe how their approach to child-rearing is shaped by current events as they attempt to prepare their sons for a life few could have predicted. The pressures on young African American men today not to achieve and the dangers they face in the streets from drugs, violence, and AIDS are markedly more extreme than what the fathers experienced when they were growing up. Other pressures are the same. African Americans have always felt at risk when traveling through certain areas. The economic situations of many remain tenuous, and a growing global and high-tech marketplace is heightening the need for advanced training in order to find employment. At the same time, the opportunities are also greater than before if a young African American man is succeeding academically. More doors are open.

Weaving the Tapestry

The fathers provide a rich diversity of experience, from the sons of sharecroppers and military personnel to the sons of the unschooled and teachers. As they tell their stories we can see commonality both among these African American families and with families of other races who have been successful. Though they are from many different backgrounds, these fathers all have sons who placed in the top 2 percent of all African American students in terms of math SAT scores and high-school grades (and all the sons have enrolled at the same university). After listening to the fathers' voices for hours, hearing them both individually and in groups, we have discovered several emerging themes that characterize their varied approaches to guiding their sons to academic success. In some cases, these themes have been mentioned by others studying the African American family. Other themes, though, we believe, are new or require renewed emphasis.

It is important to note that not all fathers we interviewed provide descriptions that fit neatly into a theme. People's lives are complex, often unchartable. We have tried to accommodate those stories where possible. What we are left with is a tapestry of three generations of African American life—the fathers we interview here, and their parents and sons.

Unfortunately, it is becoming increasingly rare for fathers in the African American community to live with their children, as we mentioned in the first chapter. Recent data reveal that only 33 percent of all Black children under the age of eighteen are living with both parents—a marked decrease over the previous generation when 59 percent were living with both mother and father.[1] In this chapter we hear from fathers who, with few exceptions, are living with their sons' mother. For these fathers even to be in the home throughout a son's childhood, as they are for slightly more than half of the sons we interviewed, has been important in the sons' success. In some predominantly African American neighborhoods, fathers are believed to be present in fewer than 10 percent of the families, though the issue of presence in the home versus presence in the children's lives is not addressed here.[2] A number of young men in the Meyerhoff Program do not have fathers in the home. Nonetheless, they found male role models in other relatives, teachers, friends, or fathers living outside of the home. We wish to make the point that while the presence of two parents in the home, especially when they are working together as a team, can be very beneficial to a young man both academically and emotionally, a two-parent family is not a necessary condition for success. Legion are the people who succeed without two parents in the home.

This chapter is divided into two parts. First, the fathers describe their own upbringing; second, they reveal how they raised (and are raising) their children. In many cases, we find that the acorn does not fall far from the tree—those values a father's parents (or extended family) stressed, he in turn stressed when assuming the responsibility of fatherhood. This also proved to be true in the lives of the mothers we interviewed.

The twenty-nine fathers bring a range of backgrounds to their child-rearing. Many come from homes where parents did not attend or graduate from college. In fact, only about one quarter of their parents finished high school, and a few fathers have parents who never finished elementary school. Most had two parents in the home, a statistic that is not surprising for Black families of that era, considering that in 1960 approximately two of every three Black adults were married.[3] By the mid-1990s, that figure has fallen to less than half (43 percent), and one-parent families are almost twice as numerous as two-parent families.[4]

The fathers, with an average age of fifty, are better educated than their parents.[5] One father does not have a high school diploma, and nine others finished high school only and do not have college degrees. Nine possess college degrees only, and the remaining ten have completed at least some graduate training. Overall, they are a much more educated group than the general African American population, among whom one in eight is a college graduate.[6] Three of every four fathers are married, a similar percentage to what would be found among African American fathers in this middle-age group.[7] (In contrast, three of every four African American fathers under the age of thirty have never been married.)

In terms of employment, the fathers' occupations range from construction workers and military and government personnel to salesmen and businessmen. Several are high-level administrators, one is a professor, another a practicing physician, and another is an engineer. This last group, of course, is more highly educated than African American men in general and other men we studied in this book.

We need to emphasize again here that over half the sons interviewed in chapters 4 and 5 lived a large part of their childhood in single-parent homes. Many of their fathers either were unavailable for interviews or refused our invitations. As a result, we gained a sample of highly involved fathers who were willing to be interviewed and were likely to be more residentially stable than other fathers. At the same time, if part of our purpose was to learn about what has worked for these sons, we believe this group of fathers can provide an enormous amount of beneficial information.

Gaining a Perspective on African American Fathers

When looking historically at African American fathers, we see immediately that their role in the family has shifted considerably over time as the result of a combination of factors.[8] Before slavery, while still in Africa, fathers were intimately involved in the community and their children's upbringing, particularly that of their sons.[9] After being brought to America, and during slavery, Black fathers continued to play a significant role unless they were separated from their families by sale to a different landowner. In the years immediately following the abolition of slavery, the vast majority of Black children lived with both parents.[10] But with industrialization of the North and its promise of jobs and a better life than the rural South offered, came great population shifts. Chicago's population, for example, grew sixteenfold from 1860 to 1900, to almost two million people.[11] With migration, which continued into the twentieth century, came family breakdown as the bonds of the smaller community were erased. E. Franklin Frazier wrote in the 1940s, "If these families have managed to preserve their integrity until they reach the northern city, poverty, ignorance, and color force them to seek homes in deteriorated slum areas from which practically all institutional life has disappeared."[12] These stressors tore at the family fabric. With the difficulty many men had in finding work, the balance of economic power in the family slowly shifted over generations to the women, who were able to find domestic and other low-paying work.[13]

Despite the sea change occurring in Black families, gaining an education remained a primary goal. According to Griswold, research undertaken in Pittsburgh on Black, Italian, and Polish fathers between 1900 and 1960 reveals that Black fathers, more than the others, encouraged personal resourcefulness with an emphasis on education. The other immigrant groups were much more likely to remove children from school to aid the family's economic resources. Black fathers, however, were aware of the limited work options open to them because of race and viewed education as the only road to success.[14]

Continued economic shifts in the 1960s away from unskilled labor, Great Society programs that were often seen as encouraging the single-parent structure, and discrimination further eroded the two-parent family.[15] A correlation has been found between rising unemployment rates among African American men in the late 1960s and a rising rate of single-mother-headed families.[16]

What, then, is the modern-day role of the father in the family? Different theorists have considered this question. According to John McAdoo, a researcher who has focused on African American fathers, the role of provider is usually seen as primary.[17] As provider, the father sustains the growth and well-being of the family economically. Because our society tends to define men by their financial contribution to the family, the father who is underemployed or unemployed is at a significant disadvantage. An African American father often shares this provider role with his wife. If his ability to provide wanes, so might his influence on the family as well as his presence. It is difficult for men to stay involved when they feel they are not providing what they should. If they have little (economic) power in the community, it is difficult to wield influence within the family.

Closely linked with this role is that of decision maker in the family. This role involves making decisions about discipline, shopping, insurance, medical care, and residence, among other matters. This role diminishes if the provider role fades.

Fathers are also significantly involved in the child-socializer role (though to a less extent than mothers, McAdoo notes). The father functions here as a nurturer and reinforces family values. McAdoo believes that this is often an underrecognized function of the African American father, as the mother's participation has received the most attention. His own observations of middle-class fathers found them to be warm and loving with their children, yet strict. Charles Willie has noted the sharing of roles that occurs between mothers and fathers in the family, with both pitching in to maintain the family in ways that White families, with a more traditional splitting of roles, do not experience.[18]

Finally, the importance of the father's marital role is noted. When fathers nurture their wives, their children benefit.[19] In fact, marriage benefits fathers, too. Married African American males have been found to be happier than unmarried African American males.[20]

These roles—the provider, the decisionmaker, the socializer of children, and the husband—come through loud and clear as we hear the fathers in this chapter describe how they rear their children. These roles are also linked to the six parenting strategies introduced at the conclusion of the first chapter. We learn here how these family roles relate to education and how family structure and behaviors within the home can positively influence achievement. We must emphasize, however, that these are not simply roles identified by social scientists and educators. Religious and political leaders, community activists, mothers, and fathers themselves are calling upon fathers to become more involved with their children. One cannot pick up the newspaper, turn on the news, or go to a religious or social gathering without hearing about the role of the father in the family. Many fathers are struggling with this role, and they need to learn, or relearn, how to help their children survive and succeed in difficult neighborhoods, school systems, and work environments.

We also note that fathering, like parenting, is a dynamic process, not a static one. Children's developmental needs change as they age. Older children need different types of guidance than do younger children. Children within the same family differ by virtue of their personalities and the way they interact with the parent or parents. A parent may need to be more authoritarian with one child than with the next, based on the nature of the child or the "crowd" with which the child is spending time.[21]

The fathers that we interviewed describe a special relationship with their sons, one in which they are clearly in charge. This unique bond is consistent with at least one theory of healthy family functioning.[22] To appreciate these men, one need only remember how difficult it is to be a parent today, how tenuous the African American father's role has become, and that not all children have the benefit of a (biological) father successfully playing these multiple roles. To learn about these fathers, we first asked them to describe their own upbringing.

When the Fathers Were Young

I grew up on a farm in Mississippi [just after World War II], and my parents were very religious, very hardworking. I think education was the thing that was stressed most. "You want to get away from the farm, you don't want to do this hard work, son, you'd better get an education," they told me. So education was always foremost. The thing I learned was you have to work hard, and you have to be focused. Those are the things I have tried to pass on to my son. You have to know what you want, you have to work for it, nothing is free. Unless you are willing to pay the price, you're not going to make it.

The education system in Mississippi was very poor, so they worked hard to get me into a private school. When they were about to close that school down, the parents worked hard to keep it open. I had to walk four miles to school every day, and my father would cut the grass along the field so we could walk there. That's how it was for my parents. Discipline, religion, education.

Now a medical technician, this father completed one year of specialized training after he graduated from college. When he was growing up, he did not feel poor compared to the families around him, although when he moved away, he realized how impoverished he had been as a child. Even more important, he clearly appreciated the values he learned from his parents.

A second father received a similar message. A college graduate who works for the government, he told us:

My parents had a strong sense of discipline and a strong belief in God, so I had to go to church, even if I didn't want to. As long as I was in their house, if I went out Saturday, I had to go to church on Sunday. School was always very important. I had to do homework before I went outside. They did not freely give me things that they didn't think I needed, in part because they didn't have a lot of money even though they weren't poor.[23] I think my parents did a good job of raising me.

When asked about the role that being an African American played in his getting ahead, he responded, "Integration was just coming into being. People would tell us you have to outdo the White guy. Whatever he'd do, you have to do one better. Good is not good enough."

The father whose quote begins the chapter was also poor as a child. Contrary to most of the other fathers we interviewed, his parents emphasized work over education because of its utility in the South's agrarian society. "In my home, you would take a person out of school to work in the fields. That was more important work than getting an education." With a high-school diploma in hand, his commitment to work followed him into his lifelong career in the armed forces.

A fourth father, who now heads an elementary school, had to make it on his own. "I lived in the Baltimore projects. My father died before I started school, and my mother only finished sixth grade. Even though she worked long hours, she always showed an interest in education. My biggest motivation, and she died when I was in junior high school, was that she felt you could be whatever you wanted to be, and education was the key." (This father's wife is interviewed in depth on page 90).

The themes in these four fathers' stories are repeated with minor variation through the words of a number of other fathers we interviewed. We see in their upbringing a dedication to work, education where possible, and the church. For many of the families in which these fathers were raised, we also see a strong drive to overcome great hardships, including poverty, limited access to employment and education, and racism. Having a closely knit family existence is another theme that becomes clear, with grandparents and children often pitching in to help each other.

Not all of the fathers are American-born. Here we learn about the role of the village in the rearing of this father.

I grew up in a totally different environment, being raised back home in Africa. The family unit is closer together, and it is not just a mother and father, it is an extended family with aunts, cousins, and even distant relatives. If you did something wrong in a small village, anyone can discipline you. Right from the beginning, you have to do right. School and religion were important, and if you didn't go to church Sunday, they had a list with your name on it in school on Monday.

Several of the fathers spent significant periods of their youth in single-parent families. This father, for example, shared time with each parent after their divorce and, before eventually becoming a school administrator, experienced a few detours along the way.

Both my parents completed high school. They separated when I was young, but I was lucky in that I spent time with both of them. My mother was a housewife and raised me, my five brothers and sisters, and her own brother and sister, who were only a few years older than me. I dropped out of high school, and that brought a lesson home that you have to complete your education. My father was a truck driver and then a foreman. I would travel with him, and we'd see all kinds of traits in people, and he'd ask me, *"Do you want to do that?"* And I'd say, *"No."* He'd say, *"You've got to get an education."* I was working when I was fourteen as a laborer, and as I got older I was doing the billing. I realized that to get a good job, I'd have to have an education, especially being a Black man in the 1950s.

Another father's experience exemplifies the nature of parental team-work, of parents pulling together and working hard for the benefit of the children. He also showed what a positive influence a father can be regardless of educational level.

My father was a truck driver and my mother a midwife. He lost his leg in 1940 and was a huge role model for his perseverance to carry on as he did. My mother supported him along the way. My mother only made the fifth grade and my father the eighth, so their push was to have us graduate, which we all did. That was a great achievement for them.

My father was a strict disciplinarian, especially for the boys. We were like Cinderellas growing up—we had to be in by midnight. He made sure we were home safe. He was from Jamaica, a proud man who wanted to keep his sons and daughters intact. I think that had a great influence on how I raised my children!

We should caution that not every father necessarily heard what his parents were telling him about the importance of education. At least one father who has a high-school education has regrets about his mis-spent youth.

I wish I had listened better to my parents when they were talking to me because it took me a while to understand the impact of education and being able to acquire the things you want in life. You understand that people who are well educated run the company. I wish I had done more.

We can see from these fathers that a premium was placed on certain values—hard work, discipline, and education. Often, with a foundation of religion and family togetherness, these tenets were the cornerstones of their early experiences.

GENDER ROLES

We asked the fathers about the role that gender played in their upbringing. We were interested in the gender issue because of the particularly precarious position of Black males in the United States today. Current research on the Black family indicates that, out of economic necessity, there is a great sharing of roles in the family unit. We wondered if this was the case and if boys in the home were treated differently than were girls.

Without exception, it seems that these fathers came from families in which the father was, in the words of one of the fathers we interviewed, the "enforcer," while the mother was the more nurturing, hands-on parent. If the father was not a presence in the home, either the mother fulfilled both roles or relatives were actively involved. From the next two fathers we hear about the roles of fathers.

On the farm, there was a strict division of labor. The mother was in charge of the household—cooking, milking cows, and things like that. The dad saw to the finances and served as sort of the disciplinarian. If my mother said to do something, behind it was that if you did not do it, your father would take care of you.

My father played the role as the person who basically set the standard, the foundation. My mother was the implementer, or the nurturer. Whatever values existed in the family centered around the expectations of my father. The way we went about implementing that was more or less orchestrated by my mother. Obviously she was the one who had the contact with us. My father, being a man of the world and a Black male, understood the importance of being the very best that you could be. He understood the significance of being able to work against the odds.

Even when a mother was described as being a jack-of-all-trades (as many were), the father still played a significant role.

I think my mother was probably the dominant one. She was a very multifaceted person and did a lot of things in the community. She'd take care of other kids, and our house would be a meeting place for a lot of the people in the neighborhood whenever different things would arise. My father was a disciplinarian also. When he came home, my mother would tell him that one of the children did not do something, and he would be, in my term, the enforcer. As I look back on it, they were a good combination—the good-guy-bad-guy team.

SISTERS AND BROTHERS

If sisters were present in the homes when these fathers were growing up, there appears to have been a diversity of approaches. Some fathers describe differential treatment, while others say everyone was treated equally. The messages given about how members of the opposite sex should be treated also varied, as these next examples show.

I know my father treated my sisters differently. He never spanked them. They could blow the roof off the house, but he wouldn't put a hand on them. It was a whole new story when it came to my brothers and me. As far as respecting them and pushing them the same way, he pushed us all in school. I think his treatment is related to the notion of a proud heritage where the sons were to be dominant in all relationships in the family, and we were to go on to do great things. Daughters were to go on to marry great men.

My father made it clear he was the authoritarian in the family and that the man ran the household. But my brothers and I have the utmost respect for women. I think we got that from my mother even though I had thought until now that my father's influence and his being domineering would have the effect of the male children growing up to be disrespectful of their spouses. In fact, it's the opposite—the male children are unusually respectful.

My family was raised to respect women. My sisters were tomboyish, and that was accepted. If they wanted to try something out that was not considered female, they were encouraged. I think that has given me more respect for women. But if the sisters or the brothers did something wrong, you got spanked.

The same discipline was for both boys and girls, but there was a higher expectation for boys in terms of education because it was felt they were going to be the family leaders. Even though the girls were in school, my parents did not expect as much from them.

Here we observe that within these traditional families, the males received the message that the mother's role is important and commands respect. In this way, the woman's role is upheld. At the same time, some sisters were protected while others, as in the last example, were not encouraged to get an education. Rather, through motherhood they would find their niche.

These fathers' stories offer a number of insights into what influenced them to become the kinds of fathers they were with their academically successful sons. Seven primary messages emerge. The six components of parenting discussed in the first chapter also are reflected here and are shown in parentheses:

1. Families placed the highest value on education and succeeding academically. Almost all of the parents of these fathers stressed the importance of getting an education and doing well in school. The message given was that in order to get ahead and avoid the poverty that so many experienced, one had to have an education. Mothers, in particular, checked over homework and were involved in school-related activities, such as the PTA. A few fathers mentioned being primed for the first grade with the preschool study of reading and math. (This is the strategy of continually setting high expectations.)

2. Fathers were raised by parents who worked hard. Regardless of the level of the parents' education and the type of work they were performing, being vigorously engaged in work was the standard. Fathers were specifically encouraged to do their best and received the message that if they could not succeed academically, they should develop a skill and work hard at that. (These are the strategies of strong limit setting and consequences, and continually setting high expectations.)

3. The fathers were raised strictly. Discipline was doled out to sons who stepped out of line and also frequently to daughters. The fathers appeared to have a clear sense of right and wrong, taught to them by their parents and, often, by the extended family. This was manifested by having strict rules about dinner, bedtime, household behavior, and schoolwork. (This is the strategy of strong limit setting.)

4. Religion was emphasized. Many of the fathers describe church attendance as a family requirement and religion as a theme in family life. This underpinned their strict upbringing. (The strategy of making effective use of available community resources is captured here.)

5. The fathers' parents, regardless of how many children were in the family, were actively involved in their children's lives. The fathers sensed that they were individuals, even in large families. One manifestation of this was that the fathers' friends were closely scrutinized. Contact with friends who had inappropriate values was discouraged, while friendships with others involved in positive activities were praised. (This is the strategy of child-focused love.)

6. Families usually had a traditional division of roles. Fathers in the families tended to be the disciplinarians, and mothers were the nurturers. Fathers set the tone, while mothers implemented family policy. The fathers were strong and often silent, and their presence was felt when they were in the home.

Related to this is the sense that parents worked together as a team. This bred in many of the men we interviewed a keen respect for women. (This is the strategy of emphasizing appropriate positive identity.)

7. Families encouraged overcoming adversity. Whether facing poverty or racism, they emphasized trying to get ahead. Education was viewed as one way to try to reach a level playing field, a theme that Blacks have historically honored. The message, as is seen more clearly in the stories that follow, was that African Americans have to work harder to get ahead because they are Black.

The parents' upbringing had a profound influence on how they chose to raise their sons. To digress slightly, we now ask what the message is for today's parent who was not raised so well, who did not receive the attention or messages about the value of education or getting ahead. As will be discussed at the end of this chapter and in the conclusion of the book, one can overcome the obstacles of the past. We believe upbringing sets the course (and the more impoverished the past, the more harshly the course is set), but the course can be changed. Past oversights, neglect, or mistakes can be undone. A parent raising a child today, who himself received inadequate parenting, may start with a deficit, but the deficit need not remain a permanent impediment. Rather, it provides one more challenge for the parent. The parent who was inadequately raised need not always repeat the mistakes of his parents. Parental education, new role models, and significant relationships can help to steer the parent anew.

Having gained an understanding of the fathers' family backgrounds, we can now turn to their own child-rearing approaches. In many instances we see consistent themes passed on from one generation to the next, a continuation of the tapestry.

How Fathers Raise Their Sons: The Weaving Continues

The fathers provide a clear portrait of hands-on child-rearing. For example, seven of eight fathers monitored, to at least some degree, the amount of time their sons spent studying in high school.[24] They monitored their sons' studying during the elementary- and middle-school years to an even greater degree. Throughout their sons' twelve years of school prior to college, all the fathers encouraged them to achieve academically and to participate in extracurricular activities.

Other aspects of their sons' lives were also followed closely. Two thirds of the fathers kept tabs on the amount of time their sons spent with their friends in high school, about the same as when they were in middle school. Two thirds kept a close watch on television viewing and video game playing throughout the school years.

Perhaps most interesting is the fathers' perception of themselves compared with other parents in the neighborhood. Seven of eight fathers believed they had been stricter than other parents, and five of six thought they monitored their sons' homework more closely than other parents.

The fathers were also asked to indicate their level of concern about their sons. We learned they had little concern about their sons' finding a job after graduation or succeeding in graduate school. Given their sons' record of success so far, it is not surprising they would have such confidence. One third, though, had at least some trepidation that their sons would associate with the "wrong crowd." The very real distractions that parents fear their children will find in high school clearly continue to haunt some fathers when their sons enter college. Most significant, almost two thirds indicated they had at least some worry that their sons would not be treated fairly at a job because of race.

The fathers' responses show the enormous investment they have made for years in their sons' lives. They also show that the fathers see themselves as exceptional within their own community. Their hopes, though, are tempered by their awareness that the job market may not be a friendly environment. How do these fathers prepare their sons for this? We will return to this question, but the answer, we believe, is found in the fathers' own upbringing.

We also wanted to know how the fathers helped their sons succeed academically, how early the fathers realized their sons were academically gifted, and what problems they encountered in terms of educating and raising an African American male. We immediately begin to see common threads repeated from one story to the next. We also see that the fathers carried with them the lessons learned from their parents. Sometimes the mother was the leader; sometimes it was the father; and often the parents worked as a team to guide their sons in their endeavors.

SUCCEEDING ACADEMICALLY

We know that the fathers, almost to a man, were involved with their sons. But what was the nature of the involvement? What do the fathers say worked? What was the atmosphere in the home and the view of education?

Regardless of the father's educational level, each contributed significantly to his son's development. For example, a father whose formal education stopped with high school told us:

I gave my son my time. I like the term "quality time." After a certain point I could no longer help him with his studies, as it was beyond my capability, but I always made sure he knew I was there if he needed me.

Another father followed the advice of his wife rather than his own early experiences.

My wife is an educator and insisted on putting the children in school as early as possible. I was resistant because I didn't start that young. But she won out, and it turned out well. He was in the wrong school at one point, and we put him in a private one where there was a lot of structure. We explained, just as we explained our jobs to them, that their jobs were to be good students. The teacher's job is to help you learn and you should ask questions if you don't know the answer. There were rewards for achievement, like going to McDonald's. Because he was not in school with kids in the neighborhood, we got him enrolled in community sports. We got involved in the school, too.

Communication is often mentioned as the key.

Maybe the most important thing is just talking to my sons, right from the beginning. Let them know that they have to achieve something. Set sights high from the beginning. Put them in school early. Maybe the best thing I did for them was to put into their head they have to be good academically.

Challenging their sons intellectually, advocating for them within the educational system, being supportive, and providing stability at home were other themes mentioned by fathers.

We insisted he be in the most challenging courses. In our county, they have a gifted and talented program, and there were very few African Americans and other minorities in it. I was one who would question why there weren't more Black students, and I got the usual: "We couldn't find enough who were qualified." I knew my son could do the work, and I insisted they put him in. We always insisted on advanced placement and told the teachers to get back to us if there was a problem, and we'd make sure he gets the help he needs. If things got tough, we would be there to say "This is going to help you in college, and to solve problems and face challenges."

We tried to allow our boys to grow in a natural way, not be overbearing, but be vigilant for those critical moments when they needed support. My son had three or four junctures in his life when he could have given up. In every stage we were there. I remember personally insisting that he not quit. It's a thin line between success and failure. We made the critical decisions when he was indecisive in terms of the courses he would take. Whenever he thought a course might be too tough, we were there to balance the focus and to get him in the frame of reference that he could do it, and we wanted him to stick with it. We were always there saying, "you can't afford to give up on yourself." I've always been there on the sidelines. We can't run our children's lives, but we can certainly be there to reinforce the values.

When he was young we tried to set some goals—we told him he was going to go to college, that he was going to get an education. I stressed to him to pick courses that would help him get into college. If you take the challenging courses, you will be better prepared for college. I also always tried to give him respect as a young man and that trying your best is all I can ask.

We paid close attention to what they were doing. They did not go out to play until their work was done. We had a set time for bed and did not bend very much on that unless there was a special on TV or something. We played a big role in encouraging them to do well in school and to help them when they needed help. He was very interested in sports, and we went to sports activities but stressed academics. We didn't care if he dribbled the ball. Our goals for him were to get an education first.

Not all fathers took credit or felt they personally had been instrumental in the success of their sons. In one remarried family situation, for example, the stepfather backed away and let the mother take charge because of interpersonal conflict:

I have known my stepson since he was five, and we have not had the best of relationships, to be honest. We only tangle with each other. When I married his mother, he probably felt the need to be loyal to his [biological] father. That never got resolved in our relationship. It might have been my fault for not trying harder. So as it relates to education, my wife has been the prime mover. I have accused her of being a stage-door mom. He has that drive from her to produce the first college graduate in her family.

RECOGNIZING SONS' TALENT: FATHERS AND SCHOOLS

The fathers recognized their sons' academic abilities at various times. Some recognized abilities immediately when the children were very young. Others thought their sons had only a modest amount of talent until they reached their high-school years.

Recognizing talent was a central issue because it affected the advocacy role that parents played. (Not all the sons described here are naturally gifted. All are high-achieving, but some are academically more gifted than others, and some worked harder than others.) Many fathers believed, regardless of their sons' talent, that they were being underestimated by the educational system. This often spurred them to work (and, in some cases, fight) with the school to provide a challenging educational environment for their sons. The fathers saw racism as the reason many of the schools did not initially place their children in gifted and talented programs. Once parents fought for and got their children enrolled, the boys were usually able to maintain their position in class. Other parents reacted to an unresponsive school system by removing their children and placing them in other schools, sometimes public and other times private (often parochial schools).

First, five fathers describe their realizations about their sons' talent, and then we hear from other fathers who report less impressive academic beginnings.

He participated in science fairs in middle school, and he had an engineering project and won first place for his school and for the county in eighth, ninth, and tenth grades. For one of his projects, I took him over to a friend's house who was an engineer, and they were just talking, and I had no idea what they were talking about. So that was something of an indication to me about his talent.

Early on I used to take him to work. In order to keep him interested, I put him in front of a computer, and he was very good at that. Then his high-school grades starting coming in and were very high.

Our son was always a show-off. Even as a toddler, he liked to get praise for knowing how to spell. I think we realized early on that he was academically inclined. It seemed he didn't have any trouble learning that type of thing. He really got into science in the ninth grade and it has been his main focus ever since.

The first thing that got my attention were the SAT scores. I thought he was just a typical high-school student with As and Bs before that.

I think he picked up mathematical concepts very quickly. But sometimes the teachers just put the kids in lower classes, classified them, and they never get out. He was in the lower class, and he was never going to do well, so I moved him to a private school. In high school he got on the honor roll. But if you belong to a certain class or group of skin, they just bring you down, they don't expect you to do well.

Despite the sons' success in high school, it was not always smooth sailing. Many had periods in their lives when they had academic problems, and their parents became involved, as indicated in the following three examples.

We moved a lot, and when he moved back into the second grade, he experienced some problems. He was always good in math and always asked people to give him math problems. But at one point, his teacher graded him down to a C because he wasn't motivated. So we talked with him about his attitude, and that helped his motivation.

Somewhere in the middle grades, his marks started to fall. We asked him if he was trying, and he would say he was, but I felt he wasn't. My wife would scold him. We threatened to hold him out of activities he enjoyed, and that helped straighten him out.

My son only had problems two times. In the eighth grade he really got into video games. It was new to us at the time and we didn't realize how addictive it was. He was hitting it in the afternoon when he got home from school. We talked about it, and he was really giving me lip about how he was going to hide them from me so I couldn't take them away. I actually cut the plug off the power cord because I knew at that point he didn't know how to wire the plug. That got his attention. I told him when he got his grades back up, we'd give it back to him but monitor it like we do TV. I told him he was not going to end up fouling up his academic career. That worked.

In the ninth grade there was a minor dip with moving to a new school and he realized on his own that he was going to have to become more serious.

Sometimes a teacher was the prime influence in the son's getting on track emotionally and academically.

He had problems at various times at his schools, mostly behavioral, but also with his grades. He ran into a prejudicial situation at one school because he was Black, and he fell behind. When he got to middle school he recovered. He worked hard and finally got into the honor society. A Black teacher came up to us and said, pointing to a White teacher, "That man is responsible for your son getting into the honor society." They had wanted to keep him out because of his behavior, but that particular teacher said that behavior didn't have anything to do with it, it is scholastics. And my son, incidentally, couldn't stand this man. I credit that excellent teacher for being significant and taking my son over the barrier.

From listening to these fathers, we found ten specific education-related actions that were mentioned by at least one of every five fathers. Included are both general and specific actions, and the strategies most freqeuntly cited are listed first: (1) talking to teachers if there was a problem with their sons' school situation; (2) paying close attention to schoolwork; (3) teaching their children at home to prepare them for school at an early age, and providing academic challenges at home; (4) making sure their sons were placed in the proper classes and advocating for them if they were placed below their ability; (5) encouraging extracurricular activities; (6) helping with homework; (7) getting to know their sons' teachers by being a presence in the school; (8) setting high standards and encouraging their sons to do the best they could in school; (9) setting limits on their behavior and not allowing playtime until after homework was completed; and (10) moving their sons to different schools when they felt the public school system or a particular school had failed them.

General Child-rearing Issues: The Other Side of the Tapestry

While the primary focus here is on academics, all parents are concerned also about other aspects of their children's lives. This is what makes the tapestry of life so rich. If all that was needed for children to be academically successful was for parents to drill them on math tables and spelling, that could be accomplished relatively easily. But the fabric of the family and how that fabric is woven are also crucial factors. To learn about child-rearing challenges and how they were overcome, we asked the following questions: What issues do parents face raising a Black male? For what types of behavior were they most apt to discipline their child, and what serious discipline problems have they faced?

How did they talk with their sons about sex and drugs? Were there family rituals that were followed at home?

RACE AND BEING MALE

This was one area where the fathers seemed to hold particularly strong feelings. Preparing their children to deal with the world is always on their minds and provides the most difficult challenge of all given the "at risk" state of African American males. One consistent message they give their sons is to always be on guard for mistreatment. We have chosen to include a variety of quotes here because we believe this is such an important issue for these fathers and sons.

I think this is a major problem because from the beginning, society thinks the Black male should achieve less. They put my child in a lower class, and then they have some idea that since you are Black all you can do is run or do sports. This is nonsense. It has come to the point, though, that even some Black kids have low self-esteem, and in some schools if the Black child is doing well, the other Black children make fun of him. These are all problems we have to deal with in the Black community. Maybe we have to organize the Black children who excel to go into the schools very early and talk to the children.

My son went to Colorado last summer to do a science project and one of the ladies asked him what he was doing there. He said he was in college, and the next thing she asks is if he plays basketball because he's tall.

I have concerns [about raising an African American male]. I've had experiences I would hope my children wouldn't have. I've made sure I've told them about them. I still tell them, "You can't be as good as, you have to be better than." I try to prepare them to keep a strong faith in God. I also taught them that I work in situations where in some cases I'm the only person from my office at many conferences I go to and there are few African Americans. So I have to say a little prayer before going to a meeting to give me strength. We've taught them there are going to be challenges in life and to put their faith in God.

I think it is always something that's in one corner of my brain, and I think it is the seed that is constantly germinating in terms of this notion of family values and learning to stick with a task against the odds. When my son was small, he was the only Black in the class-

room, and he was fine as long as he was quiet and behaved. We ended up transferring him because there were subtle things that have impacted on Black males. Since integration, if there is a Black who is highly skilled, confident, and intelligent, there is some comment made to try and discredit his competence to make it seem it is not as significant as a European.

As far as the job market and getting along in the world's multicultural society, there's a little fear in every one of us I guess. Especially the thing that happened in South Carolina. [This is a reference to Susan Smith, a White mother, who drowned her young children in her car and initially fueled racial tensions by saying a Black man had carjacked them.] Her description could fit any Black male. If there were any Black males walking down the street, they would get arrested. Our county, until ten years ago, was pretty bad. I was in New York, and a policeman walked alongside a young Black guy, put a gun to his head, and blew his head off. And he gave no reason except that the guy he killed had recurring seizures.

I tell my sons, "Don't ever forget you're an African American, regardless of how you're accepted. If the alarm goes out that a Black person committed a crime, it could fit you. You're going to be a suspect."

There's a perception among Whites that Blacks get everything and among Blacks that Blacks don't have anything. Neither is correct. I have seen the perception talked about earlier about Black kids being ashamed of their accomplishments. Overall, I would say the Black male is at a disadvantage. We have to get more Black people into college to change this trend.

Race did play a role. I've read a lot about Egyptology and going back to the history of African Americans, and I know it's important to instill those qualities in African American boys. They have to be aware of their culture and to know history in order to achieve. A lot of Black males don't know how rich a history of math and science we come from and how others have piggybacked on us. That's important for them to know, especially with all the negative things that are happening on the streets now. They could look at another person that looks like them and see more to appreciate in them other than this self-hate.

It was very important for us that our son not have any confusion about who he is because he is biracial.[25] Before we got married we *knew that because of society, our child would be raised believing he's Black. So, from the start, we raised him as a Black male. That presented a challenge for me because I'm White, so I had to learn from my father- and brother-in-law or from what I read. I always made it clear that he can be proud of what he is. He's a Black male who happens to have a White father. I encouraged him that being proud of the Black culture was no insult to me as a White father. When he has cared to, he has talked to other Black relatives. Because he was confident in his identity, he never had any problem in school.*

Because both my wife and I grew up in an environment that was more polarized than now, we have always been cautious about racial issues and the potential for discrimination. We have instilled in our children the need for being careful and aware that this is still the case, and that they have to be prepared to deal with that aspect of life. Our son has a lot of friends from different backgrounds, and we refer to him as an international person.

What we have to worry about, though, is educating him that a nice environment in any one school or neighborhood is not the world. There's still discrimination in the workplace based on race or religion and just driving around the country. When we go down south to visit relatives we make a point of saying, "You're a Black male. You don't want to get off on every dirt road in the back country of Georgia or Alabama or Mississippi, especially if it's a place where there are Klan lodges identified with their Aryan Nations." You have to stop and think about this stuff.

My biggest concerns are regarding drugs and AIDS. I think this society is really racist, but that's a reality that he has to deal with. We taught him that he's an individual, he is not a group, and he has to have self-esteem and self-respect to make others see him as an individual. The concept that he is an endangered species is a reality, and it is because of crack and AIDS. When I was a teenager it was heroin and liquor. They were the drugs of choice. I went away to college with ten friends from the neighborhood. Two of us graduated, and the rest are either dead or in jail. So I try to stress to him to associate with whom he wants, but if there is something he doesn't want to do, he doesn't have to.

What comes through in these fathers' messages to their sons is that society will treat them differently because of their race, but that they cannot let that fact keep them down. The fathers advise their sons to try harder, to take pride in themselves, and to be careful.

Another aspect of child-rearing needs mentioning here—the role of a male with a son. To varying degrees, all of the fathers endorsed the importance of fatherhood and of having a male involved with sons. This issue is at the forefront of current considerations about the importance of the father's role in families, whether fathers are absent or present. The involvement of the father in the two-parent and single-parent family is a significant factor in shaping work- and family-related policy, and important questions arise: How much time should a father be allowed to take off from work for child-care responsibilities? How should a single father who visits his child be kept involved in child-rearing decisions?

The next father speaks directly to this issue, arguing a point that many other fathers have made. His words are echoed in one of the in-depth case studies that conclude this chapter. (We see it in the next chapter, too, when mothers talk about letting a father be the most involved parent when he is available.) When he was asked about male role models for sons being raised alone by mothers, he said,

I think it is important, either through a minister, a coach, or a brother, to find some male who could be part of these men's lives if possible, someone who will be there consistently. There are certain things that males can do with boys. Mothers raise daughters and love sons, and they need to discipline them. Some mothers dote too much on their sons.

LIMIT-SETTING: HOW DID FATHERS DISCIPLINE?

The common point of agreement among the fathers is the necessity to prepare their sons for the "real world." Yet this is difficult for all parents of adolescents. To what extent should parents provide a cocoon rather than encourage their sons to be autonomous? What messages should parents give that will sufficiently warn their children about the dangers that exist, without causing them to be tempted by those dangers? For the most part, according to the fathers, the sons did not pose serious disciplinary problems (a less rosy picture emerges from the interviews with the sons). Most fathers emphasized talking to their children rather than resorting to physical punishment. Fathers attempted to set clear rules and would not tolerate behavior that would reflect badly on the family.

In these first two examples, we see the fathers' wariness about involvement in the drug culture and hanging out with the "wrong crowd." In each example the father dealt with it directly.

One incident I will forever cherish because I know I did the right thing and kept him on course. A friend of his, a girl, had a boyfriend who always had a lot of money. He had this nice coat, and my son didn't have a coat. This guy was trying to impress my son and told him he could have a coat just like it. That's how you get sucked into the drug culture. I saw my son in it, and I asked him where it came from. I knew he didn't have the money for it. So he told me he got it from this friend, and when I asked him whose it was he said, "It's mine." I told him to give the coat back.

As men, we all face personal dangers and deal with them. But when you see the potential danger for your child, it becomes indescribable. I was in a state of panic and fear. That's why I insisted he give the coat back. I understood enough about the culture in terms of how they prey on innocent, naive, unsuspecting youngsters and suck them in. Once my son began to see the bigger picture, he understood exactly why I made the decision.

I got a call from the teacher one day saying, "You'd better watch your son. He's hanging with the wrong people and fooling around." I told the teacher I appreciated that, because it went beyond the call of duty. I went up to the school and told my son if he wanted to be a clown to do it right then and there in front of the class. I really didn't know what I was doing. I was trying to figure it out at the time.

Some fathers placed a high premium on telling the truth as a foundation for building trust and being respected, important values in these families.

I was most apt to discipline him for lying and being disrespectful. If he lied to me, it really bothered me, and I tried to teach him to come to me even if he had done something wrong.

I'm very stern, but at some point, I guess when they were around ten, I didn't spank the children anymore and would talk to them instead. If something was broken and all three of them said they didn't do it, I would let them all go but tell them that if I found out who did it, he would get a double spanking for lying. I will not tolerate a liar. We also sent them to their room as punishment. I think punishment is the key to a lot of the bad things that happen today. I was raised that way, and all my brothers and sisters and I are doing well today.

I know families who lived in the same town as us—half of them are dead and the other half are in jail. And yet my family is not. There has to be some reason for that.

Punishments were swiftly delivered and were often fairly severe.

I can remember one incident when my son was in middle school. He was responsible for doing his homework when he got home, and then he could go out and play. One time he went out to play without doing his homework. I went out and found him, and his mother and I decided that for the rest of the school year he couldn't go out and play during the week. He had to wait until the weekend. That had a profound effect on him. I explained I had a job I had to go to, and he had to do his work. "Take care of business and then BS" was our saying.

From an early age, we decided if there was anything that needed discipline, it was administered immediately. If you're out somewhere, even church, and you do something wrong, you got it. I recall giving the belt to my son on only one occasion. He was five or six and he lied. That was not going to be tolerated. I never had to do it again. If they stayed out longer than they should have, they were given a stern lecture.

TALKING ABOUT SEX AND DRUGS

These fathers do not believe in protecting children by being evasive or avoiding troublesome issues (though they do encourage avoidance of certain situations). Rather, they tend to explain and discuss sensitive questions at length as accurately as possible to prepare the sons. Using verbal persuasion is characteristic of well-educated parents.

You have an ongoing conversation with your children about these things. My wife taught at the same high school that my son attended. She knew about students who were rumored to be dealing drugs, so she would ask my son about it. That helped us stay in tune with what was happening and to talk about it.

I always tried to be as realistic as possible. I told him the truth as I knew it. Sex or crime or bad influences out there—I told him of some of my experiences and some of the people in the family and friends and some of the errors they made. When someone was in the news for something he did, I pointed out to him that he wouldn't be in trouble if he had avoided the situation. If you get into a situation you should-n't be in, get away. Leave the environment. We always tried to be as real with him as we could be.

We try to keep constant communication open. Drugs or crime were never problems per se. We had a general philosophy, a religious upbringing, and he went to school where there were classes on sexuality. We were always vigilant because we heard that parents were the last ones to know.

As soon as they asked questions about sex when they were little, we used the right words for all the body parts. We tried to answer questions as simply as we could. On the drug thing, I made myself available to my kid as an excuse. If he gets to a party where they are doing drugs, I gave him the freedom to say, even if it's not true, "My dad's an ornery SOB, and he'll kill me if he knows what's going on, and I have to get out of here." Also, make a contract with your kid that you'll come and get him at any time, no questions asked, if they want to get out of a situation.

We taught our children everything about sex, and one time a neighbor told me my seven-year-old daughter was fresh because she knew where babies came from, and I said, "What's wrong with that?" We try and control our language and don't swear in front of them and don't expect them to swear either. One time they were singing a song, a jingle, "Bang-bang, you're dead, bullets in the head." I told them they didn't talk about things like that. I took the tape and wrecked it and told them to listen to something else.

FIGHTING

Instruction concerning fighting has traditionally been a father-son rite of passage. Most fathers had the philosophy that their sons should avoid fighting. At the same time, they inculcated in their sons the feeling that they had to be prepared to fight as a way to defend themselves and avoid further harassment. Variations in approach occurred by neighborhood, with fathers raising sons in tougher neighborhoods being more likely to teach them how physically to handle such difficult encounters. Perhaps uniquely for fathers and sons, as is the explicit situation with the first two fathers, their own experiences with fighting affect their advice.

My father instilled in us a sense of survival. I was taught if you see something brewing to walk away. I think that rubbed off on my son. He's big and he didn't get into fights because people don't pick on him.

My son didn't face growing up in his neighborhood like I did. I had to fight the first day I moved in when I was young. My son got pushed one day in the chest and came home mad. He didn't fight, I think, because I didn't teach him how to. It just didn't occur to me that he's going to be intimidated. He's mad at me because I didn't teach him. I taught him if you see anything like gunplay or drugs, walk away.

He was worried when he went to a tough high school and did not know anyone. But we wanted him there because of the gifted program, and we thought it would be good training about what the world is about. He loved it from the beginning, and I think that helped him learn there's an element in school that likes to fight and another that does not.

I moved a lot because of the military. Whenever my son would be new to a neighborhood, they'd try him. There were a lot of times I had to teach him to defend himself. If you're going to go out there and play, you have to deal with the fellows out there. If someone hits you, you hit him back. He did learn to protect himself, but he also learned as he got older that you can prevent a lot by evaluating the situation.

I taught him how to fight because he was getting in little scrapes. You have to stand up for yourself. If you're a weakling, they'll pick on you. In middle school, a couple of guys began picking on him. It was a racial thing, and he settled them down but I had to bail him out of the principal's office. We taught him to avoid fights, but there's a time, especially if you are male, that you're going to face a bad situation, and you've got to decide. We taught him it is better to stand up and get knocked down than to crawl away.

It is difficult to conclude that one approach is right or wrong when it comes to helping a son cope with self-protection as a rite of passage. We do know that if children fight in school, the result is often punishment and expulsion. African American males are often caught between the two worlds of having to act a certain way in one environment and a different way in another. For example, a self-protective posture assumed in the neighborhood may cause anxiety among authorities in a school environment. It is important that parents be able to evaluate situations with their sons in such a way that they can offer advice about how to cope with these contradictory contexts.

FAMILY RITUALS

Finally, we looked at the family unit as a protective factor. Research on successful family functioning shows that families that spend time together at holidays, for example, tend to cope better with life's ups and downs.[26] Family interactions that are rewarding can build a sense of comfort and stability. Rituals, such as going on vacation together, attending church together, reading together, and eating meals together, help to build cohesion and a nurturing environment. They provide a vehicle for talking about daily life and conveying family values. They also provide a buffer against stress. We asked these fathers about rituals in their families that may have helped to build this sense of comfort, stability, and ability to cope.

We felt the way to help academically was to have a stable family life. We both grew up in families where the family ate breakfast and dinner together most days. It was a regular routine, and we did the same thing with ours. There was always the emphasis on going to bed and getting your rest.

My wife and I put into perspective that we're a family now. It became a yearly thing that the kids would see their grandparents during holidays, especially Christmas. We didn't force it, like Ozzie *and* Harriet, *when it came to sitting around the table, but we are together on holidays.*

When we became a middle-class family, we could afford to do things outside of the community, so we would take them on business trips, try to make those a family affair. Though the children are independent now, I can guarantee you they will be there on Christmas.

I think it's important for families to do things together. Maybe I have a tendency to put too much emphasis on it because my family never did anything together. Every opportunity now, because we don't have much time together, I'll have food on the table if I know they are coming home, so I know they'll eat.

We did go to all of the children's dancing classes and meets when they were young. My wife came from a family where she always had dinner with her parents, and without making a big deal of it, we have tried to do the same thing.

We cannot overemphasize this sense of togetherness. The bond that is formed serves to strengthen whatever messages the fathers convey. As the family tapestry is completed, the traditions that are so fundamental to Black families are continued from one generation to the next.

An In-depth Look at Two Fathers

Two case studies provide further understanding of these fathers' experiences. The first is a single parent who raised his son alone during much of his son's formative years. We chose him as one example because, while great attention has been placed on Black females as single parents, we rarely think about Black males in this role. In fact, only 5 percent of Black children in the United States being raised by a single parent are currently living with their father.[27]

A CLEAR CASE OF IDENTITY: A SINGLE FATHER

For two years, the son of our first father was the object of an intense custody battle and lived with his mother. Being involved in a custody dispute could have possibly had a profoundly negative impact on the son, but that does not seem to be the case. The father, who has earned a master's degree, is an administrator in a large organization. A highly religious man, his faith offered clear guidelines for family values.

My father was an extreme disciplinarian and there was little affection shown. There were many times when my father would take me along on trips. I used to hate them, but it was a time he could dream. He would show me other people's homes and talk about the things he wanted for my mother. He told me about the mistakes he had made when he was young. Even though I hated the trips, I find myself doing the same thing now with my son. I've shared what my dreams are, and I'm sure he hates them as well. [He laughs.] Many of the things my father did not accomplish, I have been able to do.

In terms of education, it did not happen much in my family. My parents never talked about it. I'm not sure my mother graduated from high school, and I didn't know my father went to college until I finished graduate school. I had to pay for my own college education even though he had promised me when I was in the first grade he would pay.

Two important messages came through when I was young—we had to attend school, which was more important than what grades we received. Second, don't accept labels. I used to fight a lot in junior high school, so the school sent me to a psychologist. I was in an integrated school, and the staff was all White. They did some testing and determined I was mildly retarded. In high school I got into more fights, and they again sent me for an evaluation, this time right after one of the fights, and I didn't answer any of the questions. And again I was labeled retarded. They wanted to transfer me out of the school. My father was going to get a gun and go up there and clean out the school when he heard that, but after some coaching from my mother, he went up there and used some curse words and insisted I stay in school. That was one of the few times he was ever in the school. Then he told me I better get my grades up.

So I became the "mildly retarded" person who became student government president of a White school, the first one in history. I graduated with honors. Then I graduated with honors from college. I just never accepted their labels. There were clearly cultural issues related to all their test findings.

My father was always supportive of my mother. I remember him saying to us, "I know there's a God because he made your mother." He also said that Black women were the most beautiful women in the world.

RAISING HIS SON

Unlike many of the families here [in the Meyerhoff Program], I was a teenage parent, and I was single and raised my son alone. I didn't have much, so I used to play games with him with a deck of cards. Even before the first grade, we'd match colors and play memory games. He was not allowed to accept a gift unless it had an educational nature to it. He was never allowed to have a toy gun. I had him memorize little prayers like "My mind is the most important thing I have," and I think that helped him. I always spent a lot of time with him. I took him to my meetings at work and in the community.

I always talked to every one of his teachers and made him understand that I knew them and the principal. If he got a low grade, I would ask him for an explanation and then write a letter to the school asking for their version, because sometimes my son could be a little creative with his reasons. I wanted him to know that he was responsible for everything he said. Even now, in college, when he gets his report card, I want an explanation for everything on it

"We never had any behavioral problems with him. His problems always had to do with external factors interfering with his grades.

There was a time in his life, though, when his mother and I were liv-
ing apart, and she wanted him with her. There was a custody battle,
and she won only because she was a woman. But after living with her
for a while, they had relocated out of the country, he wanted to come
back and live with me.

"One particular hard time I had with him was in his junior year,
when we were going over his report card like we always did, and he
blew up. He said, "Look, Dad, get off of it! Leave me alone. I just want
to be like everyone else." That was the first time I experienced that he
was not going along with me. I stood back and thought a minute and
told him, "But you're not average. You were never average and never
will be. Even if you try to be average, you won't be." And he said he
just wanted to be like so and so and named some of his friends. And I
said to him, "You know those people whose pictures are on your walls?
Michael Jordan and those musicians? Those people are not average.
They tell you they are average but they are not. If they were, they
would not be making millions of dollars." When I was done talking to
him I was pleased and I said "Whew" to myself.

I kept telling him one thing when he was young—I would ask him,
"Who am I?" And I would say, "I am your father first and your friend
second. And when you become wise enough, I'll become your friend
first and your father second. And I'll decide when that time comes."

EDUCATING ABOUT GENDER AND RACE

In terms of gender and race, my son is the third-generation Muslim in
our family, Nation of Islam. We have strong feelings about gender and
race. In terms of gender, I've taught my son that he should be very pro-
tective of women, the African American woman. Times when he was
not treating a woman with respect, I talked to him about it. Given my
situation, I believe more in the concept of parenthood than mother-
hood or fatherhood. If you only have one parent, roles have to be rele-
gated to one gender, and you have to wear both pairs of shoes. I taught
him he has to survive himself, take care of himself, cook, and the
whole nine yards. When he has the responsibility to cook dinner, he
has to have a complete meal. There is no excuse for not being home
for dinner.

The only other thing I'd say is that in the United States, there is a
war on for African American males. I'm not saying there is a conspira-
cy. When I drive a car and I'm stopped, whether it be in a northern or
a southern state, I'm a little concerned. When I can't get a taxicab

downtown in any city, I'm concerned. And I've taught him that he needs to be aware that he is a target and to use that and grow from that point.

I don't consider my religion racist, anti-Semitic, or any of those things. I'm vice president to a CEO who is Jewish and very religious himself. I'm his most trusted person, and we work extremely well together. I taught my son the same thing—the virtue of working together in a world that is not perfect.

I helped to create this in him by always teaching about African American history, about how we came to the United States, and the many obstacles that we had as a race. The laws against us reading and writing and getting together and how that has all changed. And to just imagine, with all those obstacles that were there, where we will be in the very near future. His role, as the one who came after me, is to take on the challenge and create a better world for us all! [His son is quoted on pages 18 and 119].

This father did not come from a home with highly educated parents, yet they saw the value of education. Despite their own insecurities, they were his staunchest defenders as he fought against being considered retarded in school. He became a teen father, and as he grew into adulthood he became a vociferous defender of his own identity as an African American and a father. His standards for himself and his son are very clear. We can see that the support he received from his parents encouraged him to set high standards for himself and his son. We also see how, returning to McAdoo's conceptualization, he was the provider, the decision maker, and responsible for socializing his son. Although he did not fulfill the marital role, he did provide strong messages about how women should be treated.

RESPONSIBLE PARENTING: THE FATHER IN A TWO-PARENT HOUSEHOLD

The second father is married and possesses a high-school education. (Quotes from his wife appear on page 76.) A career serviceman, he became a construction worker when he retired from the army. His story was selected to be presented in depth because, though less well educated than some of the fathers in this chapter, he more closely resembled the educational level of many fathers of the sons we interviewed, and he provides an excellent example of responsible parenting.

I come from a nuclear family where my father was a longshoreman, and my mother was a homemaker. He was the disciplinarian without being physical. My mother handled everything—the love, the discipline, the morality. She made sure we went to church and she was always in our lives. Things can work with a single parent but it is easier if both parents are there.

I was raised in a home with three other brothers. My mother was the lady of the house. She taught us that boys do not cry. She also showed us how to wash, iron, sew, cook, and scrub floors, because there weren't any girls around. She said that in case we didn't marry, we'd be able to take care of ourselves. [He laughs.] But she also said that men have certain responsibilities, and if you did not take care of your family and your children, you were not a man.

EDUCATION AND DISCIPLINE

When my son was born, my wife and I were avid readers. The big thing for him was getting his own library card when he was five. He had his name on the card and felt like a big shot. We read to him all the time, so he knew his ABC's by the time he started school. Parents must do this before school because teachers cannot do everything.

When he got to the first grade they skipped him to the second and then the next year wanted to skip him again. I stopped it. They were putting too much pressure on him, and he was too young to be that far from his peers. It was not to hold him back, but I know what he can and cannot handle. I also did not accept any failing grades because I knew he could do it. He appreciates it today.

I used to tell him if he had a problem with a teacher to let me know. He did have a problem with ethnicity because he didn't understand. One day I was called down to the school because he used an ethnic slur. He called a White boy a "nigger." He thought that was the nastiest thing he could call someone. So we had a talk with him. One of us—I worked days and my wife worked nights—was always there for him. Even as he got older, sixteen, seventeen, and eighteen, we were always watching him. I wanted to know where he was all the time and why he was sleeping late the next morning. We set boundaries for him.

We had little discipline problems. One time when he was ten, he had a BB gun and it was a responsibility he couldn't handle. We had a dog who was pretty vicious, and I caught him shooting at the dog. He tried to tell me he was shooting at the tree the dog was tied to, but I saw the truth. He lied to me, so I got physical with him and spanked him. That was the first and only time I ever spanked him. And, as far as I know, he has never lied to me since.

We cracked down on his homework. One time he brought home a report card of all As and one C in business, so we began to monitor his homework in that area. We told him he could do it, and he had to take control. He used to find mistakes in his textbooks. When he was in the ninth grade and was taking physics and calculus, he found a mistake in a new book. The teacher insisted that he had gotten the problem wrong and that the book was right. So I took the question down to the Naval Academy, to a friend who ended up agreeing with my son. So I taught him to go back to his teacher and say politely what we had learned. Not to go in and say that the teacher was wrong, wrong, wrong."

RAISING A BLACK MAN TO BE SUCCESSFUL

One incident illustrates what it took to raise him to be a man. One time, he came home without his football after playing with some boys. He was about ten. He was crying, and his mother was upset. After she found out who took his ball, she was going to get on her coat and go down and get it back. I told her, "No, no, no. Leave him alone." So he sat there for awhile, got himself together, and then went down there himself and got his ball.

"There are certain things that women can't teach a Black man— and that is how to be a Black man. [Here again we see the role of child-socializer, according to McAdoo.] I know that sounds antiquated, but certain things cannot be taught. Things like, if you are driving a nice car and are stopped at night by a policeman, you don't make any fast moves toward the glove compartment because you are going to get shot, if for no other reason than you're Black.

One time, when he was seventeen, he came home with some kind of haircut, and I asked him about it, and he said it was his Black identity. And I said, "Go look in the mirror. What do you see?" And he said he saw a man, and I asked, "What kind of man? "and he said a Black man and I said, "Thank you. Now go get it cut." [In this example, the decision-maker role is being fulfilled.]

I tried to instill in him that he had to be good. You have to be around money to make money. Learn how to play golf. If you want to be successful, get out on the golf course, where deals are made. I'm sorry, that's the way it is. If you hang around the cesspool, only one thing will come off on you. Use money as a tool. After money, then you've got power and you can make changes. [The message of providing is being delivered.] You've got to get within the system to change it. And the only way is through education. No hostility, no militant stuff. You have to be exposed to a cultural environment. It is not a Black world. We would like it to be sometimes, but it is not.

I taught him about sex and to take responsibility for himself. He can't take the girl's word for it—you protect yourself. When his hormones were causing him to bump off the walls, I sat down and told him honestly what the deal was. I taught him control, and if he couldn't control the situation, to get out of it. We didn't need to create another problem. His priorities are to finish school, get his master's degree, a job, a car, an apartment, a wife, and then children. [The marital role is emphasized.]

There are certain things you don't do around your children. You don't party and drink with them because eventually they will lose respect for you. I've always been honest with him and told him he can tell me when I'm wrong, that I will listen. The emphasis is on loving and respecting each other.

Within a two-parent family, this father shows the value of the father's restraining the overprotective tendencies of the mother. The son had to deal with the football situation himself, something the father clearly understood. The father was present when other crucial events took place, from mediocre grades on his son's report card to a new haircut. His presence, firm hand, and clear values helped his son to succeed.

Summary

A number of specific points can be drawn from how the fathers handled the nonacademic aspects of their sons' lives.

1. Fathers need to prepare their sons for being an African American male. The message here is never to forget that they are Black and that Black males are often placed in difficult situations. This is conveyed through statements related to their sons' always being suspects whenever a crime is committed, and the need for their sons to avoid areas that might be dangerous to them because of their race.

2. Children need to learn African American history. Fathers emphasize the need for appreciating culture so that their sons will have even greater pride in their own accomplishments. The sense of pride in their heritage is related to combating the problems of being an African American male, as presented in the first point.

3. Do not expect life to be fair. The notion conveyed here is that their sons will be hindered if they enter situations believing everyone is playing on a level playing field. Their sons, because they are Black, have to be on guard and will have to work harder to achieve parity.

4. Do not expect all neighborhoods to be the same. The sons who were raised in advantaged neighborhoods or home environments need to be aware that the rest of the world may not be as nice a place. Related to the first point, the fathers wish to prepare their sons for every eventuality and are keenly aware that the environment their sons grew up in may give them a false sense of security.

5. African Americans need as much education as possible in order to help others. If Blacks achieve more academically, they will be able to combat the insidious message that achievement in school is not to be valued.

6. Appropriate discipline is needed. With disciplining their sons, the fathers emphasize setting high expectations early, discussing the punishment with their children when they misbehave, and reacting on the spot. Lying, in particular, is offensive to the fathers. Mirroring this is the repeated message of the need for trust and communication between father and son. Showing a lack of respect is also mentioned as something that needs to be addressed. A few fathers cited specifically the need for a parent to be a good role model in order to be an effective disciplinarian. This is achieved most easily when the father and son have a strong bond between them.

7. Fathers must teach their sons about the dangers of sex and drugs. Fathers engaged their children in ongoing conversations about sexual relations and the drug environment. The facts should be handled honestly. The message to the sons is that they need to act responsibly about both.

8. Fathers and sons must deal with fighting. Two slightly different messages were given about fighting. Some fathers mentioned teaching their children to walk away from situations where fights were occurring or about to occur. Other fathers described the need to teach their children how to defend themselves if they had to. No one discussed the need to instigate a fight to establish a reputation, but it was mentioned that unless a young man defended himself adequately, he would be victimized.

9. Family rituals are important. Family rituals, in the form of vacationing, eating meals, attending church, and reading together, as well as supporting family members at sporting events or art performances, were mentioned frequently. Yet it was also cautioned that busy schedules and encouraging children to be involved in community activities often militated against family togetherness.

10. Fathers have an important role in raising a son. As illustrated most succinctly by the second extended case example, fathers play a unique role in their sons' lives. They feel they prevent the mother's overprotection, while teaching about manhood. Given the dearth of men in many African American families, they take particular pride in the positive role they play and see themselves as good fathers. Respect for women was also conveyed as integral to mature manhood, as was sharing parental responsibilities with the mother and supporting her in her parenting. The fathers provide living examples of fathers and mothers working together to raise sons.

Revisiting the Six Strategies of Successful Parenting: What's a Father to Do?

We found that the six components of successful parenting take on greater meaning when placed within the context of these fathers' stories.

CHILD-FOCUSED LOVE

Fathers constantly encourage their sons to try hard. At the same time, there is an emphasis on accepting results if the attempts fail. Thus the children are raised knowing there is a keen interest in their accomplishments, that they will receive praise for them, that they will be accepted if their accomplishments fall short, and that they can bounce back from failure.

STRONG LIMIT-SETTING AND DISCIPLINE

The fathers clearly set rules in these homes. They hold their sons to a focus on work, respect, and telling the truth. When there is variation from this, the retribution is usually swift.

CONTINUALLY HIGH EXPECTATIONS

The fathers present a picture of setting high expectations (the sons will say, in some cases, they were too high). Homework came first, and children were pushed, sometimes with great effort, into gifted and talented programs, even though the school inappropriately thought they should not be there. When a parent goes that route for a child, it sets the goal for the child that he must achieve or else he is letting down not only himself but also his parents.

OPEN, CONSISTENT, AND STRONG COMMUNICATION

The fathers emphasize having conversations with their sons and using those conversations as a springboard for handling problems that arise. The basis for the conversation is to prepare their son for life, to teach about "the real world." Disciplining, for example, is used by some fathers as a way to teach. It is difficult to know to what extent the mother may also have been a force here, at times helping when the father felt uncomfortable.

POSITIVE RACIAL IDENTIFICATION AND POSITIVE MALE IDENTIFICATION

Taking account of the unique status of the African American male, we have combined these two components. In the United States, given their endangered position, it is difficult to consider race and gender separately. Although fathers spend considerable time preparing their sons for life as Black males who must be on guard, they also emphasize both the need for taking pride in the history of African Americans and the sons' abilities to compete in a variety of arenas. It is a significant challenge for some fathers to prepare their sons for negative treatment while teaching them simultaneously that their skills are equal to or better than the people who may treat them negatively. The fathers, strong positive role models in their own right, convey this message within the context of the other components cited above.

DRAWING UPON COMMUNITY RESOURCES

Throughout, we hear of the influence of the church as an organizing factor in the lives of these families. We also hear about friends, family members, and teachers who recognized talent in the sons or helped out with school projects. Schools are often mentioned as breeding grounds of success, though some schools are identified as potential stumbling blocks.

These components undergird, along with specific examples of parenting techniques, the support that fathers provide. They also serve to guide future fathers. It is prescriptive and reassuring to see how others have succeeded in what is often a difficult task. Many of these fathers came from impoverished beginnings but were able to succeed through perseverance. In turn, they have helped their sons to achieve. As the fathers demonstrate, the die is not cast immutably when one does not have a privileged background. Many African American males are prospering at the highest levels, despite frequent portrayals to the contrary.

Perhaps most important is the overall message that many fathers have given their sons: "Yes, there is bias in society. But no, do not let it hold you back. Push yourself to become the best that you can be." With that message drilled into them by their fathers (as it is by the mothers, too), these sons have made it.

As we turn to the mothers we have a strong sense of what these fathers brought to the family from before they were married and as they coparented. They had teachers or sharecroppers as parents. They obtained advanced degrees or only high-school diplomas. Despite this wide range of backgrounds, they have all produced successful sons.

3

Mother-Son Relationships: The Mother's Voice

I always tried to look at the world through his eyes and listen to what he was saying.

He didn't want to be the best anymore. He wanted to be accepted.

Any serious consideration of the African American family acknowledges the central role of the mother. She, more than any other person, is the core around whom the children, the father, and other relatives revolve. Whereas the father's involvement sometimes has been diminished, the mother's role has been consistently strong. Black women generally place great value on motherhood and have within their family many role models of women who have been self-reliant and have persevered to keep the family together.[1]

In this chapter, the mothers describe their own upbringing and how they raised their sons and continue to help them succeed. As the mothers reflect on their own childhoods, we see the strong hands of their own mothers and fathers working in tandem. We see the centrality of the woman's role (as mother, grandmother, or aunt) in the family of every mother we interviewed. Like the fathers in the previous chapter, most of these mothers were raised in two-parent families, which were the norm during their childhood years in the 1940s and 1950s. Roles were often shared in these families, and their parents were traditional in their values and emphasis on work. These traditions have carried over into the present generation.

Unlike the fathers in the previous chapter, a significant number, 40 percent, of the mothers we interviewed are raising their sons without another parent in the home. Even though a father was not in the home, his presence may have been felt through either visitation, other forms of communication, or paternal grandparent involvement. Surprisingly, we found a few, but not a significant number, of differences between the parenting practices and concerns of single mothers and married mothers. As we will discuss, they look much more similar than dissimilar—a sign that, whether a father is in the home or not, we have found families who have been effective in raising sons.

African American Mothers in Context

The rich history of African American women is well known. It was the Black woman who nurtured the family during slavery because the father was more likely than the mother to be separated from the children, by either the greater demands of physical labor or being sold to a different plantation. It was she who stayed home and raised the children while the father entered the workforce during the latter part of the nineteenth century. It was she who, a generation later, worked in occupations others were unwilling to accept and found employment in an increasingly industrialized society while the father, in some cases, faced the beginning of years of underemployment or unemployment in the twentieth century. Working outside of the home was not without difficulty for mothers. Torn between home and work, they often experienced great role conflict, just as today's parents feel conflicted between trying to balance career and home life.[2] Much of this is documented in the previous chapter, as is the prevalence of two-parent African American families in the post–World War II generation. We wish to reiterate that a profound shift in the African American community has, in recent years, placed the mother in such a central position. In 1970, 65 percent of African American families with children were two-parent homes. Just ten years later, by 1980, this had fallen to 48 percent. By 1990, the percentage had fallen again, this time leaving only 39 percent of African American families headed by two parents. Recent Census Bureau figures reveal that by the mid-1990s, the percentage had fallen even further. (In contrast, in 1994, 76 percent of White children and 63 percent of Hispanic children were in the home with both parents.)[3]

Approximately half of the young men we interviewed come from two-parent families. The presence of a father in some homes may have played a key part in their academic success. But again, as emphasized earlier, we do not believe that being raised by a single parent precludes academic success, as it obviously has not with the sons raised by single mothers here. We do believe, though, that the greater the number of adults involved consistently and supportively in a young child's life, the greater the potential for academic and subsequent success. Being surrounded by family members and others considered part of the family (as well as supportive teachers, religious figures, and community leaders) is vitally important to the healthy development of most children, regardless of race or culture. In research, Blacks are consistently found to be more likely to be living in extended households than Whites and to have significant involvement in extended-family networks.[4] Single African American females have also been found to benefit from contact with mentors outside of the family and to live nearer to their kin than young White mothers.[5] The importance of a solid network cannot be overestimated because it serves as a meaningful buffer against life's stressors.

One recent study of 620 married and single (divorced, widowed, and never-married) African American mothers found that over three quarters received emotional support from their relatives and that at least 40 percent interacted with them almost daily. Over half felt very close to their kin. These mothers were helped financially as well as with child care. The closer they lived to their family, the more likely they were to receive assistance.[6] The picture that is drawn is one of the Black female being engaged in, and helped by, her network. As we hear the mothers' voices in this chapter, relatives are mentioned frequently.

We also acknowledge the unique situation of single mothers. Life in a single-parent family has been linked with an increased likelihood of adjustment problems in children, as has life spent in poverty.[7] Though there are exceptions, many African American single mothers are poor and grew up in poor households.[8] Regardless of race, difficulties may arise when mothers raise sons alone. In a study of White families, a lower income among single-parent families was linked with poorer emotional adjustment in boys.[9] Higher income for single-parent and two-parent families is usually related to a host of variables that would assist in helping a child become more academically successful. Money is linked to education, employment, and the stimulation that these provide a family. Recent research has shown that when children in the lower grades lose ground in math achievement over the summer break, it is more a function of income than of single-parent status.[10] Our sample of mothers (single and married) is more economically advantaged than most, and the majority hold steady jobs or have held steady jobs, with only a handful never having worked outside the house. Thus, while the single mothers here may face greater obstacles in child-rearing than the married ones, many are better off in many ways than the typical single mother.

The Mothers' Background

The thirty-eight mothers, with an average age of forty-seven, embody a range of educational backgrounds. Almost a third reported their education stopped with high school; a handful took some courses for college credit. Almost two thirds have college degrees (similar to the fathers), and approximately half of those who finished college went on for graduate training. Despite the range, the group is clearly more highly educated than the typical African American mother. The mothers we interviewed are also more apt to be currently married (60 percent) than is typical of Black mothers.[11]

These mothers were raised in homes with their mothers throughout their childhood in all but one case. Their fathers were present throughout their childhood in 80 percent of the cases. We estimate this to be slightly higher than was typical for African American children growing up in the 1950s and 1960s.[12] The majority of these mothers reported that neither parent had finished high school. Fifty-five percent of the mothers had mothers who did not complete high school, and 60 percent had fathers who never graduated. There were pockets of significant education, though—one quarter had mothers who finished college, and 30 percent described fathers with college or graduate degrees.[13]

Half the mothers' mothers were housewives, and the remainder were teachers, farmers, or laborers. Their fathers, when their occupations were specified, were teachers, laborers, servicemen, and, in one case, a doctor.

As these mothers talk about their childhoods, we need to mention two points. First, role flexibility is common within African American families.[14] Different roles are assumed by men and women out of necessity so that tasks can be completed on a daily basis. When the mothers describe fathers who cooked or mothers who "brought home the bacon," they are describing patterns typical of the 1940s and 1950s. Second, African American families tend to be child-focused. One legacy of slavery was the need to take care of others' children and to consider neighbors with whom there was a bond as family members. Children have been seen historically as a precious commodity. The notion that "it takes a village to raise a child" underscores the importance that parents and others give children.[15] This sets the stage for families to make sacrifices for children. Frequently this child-orientation is coupled with a strong disciplinary hand.[16] Some research has noted that African American mothers require obedience to their authority and do not allow much feedback from the child.[17] This is not true, however, of all

African American mothers. One study of fifty-two African American female caregivers found that those with more education were less restrictive, perhaps because they had been exposed to a greater variation of child-rearing philosophies than those with less education.[18] These two philosophies (being highly invested in a child and being strict as a parent) are consistent when balancing the value of the child to the family against the enormous concerns that parents have about protecting the child in an increasingly unsafe world. The specific approaches the mothers we interviewed take in raising their children can be understood as both a continuation of a tradition and a reaction to the dangers in society. Just as the mothers were valued when they were young, we will hear later in the chapter the high value they place on their sons.

When the Mothers Were Young

The mothers' stories about their own upbringing at this century's midpoint highlight many of the points that were just discussed. For example, one insurance claims adjuster with a high-school diploma learned at an early age the importance of family and hard work in getting ahead.

My parents raised me in a country setting. It was very peaceful, as we did not have the business that children have in town. We enjoyed life and played in the mud, made mud pies. We had cows in the field and worked hard. We had a garden where we got our food. We had an assigned job during the summer and, as I was one of the oldest, part of my job was to help wash clothes and take care of the kids. Every Friday we went to the grocery store, and every Sunday we went to church and then visited friends and relatives.

My parents thought that education was important. My mother constantly told us that she only went to the tenth grade, and she wanted to go farther. She stressed that she could have done more and helped us more if she had more education. My father only went to the sixth grade but he also stressed the importance of education. After school we always had to study first, then came dinner. We had to finish our studies before TV. There was discipline. You just sat there and listened, or Father would put you in line. Just having both parents there meant a lot.

A second mother, who earned a master's degree in education, shared her impressions of her parents.

My mother was a fiercely independent, strong Black woman and refused to let my father tell her what to do. She didn't work outside of the home until I was in the eleventh grade. Her role was to go to school to check on the children. My parents seemed equal in making decisions about things.

A number of messages are embedded in these brief statements. We hear about the importance of hard work and education. From the second mother, we hear about the strength of her mother and gain insight into her mother's relationship with her father. We see that a number of the mothers' mothers were home-based and placed high value on the family, education, and, in the first example, the role of the church and routine in family life. This older generation emphasized keeping tabs on the children and on the education they received. Finally, the mothers quoted, to various degrees, were able to fulfill the role they wanted for themselves while also longing for something more. (There is regret in the voice of the first mother's mother for what she was not able to accomplish.)

The next mother emphasizes the importance of religion, which was a significant factor in so many of these families. She has an advanced degree in nursing.

I probably got my strength from my parents. We were a very religious family. We had support from extended family. I saw my mom take care of her mom, and that taught me something. My parents taught us very little by word of mouth. They showed us. My dad did everything—carpenter, cook, etc. Most important was religion and then education. My parents were strong proponents of education because they did not have an opportunity to go to school. They could only go to eighth grade, and after that they would have had to pay, and their parents could not afford it. They were committed to the idea that we would have it when we came along.

Though these mothers for the most part are portraying life in rural America in the 1940s and 1950s, not all the parents experienced an idyllic small-town existence in the bosom of a two-parent family. One mother, a secretary with two years of college whom we highlight later in this chapter, learned about responsibility living in the city with just her mother.

I grew up in Brooklyn. My mother was a single parent and I was an only child. We didn't have much money. My son is an only child and I

am single. My mother was very active in the PTA. She stressed respon-
sibility—doing what needs to be done first and then you have your fun
later.

This next mother also spent time in a single-parent home, first her
mother's and then her father's.

I was born in a split home. My parents never lived together. My moth-
er had six kids and did not finish high school and her mother's mother
died when she was born. She was a strong woman, never went to
school but learned how to read and would read the newspaper. There
was a lot of love, and she encouraged us to be the best we could. I just
had a high level of self-esteem even though in the community in
which we were raised we never had role models. I didn't see my father
much until I was nine and went to live with him and his wife for three
years. He worked as a foreman and was very smart, though he had an
alcohol problem. He always encouraged us to be the best also."

RACIAL BIAS

In many cases, these mothers came from homes where they had to
overcome not only economic hardship, whether in an urban or rural
environment, but also racial bias. Segregation had its impact on them
when young and, as seen in their advocacy for their own sons more
recently, left an enduring message.

One mother with southern roots, a homemaker, told us:

Growing up in Alabama and coming through an educational system
that was separate but "equal," education was very important. There
were special messages about African Americans which you got from
segregation. You had to work very hard and most of your education
had to come from someplace other than the schools. I had to go out of
state for my graduate work because I could not go in Alabama.

A homemaker from the mid-Atlantic region recounted:

"I don't feel your parents have to be educated to produce successful
young Black male children. My parents consistently stressed educa-
tion, but when I grew up in Salisbury, Maryland, there were special
messages for Black females because of segregation. My father always
said you have to get an education because you are Black, and you are

*going to have to do better. You don't have to browbeat your own chil-
dren with the fact that they are Black, but occasionally you do have
to remind them.*

Another mother gave us her impressions about race and the opportunities open to her as an African American.

*"I didn't know about college until I went to high school. The people I
saw with responsible positions, except for my doctor, were White. All
of my relatives were farmers or maids or cooks. This is where I
thought life ended. My mother went to the tenth grade and my father
to the eighth, and he had a position as chef in a country club, which
was a prestigious position for a Black man back then. She insisted that
I read and learn math, and eventually she went back and got her GED
when she was forty and began working for the airlines. She always
told us, "You can do whatever you want to do."*

All three of these women were raised to believe that education was the
best way to pull oneself up—a belief they passed on to their children.

GENDER ROLES

As mentioned, working and sharing roles have been particularly
important aspects of African American family life. Because of the economic stress on the family, more Black than White women have worked
outside the home, and more men have spent time in the home. As such,
it has been necessary for mothers and fathers to share work roles and
housekeeping chores to greater degrees than Whites. Whatever had to be
done at home was taken care of by whomever was available.

These mothers reported that when their fathers were employed outside the home and their mothers worked at home, there was a fairly
traditional breakdown of the roles and chores. Mothers tended to take
care of the home and family, and fathers maintained the exterior of the
house when they returned from work and were the stricter disciplinarians, though there were exceptions.

Sharing chores was usually the case in situations where both parents
were working, or the father was at home while the mother was
employed outside. If roles were shared, a traditional outlook on values
(obedience, hard work, education) was still maintained.

In many of the families, the mother was also described as the primary disciplinarian, the one who set the tone, although she was not neces-

sarily the stricter parent. To understand this, we refer the reader to the earlier discussion about the centrality of the mother. To a large extent, she appears to have been the mediator in the family in terms of how the children were treated. It was rare, for example, for a father to interfere between the mother and the children, even if he felt she was too strict. More often, the reverse occurred. In fact, while some fathers were described as peripheral to the family, no mothers were. This was the situation regardless of the parents' employment status. This is not to say that fathers are not also vitally important to the life of the family or that descriptions we have of participation in the family are always accurate. Rather, it is to point out the mother's central position.

As we recount the mothers' impressions of their own upbringing, it should be noted that they observed difficulty in some family arrangements. In at least one case, we learned of the role conflict facing mothers of that era. Work was possible for Black women, but it came at great expense—they felt they were not being good mothers to their children when they left home, even if the father or another family member was there. One mother remembered, "My mother would work three or four months and then stop because she would feel guilty that she should be home with the children. So my father went out and worked."

As might be expected, in families with traditional divisions of labor between mothers and fathers, there was more often than not a similar breakdown of expectations for boys and girls. If sons and daughters were raised in families with equal responsibilities, the heavy and dangerous physical work, such as pushing a lawn mower, was left to males.

The way the mothers were raised, the messages about the importance of education, gender roles, religion, hard work, and the emphasis placed on the family have a definite impact on how these mothers raise their sons. We hear again and again the echoes of past generations in their own child-rearing practices.

A number of memorable messages emerge from the interviews with the mothers. Whether they are daughters of chefs, homemakers, doctors, or housekeepers, the emphases of their childhoods are clear.

1. Education was highly valued and encouraged in almost all of the families. These mothers, though, did not seem to be pushed quite as hard to pursue education as the fathers in the previous chapter. This is hard to interpret given that in 1960, when almost all of these parents were in school, the average African American female in the United States had more education (8.6 years) and was more apt to have attended college than the average African American male (with 7.7 years of education).[19] Although these mothers do not seem to have been pushed to excel to the same extent as the fathers, it may be because there was not as much of a need to push them.

2. The church played a central role in the lives of many families and is remembered fondly as being a key factor in the family's well-being. Church attendance was an organizing factor, both in the routines it established for the family and in the respect it created for a higher being and family.

3. The mothers' parents are described as hardworking people who emphasized industry and achievement for their daughters. The focus was on personal responsibility and the completion of chores, whether it was working in the garden, taking care of younger siblings, or making sure that homework was completed before the television was turned on. The sense is that the mothers were being watched constantly and were not able to "get away" with much.

4. Universally, these mothers' mothers were described as strong, nurturing, and central to the maintenance of the family. They were the equal of the fathers in terms of the strength they brought to the family and, in some cases, were more consistent, stricter disciplinarians and monitors of the children's behavior.

5. The mothers observed great role flexibility in their parents' lives. When fathers were not working, they were engaged in daily housekeeping. When mothers were employed outside the home, they often did less within the home. The sense is that the parents helped out in whatever way was necessary to maintain the home.

6. Segregation, especially in rural areas, took its toll on the academic achievement of the mothers' parents. The mothers were also taught that they might have to work a little harder because they were African American. Some mothers believe that because of segregation, their own mothers were not able to progress as far as they could have otherwise, and that while a few were able to overcome adversity and succeed, they did so at a later age.

How Mothers Raise Their Sons

Having described the family experience from the mothers' early years, we turn now to an exploration of how they have raised their sons. Because we believe that the early experiences leave an indelible impression, the metaphor of the tapestry used for the fathers seems appropriate for the mothers, too. Like the fathers described in the previous chapter, these mothers provide a fairly clear portrait of consistent hands-on child-rearing and parental concern about the future. Their responses show, for example, that they tended to monitor carefully their sons' schoolwork, especially in elementary school. As their sons reached high school, there was a reduction in monitoring, although three quarters of the mothers still kept some tabs on their sons' school-work.[20] They also reported encouraging their sons' academic achieve-ment to a very high degree throughout school and overseeing the amount of time their sons spent with friends in both middle and high school. The mothers greatly encouraged extracurricular activities throughout the school years.[21] Video games were perceived by some as a threat to the children's academic achievement and were regulated by over half the mothers during their children's school years. A few moth-ers saw them as educational.

The mothers, like the fathers, were concerned about their sons' futures. They see themselves, as did the fathers, as stricter and as clos-er monitors of homework than other parents in the neighborhood. They worried to some degree (64 percent of the mothers versus 55 per-cent of the fathers) about their sons' future graduate-school experiences and, because of race, about their sons being treated fairly in college (82 percent versus 75 percent of the fathers) and at a job (27 percent had a great deal of worry versus 13 percent of fathers). Given the prevalence of discrimination in society, these concerns are legitimate. A recent study of more than five hundred African American males found that almost one fifth had experienced discrimination in the workplace dur-ing the previous year.[22] Despite what the mothers report later in this chapter about their sons causing them few significant behavioral con-cerns throughout the secondary-school experience, over half of the mothers (52 percent) had some worries about their sons associating with the "wrong crowd" (75 percent of the fathers had such concerns).

Overall, comparing the mothers and fathers in terms of their level of involvement and concern can only be speculative, in part because the fathers we interviewed were more apt than the mothers (40 percent of whom were single) to share in raising their sons with the other parent. Such sharing would allow for a balancing of roles that a single mother would not be able to experience to the same degree. Fathers may tend to take a more active role with their sons (when compared with moth-ers) as the sons reach high school; at this stage, the male role often is seen as more important.

Mothers clearly have more concerns about the future (though there was some variation by question).[23] The greater involvement could be related to the mothers' being more central to the families than the fathers, or to the lack of a father in some families, which may leave the mother feeling that she needs to assume more responsibility. It also may be a reflection of the adage, "Mothers raise their daughters but love their sons." This saying, often repeated in the African American community, is meant to represent the son's special status with the mother. This unique relationship has been fostered for generations.

THE MOTHERS' TAPESTRIES

We asked the mothers during their interviews what they believed was most important in helping their sons achieve academically. The mothers universally adopted themes they had acquired in their childhood. Why is that? Our impression is that they considered their childhoods to be successful and wished to continue those parenting practices that worked. The mothers' memories (like the fathers') are that they were raised with clear values; when asked about rearing their successful children, they connect the two. Did the mothers receive the messages as clearly as they remember? Perhaps certain messages were more ambiguously conveyed or were conveyed with the normal, conflicting messages that parents unintentionally give. Whatever the reason for the consistency between past and present, it may be that having a successful child and being a successful parent lead parents to put a more positive face on parenting.

What we learn from these mothers about helping their children to achieve academically falls into two categories, general and specific. The general refers to the philosophical, that is, creating an environment at home where success is emphasized and where education and hard work are cherished; the specific revolves around preparation for school, how to handle academic challenges, and how to ensure a "good fit" between the school and the child. But most important, perhaps, is a distinct and overarching quality of the mothers, which we discerned when they talked about their sons: These sons are the center of their lives. The mothers have sacrificed time, money, and energy to ensure their sons' well-being. They are the mothers' number-one project, and they take enormous pride in their sons' academic and personal accomplishments. During the interviews, all of the mothers could have talked about their sons at much greater length, had time allowed. All have thought a great deal about their sons, including how they have reached their current levels of achievement and how to continue to foster their success. The mothers' enthusiasm for their sons is enormous.

SUCCEEDING ACADEMICALLY

The first two mothers represented here describe their philosophy.

I just saw myself as provider. I made sure I gave him the space to do his studies and made sure he had everything he needed. He did not have good study habits, and I was a nag for a while, but I stopped because he did well anyway. He always knew I would be there if he needed me.

The most important thing I did to help them succeed was not in academics. I wanted them to have a vision. I gave them attention and love— positive attention when they were good and spanking when they were bad. I did everything with them, and I treated them all the same. They all got the same allowance and all heard the same things. I told them if they want the nicer things in life, they will have to work hard.

Mothers took specific steps to prepare their children and to handle the vagaries of the educational system. This next mother changed her son's school, placed him on medication, and then supported and respected him by letting him make decisions.

I put a lot of emphasis on the school environment. If they enjoy school and you've made it clear that doing well is one of the things that will make you pleased with the child, then the child will do well. John, early on, had a lot of problems in school. He was a rebel; he wouldn't do his homework. I changed his school in the third grade to a Catholic school, which was great because it was smaller. They were able to help us identify that he had attention deficit disorder. He spent the next four years on Ritalin and excelled. It has had a lot of controversy, but for him it was a wonder drug. Once he settled down, he got his work done and he started to get good grades, which made him want to work more, which propelled him to the top of the heap. I also believe that the environment you pick for your child has to have kids in it who want to succeed or it won't work. Finally, I gave him as much choice as possible about school and activities. If he wants to be a doctor, I'll try and keep him focused by saying that this is what he has to do to get there. But it is his choice.

Other approaches included bolstering confidence, exposing children to a wealth of activities, and skill-building approaches. There was never a focus solely on skills without support for the whole child. Each of these next four mothers focuses on slightly different aspects of development.

I'll use this term that I learned at a business meeting—"creative learn ing." That was most important in nurturing my children. We had all the books and educational computer material at home. These were all things the kids could do on their own. Once you nurture and put the seed there, they don't see learning as a one-dimensional process only to be gained in a structured manner, but that learning is continuous and never ceasing.

I don't think I started out to make Bob a genius. When I was reading to his older sister and doing activities with her, things just carried over. He had a lot of books, different toys, and Lego sets. We took him to museums, art shows, karate, swimming lessons, and so on. I wanted him to have the things that I was unable to have.

Teaching the children to read at an early age was very important. I realized soon after they were born that parenting was a job, and I didn't have much to draw from in my experiences. But I taught them myself. I monitored their homework, and I told them that what they lacked in innate ability they could make up in commitment. I told them there's a lack of self-esteem in the Black race and that kind of gnaws at me, and they must feel good about themselves because of something they can do. Whatever they are told, they have complete control over their attitude and what they do with their time.

I am a strong believer in the well-rounded child, and there were things we did with our son when he was little to expose him to a number of different things. We wanted to develop his artistic abilities as well as his athletic and academic abilities. I'm a math person and would read to him, but that always rubbed me the wrong way. I thought that math was more important. So we would play math games when he was little, where he would have to count out the beans on his plate before eating them. But we tried to emphasize the whole person so he would feel confident in all his skills.

Not all parents had a long-term educational goal for their children. One mother did not focus on schooling. Rather, her goal was involving her son in activities.

I never had a grand plan to get him to be a good student. I approached it because I loved him and wanted him to have things. I provided a lot of activities, like sports, family trips, art lessons, talking together, and trying to be positive when things did not go well in school. I never started reading to him in the womb, as I know some of the other mothers here have done. I just approached it as part of general child-raising.

Some parents went to extraordinary lengths, placing their children's needs above their own.

I was a single parent and was determined that he was not going to be a regular kid. At age twenty three, living in Washington, there was a lot of drugs and stuff. They talked about the reading skills of public-school kids being terrible. But I was a product of public schools and didn't think that was the case. I was determined. I took off from work for three years and went to the school board and had them show me how to teach this child to read. I took him places, like the zoo, etc. I had a plan that I was going to have this person that would make a great contribution to society. I prayed a lot that I could do everything.

Unlike this parent, who defends the school system, many more denigrated it. One mother's answer reflects a distrust for the educational system that others also expressed. They were aware that for their child to get ahead, they would have to take personal responsibility.

I changed professions from nursing to education so I could spend more time with them. I read to them when they were in the crib. I did not trust other people to teach my children. I taught them the things they needed. During the summer, we would go to amusement parks, museums, and the zoo, anyplace that I thought was academically enriching for children." [Her husband is interviewed in depth on pages 55-57.]

While all of their sons were successful enough to get into the Meyerhoff Program, we wondered what particular academic barriers had to be bridged along the way. Most telling were the stories of those who had problems being appreciated by the school system, who were placed in lower classes because of racism, or who were misdiagnosed educationally. Parents repeated, again and again, the importance of being involved in their sons' schools and of fighting for them as a protective mechanism against an incorrect class placement, as happened in the next two examples.

I ran into at least six different incident in first grade through high school where they tried to hold him back. After one test they said I should lower my expectations for him, and I said, "Oh no I'm not," and he started to get top grades in calculus. They had wanted to put him in a technical school.

I had prepared him for school by his watching Sesame Street *and the other shows. He could read in kindergarten. But a friend told me to watch out for what they do to Black boys in school, so when he went into the first grade at a new school, I waited about eight weeks and then found out he had been put in a preprimer class. I knew that wasn't right. So I called the teacher twice, and she never returned my calls. Then I caught her at the school, and she said that he didn't have the vocabulary for the first grade. I knew that wasn't the case. If she had said he was socially immature, I could understand, but not vocabulary.*

We went back and forth with this for a few weeks until they finally put him in a higher reading class. I knew he did not need the pressure, though, so I pulled him out and home-schooled him. They called and told me I was breaking the law, and I challenged them to take me to court. A lady came out to watch me teach. I didn't know what I was doing, but I had given him all these books and he was working on a third-grade level. So they agreed finally to place him in a different school. At that point I decided to place him in a private school, where he stayed until high school.

Finally, the importance of religion to the family in dealing with academic crises is a consistent theme throughout the interviews (and is mentioned again in the case studies).

Being a single parent and having to work, I had to teach myself. I would come home exhausted, and I would do a lot of praying for myself and for them. I have to credit that with not having a lot of problems.

We had prayer time together, maybe not on a regular basis but on holidays. I think that helped us to deal with a lot of things.

RECOGNIZING SONS' TALENT: MOTHERS AND SCHOOLS

Parents are often excited about their children's abilities. These mothers, though, had children who displayed outstanding academic abilities when they finished high school. Not all the sons we studied had obvious natural ability, and many succeeded because of hard work and a supportive environment. We wondered if their talents were apparent to their mothers at a much younger age, and what part, if any, the mothers or other people played in helping the boys succeed.

My son always could put Rubik's Cube together quickly. When he was in second grade, I realized he was gifted because he always did well in science and math. After the fourth grade, I couldn't help him with his homework anymore.

I noticed when he was part of a play group that he seemed a little more alert. I bought him things to encourage that. Then he was placed in a more advanced kindergarten and he seemed to enjoy doing well in school.

Not all the mothers realized their sons' talent when their children were young.

I don't think I realized that he really had any gifts in science until he was in high school and he started to do well with it. But in retrospect, I can see now that he had been building and dismantling things, or going to the library to research topics, for years.

I didn't feel that he was really gifted, though he read a lot and was interested in a lot of things.

Along the way, many people, ranging from teachers and neighbors to extended family members and role models, helped their sons. We cannot emphasize this enough. A teacher, for example, who intervenes at a time when a son is especially susceptible can have an enormous, long-lasting impact. Many sons were helped by teachers who were strict taskmasters, held high expectations, or were supportive and understanding of their feelings. Some sons were strongly motivated to succeed by a desire to escape their economic circumstances. Parents also acknowledged their own role.

I think my son's success came from his teachers who encouraged him every step of the way.

I think the desire to escape the syndrome of poverty is what motivates

John. Also, he has a first cousin who went to an Ivy League school, and everyone looks up to that cousin.

The school environment, the home environment, and the spiritual environment the peer group, the relatives, everyone is cheering him on, and that has helped him to make it. My son really was strong with the Lord [the mother starts to cry], and so I'd say it has a lot to do with the church.

With my involvement in math, he was definitely going to be a mathematician. I felt that if you could do math and science, everything else would fall into place. He went all out at a state science fair, won it, and has been excited about it ever since. That reminded us to keep on encouraging him.

A single mother told us about the support engendered among the children she was raising, that they served as a source of support for each other:

Raising three children by myself, I know they would do anything for each other. I've told them that if I died today, I wouldn't worry about them because I know that they are so close that they'll help each other out.

Not all the mothers encouraged or nurtured their children academically at a very young age.

I, unfortunately, didn't do anything with him for the first four years of his life. When he was five, we moved to North Carolina, and I began teaching him things to help him for first grade. Then I went and talked to his teacher one day when he was in elementary school and heard how easy he was to teach and how good he was in math, and being on the honor roll. It just went from there.

I think both my sons did well because they wanted to. That is as basic as I can get because when you look around at the work that people do and the problems you see, it is almost the luck of the draw. You can give it everything, and it can still go wrong.

These quotes provide a representative sample of the themes the mothers offered in raising their sons. A number of education-related messages can be summarized here. Each message was mentioned by at least one fifth of the mothers, and those most frequently mentioned are listed first: (1) preparing their sons at home for school by providing academic challenges;[24] (2) making sure their sons were placed in the proper classes and advocating for them if they were placed below their ability; (3) helping with homework; (4) providing a nurturing environment; (5) encouraging their children to read; (6) talking to their teachers if there were problems with their sons' situation in school; (7) encouraging involvement in extracurricular activities; (8) taking children on field trips and to work; (9) encouraging the children to be the best that they could be; and (10) moving their sons to different schools when they thought the current school had failed them.

These messages are slightly different from the fathers' and provide an interesting insight into the different roles that mothers and fathers play in the home. Mothers appear to be more involved in preparing children educationally for school, perhaps a reflection of either the high number of mothers in the sample who are teachers themselves, the traditional role that women have played in the education of young children, or the greater likelihood that mothers spend more time with their children at an early age than fathers. The fathers, on the other hand, seem slightly more likely to be involved with their children by serving as advocates for them with the schools. Fathers also seem to be more involved in discipline-related matters, such as monitoring completion of schoolwork and limit setting (discussed later), the latter of which the mothers did much less often. To some extent in these families, although the mother was central, she deferred when the father was willing to take a firm position with a child. In a few cases, the fathers insisted on being the primary parent with the son, and the mothers acquiesced. If the father's presence was not felt, the mother filled the gap and made sure that the son was monitored.

The mothers also credit extended family with supporting their efforts to educate their children. This is consistent with other research on African American families.

General Child-rearing Issues

What about the other, nonacademic side of a child's life? We asked the mothers about challenges they face in raising a Black male, whether they see differences in raising a Black male and a White male, and how they educated their sons about sex and drugs. Finally, we wondered about the importance of family rituals in providing a structure for child-rearing.

As is evident from the previous chapters, the task of raising an African American male is daunting. Regardless of the environment in which the sons were raised, from the predominantly Black urban areas to racially integrated suburban communities, concerns were expressed.

RACE AND BEING MALE

The mothers echoed many of the themes the fathers raised: first, treatment by the police poses a potential threat to their sons' well-being; second, treatment by other Blacks can also be problematic.

I don't worry about him in my own circle, but I worry about him in relationship to the laws of society. I am always afraid that when my boys go out that some police officer is going to stop and hurt them. I worry that someone will accuse them of doing something just because they happen to be Black and in a certain place. I always tell them, "Do not be in a situation that can be suspect. If you go into the bathroom and you know someone is in there using dope, get out of there. If they call you chicken, get out anyway. You cannot be in a situation where there is any wrongdoing. Society has given you that dishonor. That is the burden you carry."

Another mother tries to prepare her son to be on guard, regardless of whom he is with or where he is.

Racism is a two-way street. My son is now in Florida. Maryland is in the South but not as much as Florida. When he is driving back and forth, I worry. I warn him to not do anything that might make him be pulled over because you never know where it is going to end up. But I also tell him that racism is a Black issue because most of the crimes on the news are Black people attacking other Black people. That part of racism is that Black people don't see the value in their own. That's why we're victims. You have to value yourself before anyone else will. My fear when he works late is not that he is in danger from the police, but that Black people might stop him.

Mothers, as in the examples given in these next two cases, warn their sons that they are easy targets not only because of their gender and skin color, but also because of the cars they choose to drive.

When my son started to drive, we bought him a Toyota. There was a great deal on a used BMW with a sunroof, but there was no way we could get him that kind of car.

He wants to go certain places, and I tell him no. If you are in the general vicinity and something happens, you are guilty as far as society is concerned. We have a Pathfinder, which he can't drive because he'll be stopped. Even my husband was stopped driving it. Society is very cruel and, unfortunately, all Black men have to deal with it.

Some mothers are unsure how to voice the enormous concerns they feel. They do not want to "baby" their sons, yet there is a thin line for a parent raising a teenager between educating him and providing too much protection. One mother said, "I worry about making Jack a mama's boy because I was overprotective of the things that were going on around him. It bothered him, and so his dad and I slowly cut the apron strings."

As the mothers talked about their concerns, we wanted to know whether they had to be particularly assertive in finding resources for their sons as young Black males. One mother summed up the feelings of many:

You really have to be resourceful to get what your child needs. When you are raising a Black child, you always have to tell them about the obstacles that will be there just because they are Black and to know that a White child comes with a ticket already. You have to let them know that their achievement will not be looked upon the same way as a White child's achievement. They have to be prepared for that and never give up, keep on pursuing if there is something you want, even in the face of obstacles.

Two mothers spoke of the attitudes some Whites had toward Blacks:

In the school system, we have predominately White young female teachers. African American males are a threat because of their posture and how they get upset if you get in their face. When the teachers get close to them and the Black males react, they are a threat. So our males are perceived differently from the time they are eight. We're trying to teach our kids to be their own person and express themselves, whether it is with their hair or their clothes, but they are held to a White standard.

It is so bad that they cannot go to the mall if there is a group of them. They are followed to see if they are shoplifting or whatever else. And my son is one of the ones that does not look thuggish, he looks clean-

cut, and he knows he won't get hassled as much if he is with a female. That doesn't happen to Whites.

One mother gave an opposite opinion, that Whites believe they encounter more impediments than Blacks, at least in the job market.

The son of one of my White friends applied for a job on campus, and he has a Black-sounding name. When he appeared for the job, they turned him down, saying it was reserved for helping out Blacks. The mother was very upset and said that Whites aren't being treated fairly now.

The mothers handled discussions of race with their sons by emphasizing that they had to cope with and overcome the challenges that are presented. We see this, as noted earlier, as a key issue in the sons' development into successful students. Listen as these next mothers acknowledge inequities in society while urging their children to be themselves and to keep on trying to overcome.

I talk about race even to the point of how the justice system handles issues of crime, keeping them aware that it is not fair. The point, though, is that there is nothing you can do about it. You have to learn to deal with the issue and still get what you want out of it.

I tell my son that when he and a White person walk through the door, the first thing on your face is your skin. You have a strike against you already. So your credentials have to be top-notch.

For one mother, skin color was a mediating factor in what her son experienced.

I can't really recall him having any problems but it might be because with his father being so light-skinned and with me being mixed-blood, the children are sometimes confused for Hispanic or Italian. So they really don't know what they are. The only problem I can remember is when he heard some White guys talking about Black guys, and they didn't realize he was Black. He let them know he was Black.

LIMIT-SETTING

Recognizing that child-rearing is not an easy task, regardless of the academic acumen of the student or the economic status of the family, we asked what specific challenges the mothers had encountered. A single mother provides the first example.

Raising my son has been a special challenge. He's never been one to just accept something because you say so. He's got to have a reason, and it has to be negotiated. My life has not been what most people would think is necessary to raise a child in a stable environment. I've been through two marriages, and in between we have had some rough times, which left him opportunities to stray while I finished college. His sister basically took care of him in the evenings. Trying to keep him family-focused, and with the dialogue going back and forth, were what kept him from going off.

Another single mother also described her trials.

It was tough, though it was just regular adolescence . . . especially a male that feels like he wants to become more independent, and he is not getting enough space. That can be real dangerous, especially for a single mother.

These two mothers are describing typical and significant problems of single parenthood. With the first mother, the lack of consistent parental presence was compensated for by constant communication and by having a sibling assist with monitoring. From the second mother, we hear about dealing with an adolescent male as he matures into manhood. When a male figure is available, this potential developmental conflict is often mitigated by a mother who pulls back and an older male who becomes more involved in parenting. But when an older male is not available, the mother may struggle with the seemingly conflicting goals of encouraging manhood and providing a level of protection. The adolescent male, in turn, has to struggle with loyalty to his mother and the need to prove himself in the community as a man who can take care of himself.

Sometimes avoiding the neighborhood may be the best choice. A different single mother told us how she stood by her son when he was ostracized by the neighbors' children.

He was teased a lot [because he was doing well academically]. They also teased him because he didn't have a father. The children would say to him, "You must be a fag." So he stayed away from those kids and stayed in the house. I would ask him why he wouldn't go out and play and he would say, "I don't like those kids," and I would support him in that.

With all the mothers, the approaches to preparing their sons for the world tended to fall into two categories, general and specific. Broadly, mothers advise educating children and trusting them to make their own decisions. Specifically, they teach them to avoid situations that have even the appearance of danger because a Black man will automatically be a suspect; to back away from situations that look dangerous; to understand the dangers inherent in drug use; to learn from the negative experiences of family members who have drug or alcohol problems; and to pick their friends wisely.

Three different examples are provided that illustrate how mothers prepare their sons.

I think some of the major concern was whether he was going to fall in with the wrong group. I knew what I could provide at home—my concern was with the outside world. We tried to teach him things so that when he left the house, he would have something to fall back on. We tried to explain what was out there and what would happen if he chose certain paths. When he was young, I used to tell him to tell the other kids that it was his mother who wouldn't let him do something.

I think more in terms of trust. You have taught them things and given them examples of what might happen. After that, it is a matter of trusting their judgment. I have told him to stay away from drugs and to be selective about friends. So far so good. I worry most about Black-on-Black crime, and every Sunday I go to church to pray for guidance and protection.

I taught him early on you cannot be a perpetrator of a crime. You cannot steal. You cannot harm anyone. When he was fifteen, I heard a statistic that one in four males in Baltimore was not going to live to be twenty-five, so we moved to the suburbs. When he went to the city, I told him to avoid certain areas, to park his car where it was well lit.

TALKING SPECIFICALLY ABOUT SEX AND DRUGS

In part because African American males are such an at-risk population, we were especially interested in strategies for dealing with sex and drugs. Baltimore, where some of the males in our study have lived or have friends, has a particularly high teenage pregnancy rate and faces drug abuse issues on a level similar to other major urban areas. These facts wear on the mothers we interviewed. They are constantly worried about the problems of the city and the dangers that await their sons. This first mother prepared her son by speaking to him as if he was a responsible adult.

I never talked to him as if they were little people. As issues came up about sex and drugs, we talked about them. With sex I said there would be a time when they would make the decision, and I trust you will make the right choice.

Another mother openly acknowledged to her son that he would have sex and tried to ready him for it.

One time when he was in the tenth grade, I let him spend some time in the house with a young lady and he ended up with a hickey on his neck. I asked him what he thought her father would think if he saw that on her neck and knew that he did it. Her parents would look down on him for doing it. Our discussions were about safe sex, and don't do it in the park where you are going to get arrested. With crack cocaine, I told him about the statistics and that he could get addicted immediately. He told me he could get it down on the corner, and if he had wanted it, he could have had it already. You have to be open enough to have these conversations and bold enough to voice your opinion and listen to their opinion, rather than say no and degrade them.

A third mother, raising a son and daughter alone, describes the dangers her children faced every day.

I told them that we live in a Black community because I wanted them to know where they came from and maintain some Blackness. But the drugs were there. They came home saying, "We were walking down the street and someone tried to sell us crack." They've had to be confronted with that. And there was a guy who lived down the street and was an engineering major in college and was shot in a drive-by shooting.

My son was teased in the neighborhood because he did not have a father. I supported him when he didn't want to go out and play with those boys. I raised my children the same way I was raised. Education was it in my house.

Sometimes preparation does not always stave off problems. When they were encountered, this mother found a unique way to handle them.

My husband and I talked about crime, sex, and drugs, a long time before they encountered that situation. My husband's father was an alcoholic, so he would tell tales about how he was treated when he was young and what happened to people in his family. Those were things the kids learned they definitely did not want to have happen to them.

One time he was with some kids riding around in a car and smashing mailboxes, which is a federal offense. He said he didn't do it, but he was guilty by association. Another time, when he was ten, he was with a boy who stole a toy from a store and was taken and interrogated at the police station. Again he was guilty by association. Finally, when he was in high school, I got him a beeper so I would know where he was. People see him with a beeper and think he's doing other stuff, but I wanted it so I could beep him anytime and know where he was. That is how I gave him freedom but also kept a check on him.

One mother repeated a very basic message she had given her son:

About sex, I told him, "You do the crime, you gotta do the time." I'm not going to take care of a grandchild. If I had wanted another child, I would have had one. You're responsible for what you do.

FIGHTING

How does one raise a young man today to protect himself without running the risk of getting seriously hurt? The mothers agreed on the importance of their sons' being able to stand up and defend themselves but did not want them getting a reputation for starting fights. This is a complicated message to convey, and these next two mothers have different approaches to it.

I told my son that I did not want him to pick fights, but I wanted him to stand up for himself. If you don't fight back when you are picked on, you get a weak reputation.

When it came to fighting, we tried to show that you could solve problems without getting physically involved. There is a way of discussing

issues and coming to an agreement. You might not get what you want,
but a discussion is better than an argument.

One of the most unusual stories we heard about monitoring a son's
behavior while teaching about fighting came from a mother who
accompanied her son to a confrontation in the park one Saturday afternoon.

One problem in middle school stemmed from his getting taunts for
being biracial. We always told him the truth never hurts. But he was
going to get into a fight over this anyway. The other youngster was of
Asian descent. They had planned to meet in a park and fight it out. I
was happy he was able to tell us about this big event. So we piled into
the car, and I thought I better take the dog along. My husband wasn't
with us.

I figured I had to monitor what was going on. I could see there was
really no way out of this without my son losing respect. So they duked
it out for a while and then I stopped it. The next day we went over to
the boy's house and talked to the parents, and the boys were sent out
to the garage to talk about it. Everything got straightened out and they
became good friends.

Teaching responsible behavior and having open communication
about sex and drugs were the ways these mothers handled these issues.
They also acknowledged their sons' potential to be targets, either
because of their race or if they associated with the "wrong crowd." The
mothers' ability to help raise a man to protect himself is also discussed.
As we heard from the fathers, they often interceded, taking over with
child-rearing at adolescence. For the mothers with no male figure in
their sons' lives, this option was not available, and it led to a number of
concerns.

FAMILY RITUALS

All the mothers mentioned some commonly repeated patterns that
provided a sense of family. Family rituals, as we described earlier,
become the glue that holds a family together and give it a sense of identity. Rituals have been defined as "a symbolic form of communication
that, owing to the satisfaction that family members experience through
its representation, is acted out in a systematic fashion over time."[25]
With these mothers, the sense of family was built through a variety of

activities: talking during a weekly car ride, eating meals together, attending church, spending holidays together. Through repeated patterns of interaction, families build cohesion and reinforce the structure and importance of the family.

Rituals continued for some families even after divorce. A single mother told us, "We have been divorced for eight years, but I have always referred to him as a hands-on father. We still do many things together as a family and have even gone skiing together, which my friends think is weird. But we are very supportive, and I think this has made a difference."

The Child-rearing Experiences of Single Versus Married Mothers

Perhaps one of the most important points we learned from our survey of mothers was the number of similarities between the parenting practices of single and married mothers and the types of concerns they held for their children. (Differences in the family environment are discussed in the next chapter.) Specifically, there were no statistically significant differences in the mothers' reports about the amount of encouragement they gave their sons in academic achievement and in outside activities, or the amount of monitoring of homework or the types of friendships their sons formed throughout school. Further, the mothers were equally concerned about their sons' futures. The only significant differences found were that single mothers were more apt to attend school programs than married mothers, and married mothers were more likely to help with course selection and to monitor video-game playing.

What if we consider college education as a factor? When college-educated versus non-college-educated single mothers are considered along with college-educated and non-college-educated married mothers (a comparison we make with the sons in the next chapter), two significant differences are found that may be suggestive of other parents in similar situations. Unmarried college-educated mothers report monitoring their children's studying in elementary school more than other mothers, and unmarried non-college-educated mothers are less supportive of extra-curricular activities than other mothers.[26] For the first finding, it may be that these college-educated mothers deeply appreciate the importance of education and have no other parent in the house to help them to monitor the homework. As a result, an educational imperative falls on their shoulders. For the second finding, we believe that it is the non-college-educated single mothers who may have the most demands on their time and be least able financially to afford extracurricular activities and to have the time or transportation necessary to involve their sons in such activities.

We wish to interpret these findings as showing that, for these academically successful sons, the marital status of the mother does not seem to predict what types of child-rearing practices are used. In other words, single-parent status, in and of itself, does not appear to be a barrier to academic success for the child (though when it is accompanied by economic hardship, as we discussed earlier, the challenges are even greater).

Case Studies

Two case studies are included to add further to the understanding of the cases we are presenting. We chose to include these two cases—one of a married mother, the second of a single mother—to illustrate two different family tapestries that have produced academically successful sons.

CULTURE AND A SENSE OF SELF: A MARRIED MOTHER

Our first mother, born into poverty, is married, has a college degree, and works as a computer specialist. Her husband is an academic administrator with a graduate degree. Thus, both parents have at least a college degree, and one has a background in education. Their son was in the first class of the Meyerhoff Program at UMBC and is currently pursuing his doctorate at an Ivy League university. He has faced many temptations, but because of his strong upbringing, rooted in his culture, he avoided them.

I grew up in New York in the projects, and both my parents worked. They put their dreams into my brother, sister, and me. To call them supportive is too simple to describe what they did for us. They believed we needed exposure to everything in the world, and the sky was the limit in what you could accomplish. They let us know we could make mistakes and learn from them. The expectations ranged from what you did as a family member to how you acted when you left the family. We moved from East Harlem when I was ten to the Bronx, which gave me a sense of upward mobility. We were exposed to ballet, violin, and music. Both of my parents came into the marriage working and had worked since they were very young. They measured themselves by being able to bring in the bacon.

We had jobs in our house, so when our parents came home from work, there were certain things we had to do. As far as discipline was concerned, I can only remember one time when I was hit by my father and a few times when I was hit by my mom. All my father had to ask was, "Did you do that, Mary?" and that was enough. We were raised where the girls were expected to do the household thing, and my brother had to do less. My brother could go out at night and my sisters and I had to stay in.

We see that this mother was reared in a family that placed a great value on getting ahead and on preparing the children for a life of responsibility.

WHAT HELPED HIM SUCCEED ACADEMICALLY?

In raising my son, he was given all the things I was given and a little more. I always knew he was going to go to college. I wrote a letter to my best friend when he was born about all of my dreams and what I wanted to do for him. My son and I would go out, and I would point out things to him and give him a vocabulary for everything. I always tried to look at the world through his eyes and listen to what he was saying. Whatever we did outside we would then find in a book to reinforce it.

He did well academically because we tried very hard to give him a sense of self, and from an African perspective the sense of self cannot be separated from the community. He was always reminded that behind his name were his grandparents, aunts, and uncles and that there was open communication with all the family. The extended family knew about his accomplishments and would write or telephone him to compliment him. His music teacher, who was a Black male, was very influential. His teachers in the first, second, and third grades who were European were some of the best he had because they understood exactly how we were living our lives and how important being African was to us and respected that.

This importance of culture is highlighted and is reinforced by extended family. A sense is gained from this mother that a number of influential people were positively involved with her son. Yet when we asked her about concerns in raising her son, we also heard about specific problems within the family that had to be overcome. Again, an emphasis on African culture proved invaluable. It added stability to the family tapestry.

CONCERNS ABOUT RAISING AN AFRICAN AMERICAN MALE

Knowing what types of problems existed in my family when I was growing up, and knowing that I had lost my brother to violence when he was nineteen, there was a wariness that settles in, and I was determined that we would not lose any more of our family. This decision was made with the consciousness of what racism is and that we would protect and prepare our children. We sought alternatives and substituted Kwanzaa for Christmas. When he was born, we whispered his name into his ear so that his ancestors and the Creator would protect him, and then we had to wait eight days to see if this child had decided that he wanted to stay on earth with us. From that point we decided that we could never be lazy and sit back and let him be educated the way European children were. Our concern was that he could fall victim to what has happened to African American males as they are being destroyed by society.

When the decision was made to come to UMBC, it was between here and [an Ivy League school]. We had to pull on all those things that we had taught him in the past, our lifestyle, so that we could feel comfortable with making the decision to continue the bonding with African Americans that would occur here. We felt he should not go far away until he had all that he needed so he would never fail.

He is lucky. He has been in a predominantly Black [class from] preschool through high school and he has been very much his African self, so much so that he was able to choose a European friend and maintain a sense of self.[27]

SEX AND DRUGS

As far as sex and drugs, I always tell him that if you get involved, your body is going to be infected. My husband always said that if my son got anyone pregnant, he would stop school, get married, and go to work. That scared him. He has been around students his age doing cocaine. We tell him to stay away from certain places. He has been taught to defend himself, but he does not have the right to initiate anything.

Clear messages are given about the importance of culture, the family, and personal responsibility. This mother took a protective stance from the day her son was born because she was aware of the dangers her son would face.

THE "REAL WORLD": A SINGLE MOTHER

A second mother works as a secretary, having completed two years of college. She was a single mother for much of her son's early years and remarried when he left for college. She also was raised by a single mother who was poor. Unlike many of the mothers we interviewed, she was not very invested in her son's early education nor did she believe that he was especially talented when he was young.

I was raised in Brooklyn by a single mother who stressed working first before having fun. My parents divorced when I was in third grade. I do remember that my father was more lenient and my mother more the disciplinarian. She took care of the inside and he the outside. He taught me how to ride a bike and roller-skate. After the divorce, she had to do everything. My mother was very protective of me, and she taught me responsibility. She also liked to fix things and tried to encourage me in that area, though I am not mechanically inclined. She did not stress academics, though I have with my son.

THE SON'S ACADEMIC SUCCESS

The message this mother received was that she had to be responsible for herself, and education was not necessarily the route to self-fulfillment. When she began raising her son, she took a different approach, perhaps born of the realization that more was necessary to succeed.

Even in kindergarten I told him that he was going to college. I always stressed that he was going to do 100 percent. I always talked to the teachers. I had some problems with placement for him. In the fifth grade, I thought the work was too easy for him, and he was having behavior problems. So I went to the principal and asked that he be moved up, and if the work was too difficult, he could be moved back.

I did not check his homework every night, as some parents do. I did random checks. I based everything on the report card. I told him if he did not understand something, to ask the teacher. In the seventh grade he began having problems with algebra, so I asked a neighbor who was a professor at Morgan State to help him. He did not want to be tutored, but I dragged him there each week. I also told him he had to study more than what the teacher told him, so I signed him up for classes at the Science Center. I thought he was going to learn to do things on his own because the world is so hard on African American males.

He has done well in school, but he still needs to learn to seek help before the roof caves in. He's had his problems, particularly in middle school, where he would play hooky for the first two hours of school some days. I had to crack down on that. He is not gifted in math. But he has always had an interest in how things worked electronically and mechanically. He came in third in a science contest in fifth grade and participated in the National Science Olympics.

HOW AN AFRICAN AMERICAN MALE IS VIEWED BY SOCIETY

Each child, despite commonalities of race and gender, has a different personality and on that basis may be more or less likely to have certain experiences. Because of her son's preference for being alone his mother is not as concerned about him, but she is very concerned about the way he is viewed by society.

I often wonder why my son is doing well. I keep saying that we are blessed. I always taught him that he is part of a family and what he does reflects on the family. I also taught him that other people from our history have died and shed blood so that he can attend school or walk in certain neighborhoods.

I have not worried about him getting in with the wrong crowd because he is a loner. But I worry about Black-on-Black crime and that he could be in the wrong place at the wrong time. In raising a Black male, I had to not only worry about the academics but also his self-esteem and pride in his race. It is rough on the Black male. Society automatically thinks they don't achieve, that they are the rabble-rousers. We only hear the negatives, not the positives.

RESPECTING WOMEN, AVOIDING DRUGS

Discussions about sex and drugs were handled in a matter-of-fact manner.

Talking to him about sex and drugs has not been a problem. I've told him that he should respect women. With drugs, it has been more a matter of sitting down with him and watching the news and then talking about it.

Both of these mothers emphasized openness about issues, preparing their sons for the "real world," having high expectations for them, and providing the protective umbrella of African culture. They also clearly appreciate their sons' accomplishments. The mothers are keenly aware of society's dangers, of how few Black males "make it," and that their sons have been fortunate enough to be among the few who have.

Summary

Based on what we learned from the mothers about how they raised their sons to handle the nonacademic aspects of their lives, we can provide a brief summary. Although the mothers were asked the same questions as the fathers, their answers varied somewhat.

It is important to note that we gained a number of impressions about the mothers' relationships with their sons. They more than the fathers seemed to do things *for* their sons, while fathers either did things *with* their sons or offered advice from the sidelines. This is consistent with the adage "Mothers raise their daughters but love their sons." The mothers seemed very involved in their sons' lives. This may be a prerequisite for good child-rearing. But they also stood aside when they felt the father, or another man, could be helpful.

Compared with the fathers, the mothers placed greater emphasis on nurturing and less emphasis on disciplining and on the extent to which their sons have to deal with life's unfairness. It also appears that the mothers told fewer stories to their sons; instead, the emphasis was on open communication. The mothers appear to "do" while fathers appear to teach.

1. Develop a broad philosophy of life. The mothers described their efforts to create an atmosphere at home where values were discussed. This is part of a preparatory stage that the mothers see as important to handle the ups and downs of life.

2. Develop a relationship that encourages open discussion of issues. Mothers emphasized their ability to talk to their sons about key issues in their lives in a nonjudgmental way. At the same time, it was clear that they conveyed definite values. This is a difficult balance to strike for any parent but one that is key if communication channels are to stay open between a parent and child.

3. Teach specific ways of handling situations that arise. Mothers taught their children what situations to avoid, as well as what to do when such problems arise as drugs being offered or fights being started.

4. Talk about race-related matters. Mothers, like fathers, had many concerns about the situation of African American males and taught their children to be wary of the police, about discrimination at the hands of Whites, and about Black-on-Black crime. They also described how they intervened in the educational lives of their children when they believed their sons were being held back because of their race and gender.

5. Understand one's own family and learn about African culture. Whereas the fathers emphasized history, the mothers placed a slightly greater emphasis on culture and the workings of the family. For many mothers, African culture was a bulwark around which to build the sense of family. The mothers also made the sons aware that how they conducted themselves in the community reflected on the family, and that they should act accordingly.

6. Set high standards. Achievement in nonacademic aspects of life was underlined when mothers described their expectations of their children in terms of behavior and gaining employment.

7. Maintain family rituals. As the unifying influence, or glue, of the family, mothers placed great emphasis on family togetherness. Spending time together—at church outings, while driving, during sporting events—became a important occasion to engage in meaningful conversation, build a sense of unity, and convey values.

8. Maintain religious beliefs. When faced with problems that seemed insurmountable or incomprehensible, the mothers often turned to the church or to prayer for solace. The church also played a preventive role by serving to unite the family.

The Mothers' and Fathers' Suggestions

In addition to capturing the broad themes that the mothers employed at home to enhance their children's lives educationally, we also learned about the many specific educational techniques that the mothers and the fathers used to helped their sons become academically successful. (Fathers were more likely to describe broad themes, such as encouraging enrollment in challenging courses, setting high standards, etc.) We encourage other parents to consider the specific techniques listed below.

1. Focus on reading.
   - Read to your children when they are very young.
   - Take them to the library.
   - Get them their own library cards.
   - Have them read aloud to you often.
   - Encourage them to read anything, from street signs to comic books.

- Start teaching them to read when they are young enough to talk. (One father taught his three-year-old son the alphabet the day before an entrance exam into a special program.)

2. Focus on vocabulary words.
   - Have books on tape available.
   - Name objects when children point to them. (One mother, remembers saying, "Yes, that is a green leaf," in order to name the object and teach the color.
3. Discuss everything that you see in the world.
4. Look up what you see in books to draw connections. One mother, when unable to answer her son's question about the moon, went with him to the encyclopedia to find the answer.
5. Have workbooks available as soon as the children can hold a crayon.
6. Focus on math and science.
   - Prepare children for school with simple problems.
   - Send children to special science programs over the summer.
   - Start children on math at a very young age. (One father took coins and lined them up to show multiplication. One mother awarded ten correct math answers with a trip to McDonald's. She called them math games rather than math problems.)
7. Encourage children to ask people they meet questions about themselves (e.g., "What kind of work do you do?").
8. Use computer and video games that will enhance learning.
9. Talk to the children on an adult level, so they learn more.
10. Answer "why" questions with complete answers.
11. Proofread the children's schoolwork.
12. Have them watch *Sesame Street.*
13. Return to the same places at different points in their lives because they can learn from the experience in different ways each visit.
14. Provide tutors when needed.
15. Take the children to the zoo, museums, amusement parks, different cities, and on picnics.
16. Involve them in swimming, karate, art lessons, music lessons, team sports, church activities, and computer camps.
17. Buy them Lego sets, a chemistry set, electric toys, books, puzzles, building blocks, dinosaur toys, art supplies, Rubik's Cube, chess and checker games, and anything else educational.
18. Talk to them about the activities they are involved in and the educational items you have bought them.
19. Try to be creative about everything you do with them.
20. Finally, encourage and support them in their learning experiences.

Revisiting the Six Components of Successful Parenting

These components help us understand the approaches the mothers take with their sons.

CHILD-FOCUSED LOVE

The mothers, to a greater extent than the fathers, approach child-rearing with a self-sacrificing attitude that lends itself to a great deal of child-focused behavior.

STRONG LIMIT-SETTING AND DISCIPLINE

The mothers set strong limits but seem less likely to discipline in situations where the father is present, leaving that to him.

CONTINUALLY HIGH EXPECTATIONS

The children were constantly pushed to achieve academically. They were told they could achieve and often had to explain why they were not receiving exemplary grades. Teachers were contacted so that bridges could be built to schools and communication kept open if there were problems. Nonacademic behavior was also expected to be exemplary. When it was needed, the children, were pushed to reach the highest level of their ability.

OPEN, CONSISTENT, AND STRONG COMMUNICATION

The mothers emphasized this component more than any other. They communicated every way they could, talked with their sons, and tried to find out what was happening in every aspect of their lives. The importance of communicating was highlighted, as was remaining open about the kinds of issues a son would raise.

POSITIVE RACIAL IDENTITY AND POSITIVE MALE IDENTITY

The mothers taught their sons clear and important messages about discrimination. The mothers are keenly aware of the conflicting messages their sons are exposed to, as demonstrated in the words of the mother whose quote begins this chapter—there are pressures on African American males not to succeed. The fathers appeared more comfortable in discussing male identity and used their own experiences as a teaching tool.

DRAWING UPON COMMUNITY RESOURCES

The mothers drew upon the church and their extended families in meeting the parenting demands they faced. Schools, in turn, were described as helpful in some instances. The overall impression is that the African American community, in particular, was helpful in their sons' success.

It is clear that some children needed more guidance, and others needed very little. Despite enormous talent in some cases, hardships still had to be overcome. Other sons were described as less naturally gifted and, as a result, had to work harder to achieve. There are specific attitudes and approaches the mothers credit with having contributed to their sons' high achievement. This seemed to cut across the child-rearing practices of single as well as married mothers, with the two groups looking generally similar in their approaches. Certainly, other parents have tried the same things and been less successful, so there are no guarantees that what has worked for some children will work for all. Perhaps most reassuring is that there are no great surprises in what we have learned. Hard work as a student or a parent (coupled with advocacy for the child) pays off.

These mothers provide a consistent, hands-on approach to parenting their sons that demands excellence, acknowledges discrimination, focuses on competing and surviving in a biased society, and views the family and the local community as major resources. Their approach is child-centered in that parents listen to their children and try to enter their world and understand it, while also placing realistic demands on them. It is also a flexible approach, often involving the role sharing that, out of economic and social necessity, has been the standard in African American families.[28] Perhaps most important, these sons are at the center of their mothers' lives—they are seen as a treasure, a gift that the mothers have invested in and in which they take enormous pride. Hailing from diverse backgrounds and living in both two-parent and single-parent households, these parents kept their eye on the prize—their sons. And they continue to do so as these young men reach adulthood.

What we see in the next chapters, the interviews with the sons, is that while these sons are special in many ways, their parents do not always know what is going on with them. We are left with a more complex view of child-rearing as we hear from the primary focus of the book, the sons.

4

The Son's Perspective

My parents probably worry about me every night when I go out. For example, if I am in the elevator with that White woman, is she going to clutch her purse closer to herself? Am I going to be shot because I am mistaken for somebody else when I go to that club? When you raise a Black child, you are raising an endangered species. I don't have anything guaranteed to me. I have to work for it ten times as hard.

We were the only two Black students in the high school who wanted to take the honors classes, who wanted to go for the more challenging courses. The other Black students looked down on us. "Why are you guys trying to be like that? Why are you guys trying to be White?" The way to overcome that is to understand what you have to deal with, and not become blindsided or distraught over people's ignorance, perceptions. I hope that this book will shed a little bit more light on why we really need to nurture the talent in our children.

A White male doesn't have to fight society's view of you. They're already saying, "Oh, well, you can be a doctor, you can be this." But if you're a person of color, you have to prove that you can excel, can be a doctor. It's sort of like you're assumed guilty until proven innocent.

In this first of two chapters focused on the sons, we explore the challenges they faced and why they think they succeeded where so many other African American males have not. In many regards, their messages are similar to those we heard from the parents, but with a different resonance and emphasis. New perspectives are voiced about challenges faced and about factors leading to success that the parents either were not aware of or did not think were particularly important.

This chapter highlights the varied nature of the family, the challenges facing each son in school and the neighborhood, and the factors that helped the sons succeed. In the two preceding chapters, commonalities across the families were emphasized. We are now ready to portray in more detail the unique tapestries that constitute the personal stories of individual sons.

Previous research on Black adolescent males has focused on their deficits, including their academic, social, and behavioral problems.[1] A new body of research, however, focuses on the strengths, resilience, and empowerment of Black youth. The literature regarding strengths emphasizes the positive resources young people bring to bear in coping with difficult lives and hazardous environments. For instance, involvement in activities that draw upon latent skills and talents (for example, leadership skills or artistic talent) has been found to be related to positive development among urban youth.[2] The literature on resilience focuses on high-risk youth who succeed in life despite unfavorable odds. One key factor that leads to their success is the support they receive from at least one primary adult—whether inside the family or in the larger community.[3] Finally, the empowerment-related research model examines ways in which youth can develop an inner sense of competence and an enhanced sense of power in order to achieve significant personal goals in the face of environmental obstacles. One model suggests that it is especially important to provide young people with a positive, inspiring belief system that focuses beyond the self and emphasizes developing capabilities, contributing to others, and a strong support system.[4]

We first discuss in this chapter four subgroups of sons in order to portray as clearly as possible the varying life- and family-related contexts present for the sons. The subgroups differ based on family structure (single-parent versus two-parent) and parents' education (college-educated versus not college-educated). These subgroups reflect basic demographic differences that may pose distinct challenges (and opportunities) in raising African American sons.[5] Significantly, none of these challenges represents an insurmountable barrier.[6] In the concluding portion of the chapter we discuss the common parenting practices the sons experienced, and what they say their parents did that worked.

In considering the different subgroups of sons, the marital status of the parents is important because sons who live with a parent who has been divorced or has never married will likely face challenges different from those facing sons in two-parent families.[7] When the father is absent from a household, for example, the mother is likely to bear special burdens and responsibilities (that is, combining the roles of mother and father). Also, the son is likely to lack a male role model in the home (although a number of sons have models outside the home) and, in many cases of divorce, to suffer a substantial loss of connection with the father. About half of the sons we spoke to lived with only one parent for all, or some, of their upbringing.

The parents' educational level is significant in a different way. Parents without a college education will likely bring to their sons' upbringing fewer academic and economic resources than those with a college education.[8] Furthermore, they are less able to serve as a role model of someone achieving a successful academic or professional career (although, as we shall see, many were very effective in personally supporting their sons and serving as models of hard work).[9] About two fifths of the sons we spoke with grew up in families in which neither parent had a college degree.

The number of parents in the household and the parents' educational level also affect family income, what kind of neighborhood the family lives in, and the quality of the schools children are sent to.[10] The son whose parent, for instance, is not married and does not have a college education will more regularly be confronted with negative peer models and less academic support, because he is more likely to live in less-advantaged urban neighborhoods and to attend poorly funded urban schools.[11] Overall, about two fifths of the sons we interviewed lived in urban or rural neighborhoods rather than suburban communities.

In the first portion of this chapter, then, we present four sets of home- and family-related contexts in which these academically successful sons grew up. The first set includes thirteen sons who grew up in single-parent homes in which the parent was not college-educated.[12] These young males, especially those growing up in city neighborhoods, are among those facing the least favorable odds. One key question here is how these youth stayed focused on academic success, given all the factors potentially leading to distraction and deviation.

Next, we look at sons growing up in single-parent homes in which the parent was college-educated. This group of fourteen sons, it turns out, contains a sizable number of youth who deviated from the straight and narrow. They took part, for example, in antisocial peer activities or experienced academic problems. A key question is how their parent(s) helped them to get off the negative path they had started down. And for those parents in this group whose sons did not cause as many problems, what made the difference?

The third group of sons is from two-parent homes in which neither parent is college-educated. These thirteen sons vary in the challenges they faced, depending, for example, on whether their parents worked the night shift, were in the military, or lived in an urban or suburban neighborhood. Here we see the crucial importance of close-knit family ties, and for the first time in the chapter we consistently hear reports of fathers playing an important role in the youths' development. An interesting question here is to what extent the advantage of having a father in the home offsets risk factors associated with the parents' lack of college education.

Finally, the fourth subset of youths are those who would appear to have the most going for them: two-parent families in which one or both parents are college-educated. These twenty youths grew up in middle-class suburbs for the most part, and their academic peers at school were primarily White—factors that, as it turns out, resulted in special racial and cultural challenges for many.[13] An interesting question here is to what extent, and in what ways, college-educated parents in general, and college-educated fathers in particular, serve as a bridge among the cultures of home, school, and community.

We also note that within each of these four groupings, salient differences will appear for each and every son in the specific details of their lives and in the exact combination of factors leading to their success. The stories of no two sons are exactly alike. Although the groupings help us to distinguish somewhat among sets of sons, each son nonetheless presents us with a unique tapestry.

Having prepared the way, we are now ready for our journey through the varied lives of these academically successful sons. We turn first to those youth likely facing the greatest odds—sons growing up with no father in the home, and who lack a model of a parent with a college education. How did these youth succeed, overcoming these tremendous odds?

Those at Greatest Risk: Non-College-Educated Single-Parent Households

One fifth of the sons we spoke to were raised without a father in the home and by a mother who did not have more than a high-school education. Furthermore, most of these youth spent at least part of their formative years in urban areas—where, by their own accounts, they were exposed to drug use, crime, and an antiacademic peer environment. Yet these youths stayed focused—and achieved at the highest levels— in the face of such obstacles. Let's listen as four of these youth talk about the challenges that beset them and the parenting and community resources that led them to where they are today.

"I DIDN'T WANT TO END UP LIKE THAT"

Ian spent his childhood, through the fourth grade, in an urban neighborhood with his sister and mom.[14] His mother worked as a data entry operator. Ian begins by describing some of the challenges he faced.

My relationship with my father has been basically nonexistent since I was about three years old. He has been in and out of prison, and he really hasn't been in my life. Not having a man to support me and be a part of my life, sometimes it made me feel like less than a person. Seeing other kids' dads was painful.

No one in my family has ever gone to college. I lived in environments where I was exposed to people doing drugs and alcohol and stealing and so forth.

After the fourth grade, Ian's family moved out of the inner city, and lived in several predominantly African American metropolitan-area communities. Throughout his education he attended public schools in which most students were African American.

What accounts for this youth's success, given the loss of his father and his early years in very troubled neighborhoods? He focuses primarily on the positive motivation involving his mother and on the desire to avoid a fate he saw affecting others around him.

Early on I would bring a report card home and I saw how happy it would make my mom, and as the years went on it kind of got contagious. I got happy. And I saw a lot of the negative people growing up in my life—that made me realize that I didn't want to end up like that.

I guess my mom just instilled in me what was right and wrong. I saw where others ended up and I just realized early on that that's not where I wanted to go. That's not the route I wanted to be on ten years from now. So I shied away from it.

I never had any big problems with my mom. My sister is three years older than me, and I saw the stress my sister put my mom through at times, going through that teenage rebellion period. And I didn't want to do that to her.

Extended family was an important part of Ian's life.

Just about all my family lived in the city, so weekends I would go visit cousins, aunts, or whatever with my sister. And maybe once every two or three years we would go on family vacations. It wouldn't be just me, my mom, and my sister. It would be a whole family vacation, aunts, uncles, and stuff. We'd have some kind of family reunion somewhere. We would all go.

We asked Ian what he was most grateful for in his upbringing.

I would have to say the love and support my mother has given me, and all the sacrifices she's made so that I would have a better opportunity than she did.

We also asked each son what advice he would give to parents raising an African American male.

Make sure their kids know that no matter what is going on around them, the bad things that might be going on in this world, that there is always somebody there. Their parents are going to be there to love them and support them no matter what they do. Be there for them, to push them on to the next level.

This last theme of being "pushed on to the next level" was frequently heard from the sons of non-college-educated single parents. In fact, the majority of the sons in this grouping spontaneously described their parents' involvement in their education as involving some element of "pushing."

Overall, Ian did well in school and felt committed to and appreciative of his mother's sacrifices.

"BELIEVING IN YOURSELF"

Unlike Ian, Scott's family resided in city neighborhoods throughout his youth. His parents divorced when he was very young. His mother works as an office coordinator.

Since I was three, I basically lived with my mother. As I grew to six years old, my relationship with my father became almost nonexistent.

In elementary school, kids got upset about good grades. When they saw somebody's paper and they saw a 90 or 100 on it, they'd be like, "Uh, this says nerd right here." And they'd pick on you like that. And also when I was speaking correct English, they didn't seem too fond of that either. But I spoke with my mom about that, and I decided to handle that by preserving my originality, my individuality.

Why did Scott succeed? He primarily attributes his success to his mother, emphasizing the diversity of roles she played. These included guide, motivator, friend, and source of empowerment.

I'd say the most important thing that my mother did was that she reasoned with me. Like, when I was doing homework and I would find something difficult, she'd tell me why I shouldn't give up. When I was in middle school and I wanted to go to a magnet high school, she said, "If you plan on going on there, the curriculum is going to be more difficult than this, so you can't allow yourself to become frustrated by this one particular thing."

She would always make sure to say, "Are you sure you've done your homework, before you play?"

As far as I can remember, I've always been at a certain level. I haven't always been an A student. As long as she knew that I was trying as hard as I could, she wouldn't punish me or anything like that, but she always just told me to do my best and pretty much the problems will work themselves out. When I became interested in becoming a doctor, particularly from that point on, she would refer to the future. She'd say things like "And in the future when you're a doctor, you'll be able to do this, you'll be able to do that." And also, she would always bring me articles from the paper, like when they discovered a medicine or such. And she pretty much supported me with that whole doctor theme as I grew up.

My mother and I didn't eat meals together, but we took vacations every year together. And also I found that through the years my mother was kind of my friend as well as my mother. I would go in and speak to her about the day, you know, and she would tell me about her day, whatever. We'd say a few jokes or whatever. We got together on a friendly level.

My mother always told me that I had to try harder than Whites, I had to do better. She'd always push for that.

Scott is clear about the central importance to success of believing in yourself.

I'd say it's just a matter of believing in yourself. That's the main thing. You may need people to place that belief there, that would be a good thing. But basically you have to take it on and hold it yourself at some point.

What advice for parents does Scott offer?

Some of the people I know, their parents focused a lot on going out and partying or what have you, but didn't really take the time to help them with their homework or encourage them in their studies. So I'd say that's the big thing that you want to always remember—to take the time to encourage your child in his studies, so he can feel good about himself.

Ian and Scott each attended schools that were primarily African American. In contrast, the next son, Cliff, attended either mixed-race or primarily White secondary schools. In describing his mother's contribution to his success, he emphasizes her role as disciplinarian to a much greater extent than either Ian or Scott.

"MY MOTHER ROSE TO A HIGHER LEVEL"

When Cliff was growing up, his household included his mother and an adopted sister. His parents were divorced when he was eight, and his mother worked as a printer. His neighborhood contained a mixture of Whites and Blacks. Cliff describes a number of the challenges he faced:

After they got divorced, I would only see my dad once every couple of months. He really didn't have a hand in raising me after they separated. My father never liked school, so he didn't care. I think he just expected me to graduate and get a job doing something he did.

All through high school, Mom worked at night. By the time I got home from school, she was gone. When I was younger, she didn't cook—she can't cook. I grew up at McDonald's and Burger King.

Around my neighborhood I really didn't associate with anybody. The ones I did associate with are criminals now.

In high school, I didn't have many friends there. The Black people would say I didn't have the time because I was smart. The White people would say that I wasn't supposed to be smart and would put me in my place because I was Black.

How did Cliff succeed, given his challenging neighborhood and school circumstances, and lacking a male role model? As he reports, his mother was central—especially her strong discipline, the respect she demanded, and her ability to counter negative peer influence.

My mother used to give me cold, harsh punishments—usually school-related. I couldn't do anything except just sit in the house. Drugs—my mom used to tell me if I touched the stuff, she would kill me.

Everybody in my family cusses like a sailor. I don't particularly cuss around my mother. As far as slang, the only word she knows is "Yo," and if I say that, she gets upset.

It bothered me when someone would say I was acting White. I used to get very mad. I think in fifth grade, I let it get to me and that is when I slacked off from work. If I got a 90 on a test, the kids would make fun of me. The teachers never gave me any kind of encouragement, and I let my academic focus slip. Then I was punished and I went back to normal.

Cliff next describes an episode involving a kid next door who lost his focus, contrasting the other boy's downward slide with his own ability to stay on track with his mother's help.

The kid next door to me was going to private school and getting straight As. The minute his mom took him out of private school and he went around kids in public school, he got on drugs and is in jail now. I saw him go from good to bad in a matter of months. When I was young, I did well and was susceptible to the same pressures. My mother would kick me in the pants and give me that boost to keep doing well. She made me realize that there was nothing wrong with being smart.

He provides one additional perspective on his mother's role.

We don't have anybody to look up to. Some Black parents have Ph.Ds, but my mother and father don't have college degrees. I think she had to put herself up on a level higher. She has to go to the extra trouble to see that I do the best I can.

"THE PROJECTS": "NO ONE WOULD HAVE KNOWN THE POTENTIAL I HAVE"

The final son we hear from grew up in the most hazardous environment of any we heard about—a large housing project in one of the nation's largest cities. Unlike Ian, Scott, and Cliff, whose fathers played little, if any, role in their lives, Jeffrey's father played a major role at a crucial point in his adolescence.

Jeffrey lived with his sister and mother in a large housing project. His mother did not have a college degree and worked as a nurse. His description of life in his neighborhood is very unsettling.

In my neighborhood—it's the projects, it's huge—people hang outside a lot. So whenever people in my neighborhood saw me, they saw me as a different face, and they knew I wasn't really doing what they were doing. As far as crime, it was just something that we lived with. I was jumped, and I was chased by people with knives and stuff like that. I didn't belong to any group, so really I was of no consequence, so they could just do whatever they wanted. It didn't matter, there was no one coming after them to protect me. In that sort of environment, being different is not merely an oddity, it's actually a hazard. So the question is, does one hold one's ground and face that sort of danger, or does one acquiesce? And at the point at which I moved, I was trying to make that determination.

How did Jeffrey stay focused academically while living in the projects?

Until age fourteen, his mother helped isolate him from the surroundings, and his godmother helped give him hope and a goal.[15]

My mother always told me that I was smart, and that I would do something, I would go somewhere and be someone, that sort of thing. When you tell a person that over and over and over again, then eventually they start to believe it. I think the most important thing she did was use the power of the self-fulfilling prophecy, and she used that to the maximum.

My mother kept me in the house a lot, so I was never really part of the local groups. Kids did not like me. I was called a nerd, I was said to have acted White, talked White, the whole nine yards. School was my source of pride.

My godmother was an attorney. She took me to some of her classes. I could see that it was possible—not some abstract idea, but actually possible—for me to do whatever it was that she was doing. So that made it real for me. I wanted to be a lawyer for the longest time. And I saw that as being incompatible with crime and drugs and so forth. So I guess I pretty much shunned most of those things because I knew I wanted to do something, I wanted a way to get out of where we were.

Jeffrey notes he started getting in trouble as he entered adolescence.

Before, I had a very close relationship with my mother, but I was becoming somewhat unruly. So partly because of that, partly because my father was ready to take me, he offered me the opportunity to live with him.

In Jeffrey's view, his leaving his urban neighborhood to live with his father in a suburban neighborhood in a different state saved him from going down a different path.

I think the reason why I am the man I am today, in part, is due to the fact that I was able to move, to get out of the situation, and go somewhere where I could just be myself. I really think that if I had stayed, I would have changed. I don't think that I would be the person I am today. I almost went over to the other side—but no one would have ever known the potential I have.

The transition to living with his father, however, was not without its challenges and stresses.

My father was a very religious individual. He didn't allow me to participate in certain activities in high school, and I was bitter. I had some serious trouble adjusting to my father's rules. House rules. And that spurred on some rebellion.

Over time, Jeffrey reports that his father became somewhat more flexible, and their relationship worked itself out and became close. He now sees his father's household in positive terms.

Things are very orderly and very stable. If my father's not home, then my stepmother's home—someone is with the children. We usually all get together when it's dinnertime. It's very much a family atmosphere.

He views the neighborhood his father lives in as "very nice" and the primarily White high school as full of "warmth." This is in direct contrast to his descriptions of his previous inner-city neighborhood and school as hazardous and difficult.

OTHER VOICES

Some of the youth in this group who lived in urban areas attended private schools, at least for part of their education. Below are brief excerpts from two of these youth. The first son attended parochial elementary and middle schools and a prestigious private high school, all on scholarship. The second son, the son of the single mother presented in the extended case study at the end of chapter 3, attended a prestigious high school, also on scholarship.

In elementary school I guess the biggest problem was coming back to my own neighborhood, because my elementary school was in the suburbs, but I lived in the ghetto. It was difficult having to deal with other boys around me, taunting me. They would say, "Hey, what's up college, what's up college?" That isolated me. This one Black kid said I was acting White, or would ask why I spoke so proper.

In high school one time, a friend and I were coming out of Burger King and a police officer came up to me with his partner and asked me for my ID. It never happened to me before, and so I started arguing with him. Finally, I decided to give him my ID. It turned out that he thought I was a robber who had killed two people.

For this son, what was most significant in succeeding academically was "my mom not putting me in the public school system. And my grandmother [who lived with the family], because she took us to church all the time when we were younger. I guess I kind of molded myself after her, and that probably helped me."

Another son says:

I think I was blessed with having decent parents. My mom always pushed me to do well—although she never really checked my notebook, like all the teachers tried to get the parents to do. And my dad, even though he walked out, he turned out to be pretty decent. He tries to do things for me.

I have good parents; they try to make me proud of who I am. My mom talks to me about the achievements of Black Americans. My dad took me to a special lecture about African American history. And it's also me—I worked hard. And I always tried to be smart.

I did pretty well in third grade. In fourth grade, they started tracking, and for some reason I started in the lowest section in math. But by fifth grade, I made it to the highest section.

In the beginning of eighth grade, the recruiters for several private boarding schools came down. I was really impressed by the first recruiter. To get away from school seemed like complete freedom. I really wanted to go to that school, so I begged my parents, and I said, "Can I just apply?" And I was accepted. They gave me enough money, because it's done on financial need.

I've thought a lot about Blacks in general, as a race and in terms of what we're doing about the stereotypes of Black men and the statistics that one in twenty-one Black men is likely to be shot. I've thought

*a lot about how to raise the living standards, and about what we
Black men can do.*

The youths whose voices we have just heard grew up with single
parents without college degrees and experienced a range of living situations and contexts. These youth have come a long way—and yet still
have a lifetime of challenges ahead. We can say several things about the
factors that led to their success:

1. A strong maternal influence is paramount, with the form it takes
differing somewhat in different families. For many sons, the mother as
disciplinarian appears most salient; for some, maternal influence
encompasses role model and friend as well. What is common is an
enduring, close bond and commitment. Extended family, especially
grandmothers, may also be important.[16]

2. To our surprise, these sons say relatively little about male role
models, whether biological parents or extended family. A minority of
the sons mention encouragement or support from their biological
fathers, and for one son, moving out of state to live with his father and
stepmother was critical.

3. Punishment is an important theme in these sons' accounts. The
sons are especially likely to report being disciplined for showing disre-
spect, and to a lesser extent for fighting or hitting. They indicate that
physical discipline was one form of punishment used by their parents.[17]

4. Although some of the sons mention finding peers supportive of
academic achievement, most others do not. In the main, neighborhood
peers are a negative influence.[18]

5. The specific living circumstances of the various sons in this
grouping vary tremendously. Many spent all of their childhood years in
urban areas, while a few lived, at least some of the time, in the suburbs. Most went to public schools exclusively, although some attended
urban parochial or private schools. As noted above, many viewed their
mothers primarily as authority figures, while others describe a more
intimate relationship.

6. Life has clearly not been easy for the sons in non-college-educated
single-parent households. These are youths who succeeded against the
odds. They are less likely than sons in the other groupings to say that
parental "support" was a key contribution to their success, using
instead terms such as parental "push." Perhaps strong "push" from a
parent is more effective for these youths, because the obstacles they
face will not yield or a path will not be forged without more active aid

than "support" connotes. Mothers who lack a college education may support their sons in ways that are different from the traditional approaches of educated parents, who can draw upon firsthand knowledge in guiding their sons along an educational path that they themselves successfully traveled. That is, parents without a college education may need to "push" their sons more vigorously, forging a path one step at a time through new and difficult terrain in which they are not particularly comfortable. The challenges facing parents and sons in other types of households may differ—as seen in the college-educated single-parent households to which we turn next.

Close Calls and Turnarounds: Special Challenges Facing College-Educated Single-Parent Households

Parents with a college (or graduate or professional) degree carry with them a major resource for their sons' academic success. The parents can serve as strong academic role models and guides to success in education. This does not ensure, however, that the sons will not encounter some of the obstacles facing many Black males in our society. This may be especially true when the sons grow up in difficult neighborhoods, when they have a certain temperament or special problems coping with school, or when their parents' divorce is stressful and painful.

We begin with the voices of sons who at some point appeared to be headed toward serious trouble. In some cases the trouble took the form of negative peer group involvement, and in others it involved academic problems. Many of these sons lived in urban areas. The first two youths mention little about their fathers' involvement; for the third son, however, the father plays a critical role in turning around a challenging situation.

THE STRESS OF DIVORCE AND NEGATIVE PEER INVOLVEMENT

Frank lived with his mother after his parents divorced when he was ten. His mother has a college degree and worked as a manager. The breakup of his family was difficult.

We had to move out of state, and that was when we started to fall apart. My older sister has diabetes, and she was institutionalized. My father was always in and out of the house. When my mother left my father, she tried to get the family close again, but it was different.

Involvement with peers veered into the criminal.

As we got older, my friends started to get a little more serious. Things started to get more and more illegal. I have held crack cocaine in my apartment for some of my friends. I have played with guns.

One instance I remember clearly, I was in the ninth grade, and we were going to rob this fast-food restaurant. I heard something that sounded like thunder—it was a man's bones cracking. Everybody was just stomping this man, and I was just looking at him. I saw that man a week later and his face was just indescribable.

At this point Frank began to distance himself from his peers. He continues his story about the robbery and assault:

I looked at these people and thought, "They're the ones that I just chill with; they're supposed to be my friends, and they did this." That is when I started to separate myself from that crowd.

All my friends, almost every single one of them, are on drugs. My best friend just recently got out of jail.

Given these challenges, how did Frank escape the influence of the environment and achieve academic success? He describes a mother who was structured, encouraging, and persistent.

My mother was very structured. In elementary school, on the refrigerator, there was a schedule of what I was to do when I got home from school: practice my music, do my homework, chores, etc. TV was not to come on until she said it was okay. She put me in Upward Bound, and I had to take piano lessons—little things that really irritated me back then, but she always stayed on top of me to make sure I did them. I didn't appreciate it then, but I do now.

She told me the only four-letter word she wanted to hear was love. *She set boundaries, and I had to live by them. My mother would not let the TV come on until eight o'clock, and when it did come on, you had to ask for permission to watch. Even now, at nineteen, I still have to ask my mother if I can watch TV.*

My mother used to take us to museums, and we used to discuss news articles or rent a movie. We have a really small two-bedroom apartment, so we always interact.

The biggest problem my mother had with me was my temper. I would put my fist through everything I could find. My mother would sit down and talk to me about the consequences of me flying off the handle and what would happen if the county police were called in—I might get beat up or shot. So she did stress the point of controlling my temper.

In high school Frank received good grades, but he was not really trying and did not consider himself college-bound.

My junior year, I wasn't thinking about college. My mother really started pushing it into my head. I always figured once I graduated I'd join the Marines or Air Force. That was my game plan. My mom started talking about how I had to go to college, and I was in Upward Bound. I started taking home these little books with the SATs. She was really a motivating force and she really stayed on me.

Beyond his mother, others also expected him to succeed.

My older brother and my mother pushed me the most. I guess I can say I caught it from every angle, because I only heard from my father every three, four, or five months. But the first thing he always asked me was how my grades were, what was I doing in school. Even my community talked about how smart I was. It had just become an expectation, since childhood, that I am supposed to do well in school. I might not live up to that expectation, but I am trying.

And his peers were a source of motivation—in their way.

A friend of mine works at a barber shop and sells crack on the side. He's telling me, "You don't have to do what I do just because we're friends. You have a chance to do something better. You'd better utilize it." And I get that message every day from my people at home.

What is Frank most grateful for, regarding his mother?

I'm grateful for her guidance, her love, her just allowing me to be myself and just always being there for me whenever I needed her.

A SON WITH A TEMPER

Richard spent his first fifteen years growing up in an urban area, where he attended primarily African American schools. His mother has taken some graduate school coursework and works as an administrator.

Richard is similar to Frank in some ways, having problems with temper and negative peer group involvement—problems that are often found in children who later progress to a life of crime. In contrast to Frank, however, Richard had major behavioral problems in school; his mother's influence was essential in this context.

As an example of Richard's temper problems, he describes a situation in elementary school after he and his teacher argued.

She was just sitting there not doing anything, and I picked up a chair and I hit her upside the head with the chair.

I lied too much. It got to the point where I couldn't control it; it was getting out of hand.

When I was a kid I remember an incident when everybody was going to the 7-Eleven, and stealing. I took boxes of stuff.

Another time it was ten at night—my mom, she would go to night school—and we went down to the harbor and picked up all those little metal concrete trash cans, and we were throwing them at boats and stuff. Just being destructive.

Since Richard was doing so poorly in his first few years of elementary school, his mother transferred him to a Catholic school in third grade. As a result of his continuing problems with conduct, his third-grade teacher kept him in during recess regularly—and began to notice his intellectual capability. The teacher, and his mother, helped to turn his concept of himself around.

The teacher talked to my mother and it was like, "Richard is a bright kid." Well, my mother eventually started talking to me, started telling me that I was bright. And for some reason, after fourth and fifth grade, it eventually started sinking in.

Also, my mother started helping me with my homework. And she started showing me a little more organization because I was not very organized. When she started showing me the things I was doing wrong and better ways to do them, that helped me a lot.

My mother got very involved in the PTA. She always knew what was going on in school.

He also describes his mother as a strict disciplinarian, and someone who encouraged extracurricular activities.

The punishment was just automatic. It depended on what meant the most to me at the time. If it was my Nintendo, she would take that Nintendo. My mother was rough—she was always the hard, cold, fast force.

She did encourage me to do some hobby, like swimming. She got me really involved in swimming. She would always take me to the Y and so forth and sign me up for swimming camps. And she was also very instrumental in getting me involved in martial arts. She kept me with it. So she would always push me to those things.

As positive influences in his life, Richard also includes his father, his sister, and God.

I never felt like my dad was going to overjudge me, or that he was going to flip out. He would just talk to me like a friend and say, "Why are you doing that?" I didn't have my guard up, and so I would honestly have to ask myself, "Why am I doing this?" My dad, I felt like he was my friend.

My sister would help me and say you know, "This is that, this is this, this is what we are doing in my class." And sometimes she would let me help her with her homework. She was definitely influential.

My mother introduced me to God. I was always very, very spiritual as a kid. The church is important because it also instills a hope that even when you're down and out there is always a way.

Richard's mother later remarried, and they moved to a more advantaged area in the county when Richard entered high school.

MOVING IN WITH FATHER

Whereas their mothers played the central role for Frank and Richard, and for most other sons in this grouping, for others it was the father who played a critical role at times of major challenge. The next story is that of Patrick, whose father's perspective is presented in the extended case study material at the end of chapter 2.

Patrick was living with his mother during his first two years of high school, at which point his academic performance was poor.

The first two years of high school, I was with my mother. My mother is the type of person that will let you have your freedom as long as you show her you are responsible. Basically, that is what she did. I could talk to her, we became very close, but because I was living with my mother, I got mostly Ds. I remember seeing friends of mine who were not doing well and just thinking about what was going to happen to the future.

Patrick's academic focus and performance changed when he went to live with his father, who has a graduate degree.

Then I went to live with my father. He would tell me, "I am your father first and your best friend second." Once I began getting As, then he would be my best friend first and my father second. When I first went to live with my father, we had our disagreements, but we ironed everything out. Now I like to think he is my best friend first and my father second. But every now and then he might let me know otherwise, and bring in the discipline.

Patrick also attributes some of his success to his innate interest in math and science. "My parents fed off of that and knew that I was interested and enjoyed it. They encouraged me and gave me motivation."

CLOSE RELATIONSHIP BETWEEN CHILD AND MOTHER

Many of the sons living with their college-educated mothers grew up in urban areas, and most report special challenges related to the urban environment, especially concerning peers. A smaller number, however, grew up in middle-class suburbs, where coping with White culture presented its own set of challenges.

Sean lived in the suburbs with his mother, who has a graduate degree. His relationship with his father was nonexistent until he was twenty; his father died shortly thereafter, before Sean was able to have much contact with him

One of the greatest challenges Sean faced as a child was his experience with racism.

I went to a predominantly White school, and one of the kids in my third-grade class, his father came to teach us, and he asked us to do a little paper or something. I'd been an outstanding student in class, but for some reason I needed more time to do the paper. So I explained my situation and I said, "Can I have more time?" And he gets mad and he says no. Then a little White kid, offering no explanation, says, "I can't turn my paper in," and he is like, "Okay, fine, don't worry about it." And really, I just could not understand at all what had occurred.

Another challenge he faced was his temper.

I had a temper. I would yell at my teachers, whatever. I really think I had a whole lot of little deviations—hyperactivity, my social nature, my temper.

Why did he succeed? His mother stressed the importance of education and of believing in himself.

My mom has been incredibly instrumental with regard to championing my cause. She's always been very proactive—interacting with teachers, etc. She provided me with an environment that fostered and nurtured that curiosity. My mother went out and researched, asked her friends who were educators, etc., what school I should go to.

I was instilled with a sense of self. I was given an understanding of self and a pride in myself.

Sean also describes what appears to be an unusually open and rewarding relationship with his mother.

It was only my mother and myself, and so every time when she wasn't at work and I wasn't at school, we were together. I can say that we spent a lot of time talking with each other. I mean, she made an active effort to talk to me, to sit down and see how I was doing and really interact with me.

OTHER VOICES

Although a number of sons in this grouping posed special problems for their parents, others did not. The two brief excerpts next are from sons who grew up in middle-class suburbs and who have benefited from more nurturing environments and greater father involvement than some of the sons just mentioned.

I would say my mother was very persistent. She was always on the backs of my brothers and me to be successful in our schoolwork. Whenever we would slack off and not do as well as she believed we could, she would always be on our backs reminding us that we could do better than we were doing. I saw that we just had our priorities straight. I mean, we all were looking toward the future, and we all planned on going to college and things like that. Whereas the other people who were not doing so well just kind of were getting by day to day. You know, not caring. So I think the difference is that we were looking toward the future.

I was about six when my mother remarried. I knew that he wasn't my biological father, so it took a while—but now, over the years, we have become a lot closer. I don't have any problems discussing much of anything with him. I have had a tremendous amount of support from my parents and outside support such as teachers. I've had some positive role models all throughout my life, and I've always been in a nurturing environment. I have always been in a clean, safe environment, never really exposed to much violence.

Living in the suburbs and going to high-quality schools do not necessarily ensure an easy pathway for sons. The final excerpt is from a son growing up in a middle-class suburb who did very poorly academically at first.

My parents have been divorced for about eleven years now. I was raised mostly by my mother. My father was a graduate from a prestigious university. When I was twelve or thirteen, my plan in life was when I turned sixteen to drop out and get a job. In seventh grade, I had a 2.0 average or a little above it. I failed a couple of classes, but I got A's in gym, so it balanced out. I was just lazy. I did bad because I skipped class and everything. I realized in eighth grade that it was no way to live your life. People tell you to stay in school, but I had to realize it myself.

We can draw a number of conclusions from the interviews with sons who grew up in college-educated, single-parent households.

1. These sons represent an especially diverse group in many ways. Those living in urban areas, or whose parents were divorced during their preteen or teen years, seemed to face particularly challenging situations.

2. As with the sons from non-college-educated single-parent households, for the most part it was mothers who played the central role in the child's life. In most cases, mothers developed quite strong, close, and supportive (both emotionally and academically) relationships with their sons.

3. We hear more about fathers than we did in the previous group of sons. Fathers appear more often in the role of friend than authority figure, although in some cases they take on that role also. The college-educated fathers in the group appear to have high expectations of academic success for their children, which appeared to contribute to their sons' motivation.

4. The parent's empowering influence—helping sons to develop self-confidence and a belief in themselves and their capabilities—is emphasized by a number of the sons in this group. Being pushed is also mentioned by some, although not as frequently as by the previous group of youths. In more cases the parents played a helping, guiding, and modeling role, rather than one primarily of disciplining and pushing.

5. The strong discipline used by non-college educated single mothers seems generally, although not uniformly, to be used by college-educated single mothers as well. Sons in this group are more likely than sons from the previous group to indicate that lying was the behavior for which they were most often punished. They also were more likely to report receiving lectures or discussions and less likely to indicate being disciplined with corporal punishment.

6. Extended family and church are important resources. In fact, every son in this grouping indicated that his family attends church often, compared to less than half of the sons in non-college-educated single-parent households. In addition, more than half say they visit their relatives frequently.

7. Although many of these sons presented major challenges to their parents, others used their intelligence and drew upon the strong emotional and academic support from their mothers to stay focused throughout their upbringing. Rarely, however, were both mother and father central strands in their lives, a situation which is markedly different from the two-parent families to which we now turn.

Family Ties Which Bind: Two-Parent, Non-College-Educated Households

In contrast to the preceding group of sons, in which it is rare to see both mother and father as central strands in the tapestries of their lives, close-knit families and strong parenting roles for both mother and father characterize many of the families in this group. Overall, these families reflect the positive strengths traditionally associated with blue-collar or working-class families: a focus on structure, rules, extended family, religion, discipline, hard work, and respect. For these successful sons, it is the close family ties—to the nuclear family and beyond—that seem to anchor them against the varied challenges they confront: parents working the night shift, a continual change in schools and friends for those in military families, urban neighborhoods with negative peer influence, or rural neighborhoods replete with racism.

"IT'S IMPORTANT TO GO FOR WHAT YOU WANT"

Samuel is somewhat representative of the group, in that his ties with his mother and father differ: The mother is more important as a confidant, while the father is more significant as a role model of masculine initiative.

Samuel's mother works as a secretary, and his father is in the military. The family lives in a racially mixed neighborhood immediately adjacent to a large urban area. Although both his parents are important in his life, Samuel describes their very different roles.

My mom was more of the confidant—if I needed to tell her something, I could always go to her. My dad always got paranoid when you came and told him the wrong thing. I would always go to my mom first before I had to go to my dad. I guess my dad was more like a role model type, though. I guess I hung out with him more, and we did more stuff together. He kind of raised me and my mom's job was to raise my sister.

My dad drilled into my head how important it is to be aggressive and to go out for things yourself and not to just sit around and wait. My dad would stress being aggressive. He would also try to teach me when to back off. So, learning that from my dad, about when to be aggressive and when to back off, has helped me out.

His parents emphasized the importance of education and, in particular, that one could no longer get a good job without obtaining a college degree.

My dad just barely graduated from high school but he still managed to have a career in the military and be successful. They made it clear to me that those days are over now. You need to get an education and go on to college. By the time I got to high school, I knew how important it was. At that point I kind of motivated myself.

One challenge he faced were friends who were negative influences:

Peer pressure brought me down a little bit. A lot of times, friends of mine would skip a class or something, and they'd ask me if I wanted to, and a lot of times I would.

But other friends, including White friends from the magnet program in his high school, were an important source of positive influence.

We always tried to outdo each other. When we got to high school, we would rub it in each other's faces. We were best friends—we were just competitive. Having friends who did just as well as I did and better than I did, it gave me a reason to want to do well so I could keep up with them.

"LOVE COMING FROM ALL SIDES"

Beyond the nuclear family, other sons of working-class families emphasize additional ties that bind them to extended family, church, and Black culture as well. Dwight's story exemplifies this larger network of ties—and again underscores the significant, and somewhat different, roles of mother and father. Dwight's description echoes what we heard from the parents in the previous chapters.

Both of Dwight's parents were service workers. He notes that both parents were important in his upbringing, although he felt closer to his mother.

I think I grew closer to my mother because we have a lot of the same characteristics in common. My mom was the person who was very close to me, who really got to know me and understand me, and she could relate to me a lot better than my father. But that's not to say I wasn't close to my father, because my father was always in my corner. He was just as loving and influential.

I was always kind of rebellious. When I was about fifteen or sixteen—I didn't want to listen to anybody. I wanted to do my thing, and I didn't feel like I had to be under their wing all the time or do what they said. And so there was a lot of tension. That ended up with a confrontation between me and my dad. He threw me on the floor and put his hand around my neck—not to really hurt me, but he was like, I mean, he just broke it [my rebellion] down.

I think I've done well because of a strong family structure and their love coming from all sides onto me. Through family outings and vacations together, we get to renew bonds that seem to weaken during everyday life, when we might not see each other as much.

My religion pushes me to do everything for the glory of God. I try to do everything as best I can to please him.

Self-esteem, gained through cultural pride and self-identity, has allowed me to respect myself and to realize I have a legacy to uphold.

As with Samuel, Dwight also notes the importance of academically oriented peers in school: "Friends also support you in school and motivate you to do well."

"MY PARENTS WERE BIG MOTIVATORS"

In many of these working-class families, parents' roles appear to focus on enhancing motivation and instilling respect in their children; there is less focus on some other aspects of parenting such as direct academic support, role modeling of academic or professional success, or a close friendship with parents. Tom's relationship with his mother, an adminstrative assistant, and his father, who is in sales, exemplifies the nature of these family ties. Furthermore, for Tom, an older sister was important in learning not only what to do, but also what not to do.

My parents were definitely very big motivators. My parents always told me, "You can do this; you can do whatever you put you mind to."

My parents harped on race. They have always said that I have to be better than the best just to be equal. I have had to excel at everything that I have done in order to partially get the recognition that I deserved. They stressed that because I am Black, I will have to work harder for the same things that someone of a different race may have to work less for.

His parents did not provide much hands-on academic help, but nonetheless played a major role in helping him achieve his potential.

My mom — it may not have been her helping me with the work, but it would be encouragement, telling me that I could do something. Just saying that maybe the work I was doing wasn't the best that I could do.

They would always be there for me and support me. I had a problem in high school with a teacher. They called the teacher up and we all had a conference. They are definitely looking out for my well-being.

Tom stresses that he does not share deep feelings with his parents; they are more authority figures than friends.

I don't know why, but I have never told them things that are really deep. It's more of a parent-child relationship. I don't really call them friends.

My parents set down the law real early about what is right and what is wrong. My parents had the three levels of discipline. There was the yelling at you, then there was sending you to your room, then there was the beating you. My sister would get all three almost constantly. I guess, kind of luckily, I learned from my sister's mistakes what to do and what not to do. Later on, it was a combination of either not doing it because they say not to do it or doing it and being sure you have your back covered so that you don't get caught.

Finally, and significantly, as with Samuel and Dwight, motivation created by academically oriented peers was also an important influence, in this case in the context of a magnet high school where the emphasis was on science and technology: "It was peer pressure, but good peer pressure to do the best I could."

OTHER VOICES

Several other sons remarked as well on the value of close family ties and high standards, support, and learning respect for self and others.

I really have a very close relationship with my parents. They have always been there for me. My father is more the accepting one because he knows I work hard. My mother knows I work, but if I come home with a B in a class she thinks I'm slacking off. She has been the one to want to fight me and push me to get an A—she even threatened to kick me out of sports. But they have always been there for me, and they have always pushed me.

My father worked from four to midnight, and my mother worked from midnight to eight. My parents were real, real protective—They always wanted me to be a high achiever and to make something of myself. For all the arguments between me and my parents, I have to thank them for their understanding of me and giving me my space and the respect that I know some of my friends probably didn't get—all the support that I ever needed or ever wanted, and I think without that I probably would have gone onto a different path.

When I was younger, my father would take me and my brothers out every weekend, somewhere downtown. That was especially satisfying.

We always spent the time with my father. Both of my parents encouraged me to do the best that I can be because neither one of them went to college, and their goal was to have all their children go to college. I would have to thank my parents for the support and the love that they've given me and for instilling in me respect not only for others but for myself—because the first thing you have to do is respect yourself.

This next son describes a father who clearly was in the role of parent, not friend. He details a set of behavioral problems his parents did not know about, and he presents some thoughtful advice for parents of Black males. His father's perspective is described in the extended case study of the married father at the end of chapter 2.

My father was never my friend, he held that parent responsibility role. Whenever I made a mistake, it was my fault. But if my father hadn't pushed me as much and as far as he tried to push me, I would not necessarily have done as well, because some of the times when I did work hard, it was because I didn't want to hear his rap or whatever. Otherwise I would have had more failures than successes.

In high school I used to drink, get totaled. When we got out of school early, I would go over to the girls' houses from noon to four. Other times I would sneak out of my house to the girls' houses when their parents were not there. I was addicted to gambling, mainly because I never lost. These types of things, my parents still don't know.

I would say it's important for parents to listen to their kids. A lot of times they have something important to say, whether they are three years old or thirteen or twenty-three. They might not be effective in their presentation of what they want to say, but if you have a kid constantly getting into trouble, always fighting for attention, that might be saying that he has some sort of a problem. Or if you have a kid who is taking things apart when he is young, you want to nurture that type of ability. You want to listen to them so that you can be the most effective parent that you can be.

Some characteristics of these sons' upbringing are quite distinctive.

1. The majority of the sons in this grouping report a central and positive role for both father and mother. Although many sons report feeling closer or more able to confide in their mothers, they also emphasize the important contributions of their fathers to their development and success. Fathers help set limits, model initiative, and help motivate youths to achieve beyond the fathers' own level.

2. Family in general, and parents in particular, are very important. Family ties bind these parents and sons in a positive sense.

3. Respect is important. Parents insist that the sons learn to respect others—and respect themselves as well.

4. Extended family and religion are important. Four fifths of the sons indicated that the Bible is very important in the home; this compares to only one half of the sons in college-educated two-parent homes. Three quarters say they visit relatives frequently, compared to less than half of the sons in college-educated two-parent families. Extended family and church appear especially important for those growing up in urban areas.

5. Most of the sons report receiving a very strong dose of discipline. They are more likely to be yelled at for transgressions and less likely simply to be grounded.[19] Most report physical punishment when they were young.

6. Taken as a whole, these families uphold many of the traditional characteristics of the working-class family. For instance, every one of the sons indicated that there is a "strong emphasis on following rules" in their households. Additionally, the sons indicate less intellectual discussion, less active academic involvement (such as parents helping with homework and visiting school), and less discussion of racial obstacles to success than do the sons in college-educated two-parent families.

7. In some regards, there is notable variety in the environments in which the sons were raised. Some grew up in urban areas, others in suburban environments. Some parents were not present much due to job demands, while others were more available. Relationships with fathers were more important for some youths than for others, and personal problems among sons were more an issue for some than for others. Although general themes can be drawn, the specific family tapestries are varied indeed.

A Bridge Between Cultures: College-Educated Two-Parent Households in a Predominantly White World

The final group of sons are from two-parent families in which at least one, and in many cases both, of the parents are college-educated. Almost every one of these sons grew up in a middle-class suburban neighborhood. Many attended special math/science magnet programs in public schools; others attended private schools, especially in the pre-secondary years.

In general, it is striking how consistently and actively involved these parents are in their sons' education. Also striking are the special racial challenges some of these middle-class sons faced. We begin this section with the stories of two sons who tell distinct stories about growing up and succeeding in predominantly White towns and suburbs. One son experienced racism growing up, while another son comes from a mixed-race family. These two sons also differ in the nature of the contributions their mothers and fathers made to family life.

"MY DAD INSTILLED IN ME A DESIRE TO LEARN AND ACHIEVE"

Jesse grew up in a small White community. His father worked as a contracting officer, his mother in the human resources area. They both have master's degrees.

When I was in elementary school, there was a bunch of kids that would beat me up because I was Black. I used to dream up ways to kill these kids. The principal would get on me, suspend me, and do nothing to these White kids—the principal was as racist, if not more so, than some of the kids. To this day I always feel on the edge—thinking that you always have to look out for yourself because there will be somebody who will try to stop you.

My parents explained racism to me—racism comes from lack of knowledge of people. It comes from believing stereotypes, or just not being informed about the world around you.

In high school, race continued to be a factor affecting his relationships.

I wasn't really that social in high school. I didn't have any real close friends that went to that school. When I was in high school all the White kids would do schoolwork with me. Come Friday night, when everybody was going out to parties, I was never invited. All the Black kids, they would come to me, and I would help them with some work or we would hang out, like talking in gym class—but in the hall, they would never talk with me. Some of them would acknowledge me only when it wouldn't intrude on their own friends, or their own little group. In gym class with those Black guys I was all right to hang out with, but come lunchtime they were sitting at the cool table—I wasn't the guy to be with. For the White kids, it was all right to ask me ques-

tions about chemistry, but come Friday night, they wouldn't think about going to the movies with me. After a while I just did my own thing.

Generally, his father played an influential role.

Like I said, I never really interacted with any of the kids in my neighborhood. I spent most of my time with my dad when I was growing up; also, I did a lot of reading. I spent most of my childhood either reading books, comic books, or tinkering in my garage with my dad.

Since my dad was into the sciences and math, I got interested in it too.

My dad is the reason I am doing so well. He instilled in me to do my best to excel. He instilled in me ambition and a desire to learn and achieve. I always want to go beyond. I can't see just sitting and not having the desire to do better.

EDUCATION, DISCIPLINE AND SUPPORT IN A MIXED-RACE MARRIAGE

George is different in many respects from Jesse. George's mother's role in the family focuses on day-to-day involvement, and the father is very much the disciplinarian. George is one of three sons in this group from a mixed-race family.

George's mother is a teacher, and his father is a principal. Each has a master's degree. George comments on the very different roles that his parents play in the family, and their differing relationships to him:

I was closer to my mom when I was growing up just because I saw her more after school, before school, and getting up in the morning. I would probably be inclined to discuss something with her. Also, my father was a disciplinarian, so most of my emotional upbringing came from my mom and the discipline came from my father.

However, when it came to racial issues, the father was the key person. Discussions of race were a prominent aspect of life in this household.

My mother has a different perspective on life than my father and I. She can't see the things that my father and I see. She is White, so she has never really experienced racism like I have.

We could be up all night talking about race. We talk about it all the time. There was a time when I was growing up when I was real young and I wasn't really accepted by either Black or White kids. However, the Black kids accepted me a lot quicker, a lot sooner. So, I went to the Black children, and experienced the Black culture with my parents and Black children in the neighborhood. I would always have problems with people having certain attitudes about White people, and I would take them personally. This one White kid said my mom was a "nigger-lover," and I remember picking him up and throwing him down on the ground, and his collarbone broke and came through his skin. It was very nasty. Sitting down with my parents and discussing why I did that, it was hard for them.

His parents stressed education continually. Extracurricular involvement was important also.

They are both educators, and grades came first before I could go out to play—anything. They would give me special tests to take. They would enroll me in programs over the summer—they thought it was too long a stretch of time not to be doing anything. I used to hate that! They would go over my homework with me every single night to make sure everything was correct.

They put me in swimming at a very early age. I would get up at four A.M. and have practice, go straight to school, and have a bagged breakfast. After school, I would eat a snack. I packed everything to eat. After that, I would go to practice, and I wouldn't get home until eight-thirty. By that time, I would just do my homework and go to sleep. I learned a lot of patience, discipline, and most importantly, time management from swimming, and that helped me and carried over to my academic career. My parents knew what they were doing; they are very smart people.

Physical punishment was an integral part of life when he was younger.

I was a very unreasonable child and hard to get along with, so it was physical when I was a lot younger. My father ruled that house with an iron fist. He would not hesitate to use it. I had strict rules when I had to be inside, where I could go, and whom I could be with and when.

I have a couple of cousins who had trouble with the law, and I used to be very close with them. We used to steal cars, and my parents don't know about that. I didn't think about what the law would do to me if I got caught, but what my parents would do to me.

I remember one time my parents both sat me down. I knew it was very bad. It was around ninth or tenth grade. I had betrayed their trust, and they said it would take a long time to earn it back. That was the worst punishment I got from them. They didn't punish me at all. But what they said, it stuck in my mind. They were basically all I had in this world, the only ones who really loved and cared for me. I felt alone, and I straightened out from then on. I never wanted to hear that again.

In terms of peer relations, George benefited academically from positive relationships with a handful of other Black males, and also maintained good relationships with non–academically oriented peers.

I went to a math and science magnet school, and there were maybe a handful of African Americans in my class and maybe two or three of us were males. We became very tight. We motivated each other, and we had to represent our race, and do very well just to be equal. I had friends also who weren't as academically inclined or as motivated as I was, and they would joke with me and say I was a nerd.

George drew inspiration from both of his parents—and especially from his dad.

Just hearing what they went through, especially my father, because he grew up very poor, and he had to work his way through college. It took him eight years to get his master's because he had to work and pay for the class. It was his inspiration that guided us.

PARENTS AS AUTHORITIES, FRIENDS, AND ROLE MODELS

Many of the sons in this group note very positive, differentiated relationships with both parents, in which the parents are viewed as both authority figures, friends, and in various ways as role models. The next son describes this type of mutual, differentiated relationship with his parents. Interestingly in this case, the parents also had some concerns about development of a racial identity that affected their selection of schools for him.

Oscar's mother has a Ph.D., and his father has a college degree. His mother stayed home to help raise the children. Oscar begins by describing his relationship with each parent.

When I was younger my dad wasn't around much—he was working a lot. As I grew older, I looked to my dad more as a role model. Both my parents were a role model and a friend. Not only did they know when to switch roles, but I also knew when they switched roles, and I understood. I understood that back when I was getting disciplined, that was their job. They were doing it for my own good. We are supposed to learn from our parents. The older I got, the more responsibility they would give me and the more freedom I got. The amount of freedom and responsibility I received, it grew with maturity.

For elementary school, I went to private school. There were two other Black people in my grade.My parents used to read stories to me from kindergarten through seventh grade—African American children's stories. Then they wanted me to be around more Black people, so in sixth grade they put me into a public middle school. I would see and socialize more with Black people. Still, a lot of people in my classes were White. My parents wanted me to understand that just because you are around a lot of White people, it is not necessarily a bad thing. They...wanted me to have a sense of who I was and my identity.

I got into a lot of fights. My parents told me if I got hit to hit back hard. One time I got into a fight and I got beat up, and I never got into another fight again. I learned my lesson then.

Discipline could be physical.

My mom would send me to my room for things, or she would say to wait for my dad to come home. I liked to wait for him because he would just hit me with the newspaper or something like that. But my mom, she had a paddle. When that broke, she got something else.

Why did he succeed?

I think it is growing up in a family environment. It is not necessarily just my parents drilling it into my head every day. The way my family works, we always have to be doing something. Everything we do, we are learning. If you can, turn everything into a learning experience and do the best you can.

"YOU HAVE TO BE BETTER THAN THE PREJUDICE"

Many of the sons in this grouping reported that their parents discussed racial issues with them. Some of the parents emphasized cultural pride and heritage. Still more noted the barriers and obstacles they would face as Blacks, the importance of serving as a Black role model for others, and the necessity to excel in order to succeed in a predominantly White world. This latter perspective was remarked on by many sons when we asked them to comment on what they thought the difference was for parents raising a White versus a Black male. Below are three representative excerpts.

I think when you are raising a White male, doors are going to be open to him. Barriers are not going to be there. He can do whatever he wants to do because it is the White man's world. When you are a Black child, my parents probably worry about me every night when I go out. For example, if I am in the elevator with that White woman, is she going to clutch her purse closer to herself? Am I going to be shot because I am mistaken for somebody else when I go to that club? When you raise a Black child, you are raising an endangered species. I don't have anything guaranteed to me. I have to work for it ten times as hard.

If you are Black and intelligent, you have to be better than the stereotype of a regular Black person. They will automatically assume that you are not on their level. It is more difficult for a Black male. You have to shoot higher to get to where you want to be.

I think the difference is that each one of us, Blacks and Whites, is born into a different set of stereotypes. It is easier to uphold a stereotype than it is to break one. It is easier to fall into your group's stereotype because those doors are going to be open for you. If you are trying to open doors and knock down walls, it is going to be a whole lot harder.

When providing advice to parents on raising Black males, these sons focus on a number of different topics. The advice quoted below covers several different areas, including racial attitudes.

I would say support is very important. But I think that the most important thing is children be instilled with pride and confidence, because if they believe in themselves, then they can accomplish anything. You have to teach the child to hope and to dream and to never be afraid of dreaming too high—that the sky is the limit, and they can do anything.

You should make them aware of the race issue without becoming too preoccupied with it. You need to let them know that all people have basically the same goals in life, no matter what color they may be. Teach them that they should learn to love everyone, do their best, and to just keep the hate out of their hearts.

What were the distinctive features contributing to the success of this group of sons?

1. These sons, more so than the sons in any of the other groups, were expected by their college-educated parents not only to succeed, but also to excel. This was especially the case when both parents had college (or advanced) degrees. These sons do not want to fail. For instance, sons in these families are more likely than those in the previous group to indicate that it would bother them to fail to meet their parents' expectations. Interestingly, three fifths of the sons indicated that family members are compared with each other in terms of school and work, in contrast to one third of the sons in non-college educated two-parent homes.

2. For many sons, the father has special influence as a role model of a high-achieving and successful Black male in a primarily White world. These sons see fathers who generally are successful in professional careers and who are adept at problem-solving and meeting substantial responsibilities. As role models, these highly educated fathers are more likely to guide, mentor, and inspire their sons, rather than push or exhort them, as we saw with many of the non-college-educated parents.

Of note is that three fifths of these sons report that their fathers influenced their choice of academic discipline to pursue, compared to virtually none of the sons in non-college-educated two-parent families. Also of interest is that when these sons were young, three quarters of their fathers read to them, compared to slightly more than half of the fathers in non-college-educated two-parent households.

3. The sons are likely to see their parents simultaneously as authority figures and friends. Two thirds of these sons see their parents in both roles, while virtually none of the sons in non-college-educated two-parent homes did so. This view of parents reflects a more differentiated and mutual relationship between son and parent.

4. The parents consistently and actively contributed to their children's intellectual development and schooling. Most of the sons report, for instance, that their parents were involved with their teachers at all levels of education. Three quarters of the parents had quite a bit of contact with their sons' teachers in middle school, and more than half of the parents still did so in high school. Ninety-five percent of the sons reported that their parents showed a significant amount of interest in their homework in high school—more so than for the other groups of youths. These sons are especially likely to indicate that their parents helped them with homework, and several indicate that their parents' initiation of home schooling was useful. Four fifths of the sons attribute their success to parental support.

5. The mothers played a central role in raising these sons. The mother was more likely than the father to spend time in the "hands-on" aspects of the son's educational and daily life. In several homes, the mother was a full-time houseparent; in a number of others, she worked full time but with less demanding hours (e.g., as a teacher) than the father.

6. Discipline was extremely strict in many of these homes. In some households the father was primarily responsible for discipline, and in others the mother. Physical punishment was not avoided in these middle-class homes.[20]

7. The sons are likely to report that their families spend time together as a family unit. For instance, whereas only one fifth to one third of the sons in the other groups report regularly spending time together as a family over meals, fully two thirds of the sons in this grouping report regularly having meals together.

8. Although religion and extended family are important in many cases, they are not as consistently cited as factors central to success in this group as they were by sons in the other groups.

9. This group of sons more consistently interacts with the White world than any other. The vast majority live in mixed-race or primarily White neighborhoods and attended primarily White or mixed-race schools. Two thirds of the sons engage in frequent discussions of race with their parents.[21] Race is especially likely to be a source of motivation for success in these youth. Their parents emphasize the necessity of having to work harder than White youth due to stereotypes and discrimination, and of serving the Black community by becoming a positive role model of a successful Black male.

10. These sons differ widely in the specific combination of factors, including personality, home, neighborhood, and school, that formed the context of their lives. Some felt especially close to one parent, whereas others felt strongly connected with both parents. The relative importance of extracurricular activities, of religion, of extended family, and

of natural aptitude in math and science also varied. In this sense, the idea of a "typical" Black son in the "typical" middle-class Black family has no meaning as applied to these youth.

11. Finally, these sons are keenly aware of the disregard for Black males in society and the negative expectations and stereotypes surrounding them. They note the special costs and challenges these entail, and the greater number of obstacles and distractions that may lead young Black males, more so than Whites, to "fall off the path"—that is, to succumb to negative influences, expectations, and stereotypes.[22] However, their parents, and perhaps especially their dads, serve as immediate, in-the-flesh embodiments of the reality that African Americans can overcome stereotypes and negative peer influence and forge rewarding paths toward personal, academic, and career success.

Summary

We highlighted a number of distinctive features of four subgroups. Sons growing up in households with a single parent who did not have a college degree, for example, emphasize parental "pushing" and discipline, negative peer pressure, and strong maternal presence as primary themes. Sons growing up in households with a single parent with a college degree highlighted the importance of parental academic help, extended family, and religion, along with negative peer pressure and a primary maternal bond. Among sons growing up with both parents, neither of whom had a college degree, distinctive themes included the mother and father playing different roles in the family, the importance of respecting parents and other adults, and the central roles played by religion and extended family. Finally, among sons from college-educated two-parent families, themes emphasized included parents serving as both authority figures and friends, fathers serving as professional role models, and the sons having to cope with mixed-race or primarily White schools and neighborhoods.

The tapestries of the sons' lives are quite diverse in terms of the specific combinations of challenges they faced and the particular sets of factors that contributed to their ability to meet these challenges and beat the odds. No two sons faced exactly the same circumstances or succeeded due to the same combination of factors. The marital status of the parents and their level of college education helped to differentiate among groups of sons in terms of the challenges they faced and the parenting resources available to help them overcome these challenges. Within each grouping, the unique qualities of the sons and parents, together with the distinctive aspects of the sons' living situations, produced different patterns of coping and success. No two life tapestries are exactly the same. On the other hand, woven within these different patterns is a set of common textures, colors, and markings.

Having emphasized the differences between the groups, we can now turn to the common factors the sons describe in their parents' behavior that contributed to their success. We learn from the sons what worked.

Common Factors Leading to Success: The Sons' Perspective

For all the arguments between me and my parents, I have to thank them for their understanding of me, giving me my space and the respect that I know some of my friends probably didn't get, especially in their later high-school years. I just feel that my parents gave me all the love and all the support that I ever needed or ever wanted, and I think without that I probably would have gone onto a different path.

We wanted to know what specific actions parents had taken to help their sons succeed academically. It turns out these actions cut across parental marital status, their level of education, and geographic locale.[23] The sons' most consistent interview themes and their most frequent responses to questionnaire items are the material from which we develop this portrait of common factors contributing to success. We believe an awareness of these commonalities can serve as a guide for parents and educators in helping African American children achieve their fullest potential. We target six specific practices of parents that appear directly related to academic achievement. Many of these themes were articulated in earlier chapters by these sons' mothers and fathers, though with somewhat different emphases and from somewhat different points of view. To some extent, these practices constitute a "how-to" approach to parenting.

PARENTAL ACADEMIC INVOLVEMENT AND CONTRIBUTIONS

The sons' interview and questionnaire responses indicate clearly that their parents actively and persistently contributed to their academic development and positive school experience. Six noteworthy facets of this academic involvement are listed below.

A FOCUS ON READING

Parental focus on and involvement in reading began early in the sons' lives. Nearly 90 percent of the students indicated that their mothers read to them when they were young, with slightly more than half reporting that their fathers did so. More generally, three quarters of the sons indicated that reading was more important than TV watching in their family. Reading's positive contribution to cognitive development and the negative contribution of watching too much TV have been well documented.[24]

LEARNING AND SCHOOL ACHIEVEMENT AS FAMILY PRIORITIES

Every single son indicated that his parents viewed education as both necessary and valuable. Furthermore, almost every son reported that his parents encouraged him to do well academically; only a handful did not indicate this to be completely accurate.[25]

Each son we talked with was extremely aware of parental expectations regarding his education. The message was clear: Education is important.[26] In many cases, parents were not the only family members providing encouragement—extended-family members (cited as important sources of support in previous chapters), especially aunts and grandmothers, also reinforced the message that education was essential.[27] In this way, the intergenerational support that the parents described was clearly appreciated by the sons also.

Active parental support for education was emphasized more than any other factor by the sons as central to their academic success. Many students highlighted in particular the importance of praise and encouragement to do one's best. Consistent praise for academic efforts directly contributed to the sons' motivation to do well and to their self-concept. Consistent encouragement to do one's best similarly generated high levels of motivation, and during times of uncertainty or difficulty helped to maintain persistence and positive focus as well.

In many families, the focus on learning extended beyond school per se to a more general attitude about what makes life important and interesting. It is noteworthy that almost three quarters of the sons agreed with the statement "Learning about new and different things is very important in our family."[28]

HOMEWORK: PARENTAL INTEREST AND MONITORING

One of the concrete ways parents channeled their determination that their children would succeed academically—and a way that sends the clearest message of the importance of school and learning—was to show a consistent interest in homework and schoolwork, and to monitor the time their son spent on homework.[29]

Through all levels of schooling, according to the sons, their parents focused on the importance of homework. Beginning in elementary school, all but a handful of parents showed quite a bit of interest in their sons' homework. In middle school, over eight in ten parents continued to show this level of interest, and almost seven in ten still did so in high school. One son in ten reported that his parents showed "too much interest" in his homework.[30]

About three quarters of the parents, according to the sons, monitored to some extent the amount of time they spent studying in elementary and middle school, with almost half of the parents still doing so in high school.[31]

In addition to parental interest and monitoring, providing help with homework when needed was an activity valued by a substantial number of students. Furthermore, beyond homework, four fifths of the sons talked regularly about their schoolwork with their parents, either once or twice a week or almost every day.

If I didn't have a certain amount of homework, I had to find something to do because I had a minimum of two hours of work to do every night. If I didn't have enough, I would have to read.

I think the biggest thing my parents did was make me do my homework before I went outside to play. That is a lifelong lesson. Even now, I try to get my work done before I have fun because I know work is my first priority.

PARENTAL INVOLVEMENT IN THE SCHOOLS

The parents, according to the sons, did not limit their involvement in education to activities in the home. They actively engaged in activities in the school as well.[32] One primary form of parental involvement was contact with the classroom teacher. Almost three quarters of the parents had quite a bit of contact with elementary-school teachers, with more than half continuing to maintain this level of contact in middle school. One third sustained this degree of contact in high school. In addition to parent-teacher conferences, nearly two fifths of the sons report that their parents made visits to observe their classroom. Telephone contact was important as well—during their senior year of high school, more than three fifths of the sons reported their parents had phone contact with a teacher, counselor, or principal.

Several other forms of school involvement were reported by one third to one half of the sons, including parental involvement in the PTA and volunteer work. Also critically important from the sons' perspective was involvement with administrators to ensure appropriate placement in the school and in special programs.

The critical importance of parental contact and involvement in the school to academic success cannot be overstated.[33] It is important to remember that the sons' parents made the same points. As reflected in the account of one son:

They wanted to put me in a slow program. And my mom wouldn't accept it, so she fought the administration and kept pushing until they eventually let me stay in the curriculum I was in. My mom gave me the support I needed. Homework, PTA, whatever it was—if she wasn't there supporting me, I probably would have fallen flat on my face.

EXTRACURRICULAR ACTIVITIES

From the sons' perspective, one of the most important parental contributions to their success was encouragement and support for involvement in extracurricular activities. Over four fifths of the sons indicated that their parents always supported their involvement in these extracurricular activities. A number noted that participating in these activities helped them to develop positive traits and habits, and at the same time it helped keep their attention and time meaningfully focused during nonschool hours. During their high-school years, almost four fifths of the sons participated in a school-based or community-based athletic team; three fifths took part in community service activities; one half were involved in church-based activities; two fifths participated in a math or science club; and one third participated in student government or were involved in a hobby club.

Parents clearly believed that it was important to balance their sons' academic involvement with extracurricular activities.

My mom encouraged me to play everything. Every Little League sport, every sign-up time, I was always playing something whether it was soccer, football, basketball, or baseball. She encouraged me to do that to keep me out of trouble, so I wouldn't be outside in the neighborhood all hours of the day.

This comment is especially poignant given parents' and children's concerns about their neighborhood environments and the dangers that exist there for young Black males.

ARRANGING FOR OPTIMAL ACADEMIC ENVIRONMENTS

Many students emphasized the importance of their parents' arranging optimal academic environments and placements. For some, this included finding a special academic program or a private school.[34] For others, it involved relocating so that their son could attend another public school system. In several cases, parents actually took on the task of home-schooling.

I was really a terrible student all through elementary and middle school. I was basically screwing up. I always felt that one of the main reasons my parents moved out to the suburbs was to get to the better schools.

My mom had enough foresight to see that both my sister and I were intelligent and that we needed an environment that would help us grow and encourage our intellectual endeavors. She put us in a private school and stayed with it and didn't listen to other people tell her to save her money.

REVISITING THE SIX GENERAL COMPONENTS OF PARENTING: THE SONS' VIEW

Drawing from the previous chapters, we see again six common themes, only now expressed by the sons rather than the parents.

CHILD-FOCUSED LOVE

Many of the sons emphasized the love they received from their parents. Mothers, in particular, were viewed as providing love, nurturing, comfort, guidance, and understanding.[35]

One son describes how his mother supported his interests, although these interests differed from her original hopes for him:

My mother wanted me to be athletic, and she wanted me to be able to socialize and come out of my introversion. But I liked playing chess, I liked to study college civic books, I liked teaching myself. She didn't ever come to me and say, "Okay, no other Black child is doing this—why are you doing it!" She let me grow to be me—she let me be myself.

STRONG LIMIT-SETTING AND DISCIPLINE

Discipline emerged as an important factor in the parenting of these successful students.[36] Parents consistently employed limit setting to guide their sons' behavior and to instill in them a sense of right and wrong. In the interviews, two themes that emerged frequently were family rules governing honesty and respect toward adults.

One son poignantly describes his mother's disciplinary technique:

For me, my parents instilled at an early age the difference between right and wrong. My mother is five feet tall. I was six feet tall when I was in middle school. My mother was a teacher in the city school system for twenty-five years. She didn't take anything from anybody. She would not hesitate to stand up on a chair and yell at me. My mother did not play games at all. If I did something wrong, I was in trouble. There were no ifs, ands, or buts about it.

CONTINUALLY HIGH EXPECTATIONS

The sons generally report family environments in which very high expectations were the norm. For instance, more than nine in ten of the students agreed with the statement that in their family, "we feel it is important to be the best at whatever you do."[37] High expectations for success and doing one's best, but not success at the expense of others, characterize the family environments in which most of these sons were raised.[38]

As described by one son, "My mother knows and has seen my potential and talents. She expects me to do well. And I expect myself to do well in turn."

OPEN, CONSISTENT, AND STRONG COMMUNICATION

The students generally felt that they had strong and open lines of communication with their parents. Many spoke with them about such difficult issues as sex, drugs, and crime. Among sons with two parents in the home or nearby, some said that they could go to either one of their parents with problems they faced, while others felt more comfortable approaching one parent than going to the other.

High-quality communication channels are described by one of the sons.

My dad never scrutinized me. No long lectures and that kind of thing. He would just talk to me like a friend and say, "Why are you doing that?" So, I didn't have my guard up.

POSITIVE RACIAL IDENTIFICATION AND POSITIVE MALE IDENTIFICATION

The parents clearly communicated to the sons we interviewed, both through words and through actions, the perils and the positive features of being a Black male in American society. To best illuminate these issues, we have split off race and male identity.

Racial Awareness and Identity

The parents of four in five sons did or told them things to help them know "what it is to be Black."[39] Some sons reported that their parents emphasized the importance of "knowing your roots." They exposed their sons to African American culture and conveyed to them the idea that being Black is something to be proud of. Parents not only wanted to ensure that their children were aware of their racial identity but also wanted to make sure they were aware of possible barriers and discrimination. The majority of sons were taught that they had to work much harder than Whites to succeed at the same level. The message was that because of discrimination, an African American male will have to stay two steps ahead of his White male peers. This message has important motivational implications for the sons, as it encourages them to put extra effort into succeeding academically. They develop the mind-set that they have to be better—and that they *can* be better. Although as young African American males the sons inevitably and continually face negative stereotypes and various forms of racism, they can overcome them by achieving academically.[40] Several representative excerpts portray some of the messages about racial issues that parents communicated to their sons.

My parents used to read stories to me from kindergarten through seventh grade—African American children's stories. Then they wanted me to be around more Black people, so in the sixth grade they put me into a public middle school. I would see and socialize with more Black people.

My mother would tell us little stories about when she grew up. My grandfather is in the military and they traveled a lot. Once she told us how she had to get a police escort when they were driving through the South so no one would stop them and do anything to them. She encouraged me to do my best—both my parents have. They never got to college, and they wanted us to have that opportunity.

My mother and I talk about race extensively. She got passed up for a raise due to her race. I was disgusted. She tried to impress upon me not to become bitter and to just take the higher path, not to let that affect how I view White people in this world.

Identity as a Black Male

Not all of the sons had a father figure or male role model in their lives. With a few exceptions, however, those who had a relationship with their fathers spoke positively about them. Some students explicitly spoke of their fathers as primary role models. They described how hardworking their dads were and how they often learned from their fathers' experiences—at work and out in the world.

One father taught his son the importance of being aggressive. Another told his son not to back down from a challenge. Still another father taught his son about responsibility. These sons heard important messages about being a man. Indeed, some of the sons credited their fathers with instilling in them the ambition and the desire to succeed. The most frequent portrayals of positive male role models were those fathers who went to work everyday to support their families but were also at home helping to raise their sons—going to sports practices and helping their sons with homework.

I think I kept my focus because of my father. I noticed things he was doing—going to school to get his master's so he can be more of an asset to his corporation. He plays racquetball every morning. He is a deacon at the church. I saw all the things he was doing and he was still there for the family. So I understand focus—watching my father really helped me to stay focused.

It is good for young Black men to have an older Black role model. I know for me there was an uncle—as I grew older I saw what a real man is supposed to do, as far as taking care of your children. That really made a big impact on my life.

DRAWING UPON COMMUNITY RESOURCES

Besides parents, sons also report the important influences of extended family members, churches, teachers, and friends.[41] In terms of extended family, nearly half of the sons visited their relatives at least once or twice a month. Grandmothers and aunts were identified as being especially influential in the sons' upbringing and in their academic focus. Another important community resource was the church. For most sons, church attendance was a regular, shared family activity, with two thirds indicating that their family attended church often; indeed, even in high school, more than half attended church with their families three or more times a month.[42] Some saw the church as providing a crucial structure and being a source of support in their lives. Friends and teachers were also mentioned as a frequent source of positive influence.[43]

The sons we spoke to credited many factors for their academic success, including positive neighborhood or school environments, self, and religion. However, parental support was by far the most frequently cited factor. Many social science research studies have linked greater levels of parental involvement in education with higher educational achievement. Here we find that for African American males, in particular, parents put forth extreme efforts to help ensure that their sons successfully overcome the barriers and temptations that have tragically undermined and derailed the academic focus of so many other capable Black youth.

The similarities between parents' impressions and sons' impressions about effective parenting are striking. To some extent this may be due to the passage of time—families may communicate about and develop shared, common interpretations of what has occurred during the course of child-rearing, and why. For the most part, however, we see the convergence of the accounts of sons and parents as confirmation of the general validity of the information provided. In interview after interview, when we directly compare the accounts of the sons and the parents, we find many more areas of convergence than divergence regarding both specific details and general themes. This is certainly not true in all areas—parents' and sons' accounts of the extent of the sons' deviance from family (and societal) rules, for instance, certainly vary in some cases, as one might expect. Overall, however, we view the tremendous overlap in the perspectives of sons and parents as confirming that the components of parenting we have presented reflect to a considerable extent the actual child-rearing experiences of these successful African American males.[44]

One very special and important facet of these sons' academic involvement that we have not yet examined is their achievement and interest in mathematics and the sciences. In the next chapter, we focus explicitly on how parents and others helped prepare these sons for success in the math and science disciplines.

5

Parenting and Educating for Success in Math and Science: From Early Childhood to College

My father was a carpenter . . . When we first learned area in math class I remember he was talking about digging a hole for concrete, and he gave me the dimensions and told me to figure out the volume and stuff like that. He asked me how much cement we would need. Just little things like that, which intrigued me and jogged my interest. And I always knew that I didn't want to be a carpenter because I didn't want to work out in the sun, but I wanted to do something like that. And then I found out that engineering was that field.

The young males we focus on in this book have generally been high achievers in all disciplines. In this chapter we explore in depth what has led to their success in math and science, where they have achieved at the very highest levels. However, the lessons from this chapter can be applied to academic achievement in general. Yes, strong coursework and high grades in mathematics and science courses in high school, along with high SAT scores in math, are two of the primary criteria that led to their admission to the UMBC Meyerhoff Scholars Program. But these youth have often achieved across the board.[1]

As discussed in the first chapter, education and careers in math and science are becoming increasingly important in our technical and technologic society, and African Americans are extremely underrepresented in these fields. To help increase the representation of Blacks in math- and science-based occupations as well as other professions, we consider it important to identity the factors that led to the success in math and science of the Black students with whom we spoke. Our hope is that such understanding will contribute to the success of future generations of African Americans in these disciplines.

In this chapter, then, our focus is on parenting and educating for success in math and science from early childhood to college. The chapter is divided into two sections. The first covers the years when the child is still living in the home, up to high-school graduation. The second section describes building academic success in the college years. Parents interested in programs that help enhance student success in science at all levels of the educational pipeline may find the material in Appendix B useful.

Starting Sons on the Journey

The research literature indicates that a number of factors influence interest and skill development in math and science in childhood and adolescence, including parents, teachers, curricula, special programs, cultural beliefs, and a student's natural aptitude and interests.[2] Our primary focus in this first section is on the contributions of parents, and we hear from both sons and parents about these issues. For the vast majority (80 percent) of the sons we spoke with, their skill development, interest, and success in math and science reflect to a substantial extent the primary influence of a parent.[3] The nature of this influence varied across age and families. It included the parent serving in the role of teacher, resource person, and source of encouragement or inspiration.

To a lesser extent, schools and teachers, and the sons' natural aptitude, were mentioned in the interviews as factors influencing success in mathematics and science. Although we did not interview teachers or visit schools, the information offered by students and parents about schools, teachers, and special programs is nonetheless of interest and very instructive.[4]

EARLY-CHILDHOOD AND ELEMENTARY-SCHOOL YEARS

What factors in the early-childhood and elementary-school years constitute the foundation upon which future success in mathematics and science was built?

Many parents emphasized the importance of planning ahead, of ensuring that their children got off to a good start early on, so that the later years would be successful. As discussed in chapter 4, for many this begins in the first five years of life. This early learning included, though was not restricted to, a focus on basic skills in math and science.

PREPARING FOR KINDERGARTEN

Many parents committed themselves to preparing their sons for kindergarten. In a number of cases, teaching children before they were five was a critical part of parenting, as indicated by the following two quotes, the first from a mother and the second from a father.

I'm a math person and would read to him, but that always rubbed me the wrong way. I thought that math was more important. So we would play math games when he was little, where he would have to count out the beans on his plate before eating them.

I would like to give credit to my wife. She made the decision when our son was born that she would leave work and stay off for a few years until our children were in preschool. So she worked extensively with them during the daytime. She's really the one who taught them their alphabet and how to do simple reading, and to recognize all the numbers and colors and shapes and animals. I think she gets the credit for really working with them extensively when they were preschoolers so that they were well prepared for kindergarten.

Single parents and parents with fewer economic resources also found means of contributing to their children's education in the pre-kindergarten years, as indicated by the next two excerpts, one from a single mother and one from a single father.

I was very blessed that my children grew up in an extended family. My mother used to read to them when they were infants. She used to watch them while I worked, and she would read to them when they were one, two, and three. So when they went to school, they knew how to read, and they knew addition and subtraction, much of which they had learned at home.

I was a teenage parent, and also I was single and I raised my son. Early on, I didn't have a lot of money, so I used to have cards, playing cards, and we would play games with them. This was years before he even started first grade. And we'd match colors, then later on we'd match numbers that looked alike. And all his games were educational. I wouldn't let him accept a gift from anybody unless it was educational.

PARENT AS TEACHER IN THE ELEMENTARY-SCHOOL YEARS

For a sizable number of parents, an explicit teaching and educational role continued beyond preschool, through the elementary-school years. For the next mother, teaching math to her son was a primary project, and it included rewards for his ongoing math learning.

I would always teach him what they were going to learn in school before he learned it at school. So when he went into first grade, he already knew basic addition and subtraction. He was doing algebra in second grade, but I wouldn't tell him. I would give him problems and tell him they were math puzzles and he would do them to go to McDonald's.

In this next family, a creative array of science learning experiences was the norm.

Well, we have always done scientific things that weren't done in a scientific way. We would dye Easter eggs, and I would get a book and find out which vegetables would give different colors. And you would put a vegetable in, and when he dyes the egg you get a whole different color. You know, that's science. Or we could collect insects and study them without killing them. Or the kids always wanted ant farms. We had many animals that came into the house—they taught a bird to fly. We would also jump in the car and grab a map and decide to take a trip, and they would read the map and tell me which way to go.

Interestingly, the above ideas are similar to innovative ways recommended by early-childhood experts for parents to engage their children in science and mathematics learning, including science and mathematics backpacks, home-based mini-museums, and experience excursions.[5]

It should also be noted that siblings or extended family contributed to the early math or science learning of the sons in a number of cases, as indicated in the following excerpt:

I have an older sister, four years older than me, and I know that when I was younger, she was the one who would teach me how to read. She helped me with math, addition, subtraction, and all that.

EDUCATIONAL TOYS AND RESOURCES

Providing educational toys and materials is a central aspect of the teaching and resource role of parents, emphasized by more than half of those we interviewed. Examples of this influence are presented in the following two quotes, the first from a mother, the second from a son.

The important thing for them to succeed is giving them items that will help them. When my son was five or six, he liked Legos, and he was interested in electrical things. When he was eight or nine, he started taking the electrical toys and mixed them with his Legos. He would make elevators, and he made little doors, doors that would open and shut. We gave him a chemistry set just to help him out in the learning process—that would be fun for him, yet related to education. A lot of encouragement is good for whatever they do; whatever they are interested in, the encouragement should continue.

The primary influence was most definitely my dad. When I was young one of the toys that he bought for me was a multiplication table board. And he would get me flash cards and stuff like that. He also gave me math books when I was young.

One special resource is the computer. Many parents emphasize the importance of computers for their sons even at a young age, as reflected in this quote from a father.

Early on I used to take my son to work, and in order to keep him busy I'd sit him down at the computer. Kids take to computers, especially if there are games. I knew he was very good at what he did; if it wasn't a PC it was the mainframe at work, and he managed to get through the various things and remember all of the commands.

This son's mother independently emphasizes the same influence—and the final outcome years later.

As a little fellow about five years old, my son used to follow his dad, who does a lot of work with computers, to work. . . . My son has been doing that sort of thing, that is where he really blossomed. When he graduated, he got outstanding awards in computer science.

A GRADE LEVEL ABOVE

Some of the parents provided workbooks a grade level above for their children, as indicated in the next two excerpts, both from sons.

I remember when I was in kindergarten, I used to have to come home and do workbooks that dealt with first-grade math. When I was in first grade I worked with second-grade math. I always used to have to do that after my homework. I didn't like it at the time, but I think it definitely proved to be a good idea as time went on. And so it always fostered strong math and science.

My mom used to buy my sister and me these math books. We were in the second grade, and she would buy us these third-grade books. We would be in fourth grade and she would buy us fifth-grade books. And we really couldn't do all the problems. Our older cousin would help us do the problems. That helped me become interested in math.

GENERATING AN EARLY INTEREST IN SCIENCE

Some of the parents (about three in ten) had science- or math-related occupations, backgrounds, or interests; these were a natural, ongoing influence on the sons' emerging interests in math and science.

My mom is a science teacher, and she introduced it to me early on within my childhood. At that time, I guess I started developing this feeling that I didn't want to just use things. I wanted to understand how they worked and how they came to be. And that is what I saw science as, and that is something that I wanted to do.

I would say that my mother was probably the biggest influence with math and science. Early on, in early elementary school, she always laid it out for me that the way to the future is science.

My dad is an electrical engineer. As long as I can remember that is all I used to see around the house—electrical engineering books, calculus books, all that kind of stuff. I remember I used to ask him what he was working on, and he would show me a page with equations all over it and stuff like that.

It should be noted that most of the parents did not work in math- or science-related occupations. Nonetheless, many have been very effective in encouraging their sons in these areas.

COMMUNITY RESOURCES AND PROGRAMS

Providing access to special math or science resources and programs outside the home represents an additional means of influencing a child's interest in science. To the extent parents also take part in these programs, they represent important opportunities for a positive shared family experience. In these settings, students could learn about and be stimulated by science demonstrations, movies, and hands-on experiences.

When he was in first grade, I signed him up at the Maryland Science Center. We would go there on Saturdays.

When I was really young, my grandmother took me a lot to the Lawrence Hall of Science in Berkeley, a part of the Lawrence Berkeley Labs at UC Berkeley. And that's where I first got an interest in science.

SCHOOLS AND TEACHERS

In addition to parents, a second major influence on the development of early capabilities and interest in science is elementary school.[6] The students attended elementary schools that varied greatly in terms of location, racial and economic mix of students, and quality of teachers. More than four fifths of the sons attended public elementary schools, with the remainder attending private or parochial schools. Among those in public schools, at least a third indicated that they took part in some type of gifted and talented program. In such programs, enhanced instruction in math and science was generally present.

As noted earlier, we did not interview teachers or visit schools as part of our research. Nevertheless, parents and students spontaneously provided information about schools and teachers. In particular, a number of students indicated that their interest or capability in math and science was influenced by a specially talented teacher. Below are three representative excerpts.

In fourth grade I was in the gifted and talented program in my elementary school, and there were only two Black males in the class. I think the teacher took it upon herself to let us know that it was very important to do well in math and science for the future, so we would be on an equal standing with everybody else.

I would have to say my fourth-grade math teacher also [was a primary influence] because we would always laugh and joke, and math was just fun with him. He was a real good teacher, and he would always give me challenging problems.

When I was in the first or second grade, my math teacher made math real interesting. I was excited about math. I was always in favor of math and science classes as opposed to English classes, all the way through school. So that is the person who was influential.

PARENTAL CHOICE OF SCHOOL AND ADVOCACY IN THE SCHOOL

As emphasized in earlier chapters, many of the parents had to advocate early on for their children to ensure that they were placed in the proper classes. Furthermore, some had to find special schools for sons who had special needs or special abilities. This school-selection and advocacy process represents a major—and essential—role for parents. Without such placements, many students likely would not have progressed to where they are today in terms of academic success generally and high levels of achievement in math and science in particular.

EARLY CAPABILITY IN MATH AND SCIENCE

The students vary tremendously on whether they showed early capability in math or science and when they developed a primary interest in the area. For some students, the capability was clear at a young age. The first excerpt is from a mother; the second is from one of the sons.

I first realized he had a special talent for math when he was in the fourth grade. They were learning about theories then, and my son came up with a new one. I don't know anything about math, so I thought it was new. . . . When my kids would go to the library, they would come home with statistical books. For fun reading, they came home with statistics. I always thought it was different, but that is where their interest lay.

Ever since I've been little, my parents had me tested, and they said I had an aptitude for math and sciences. Ever since then, they have given me an environment where I can go and ask questions.

One of the more dramatic stories of mistaken early diagnosis of capability involves a youth who was initially diagnosed as mentally retarded, as indicated in the following account from the mother.

At two and a-half or three, my son wasn't talking. He had about a five-word vocabulary. So we went over to Johns Hopkins for a week, going through all kinds of tests. There was a doctor in front of me with a ruler saying, "This is a ruler. This is a normal kid's intelligence— here's yours. Don't look for him to ever go any farther—he's mentally retarded."

However, the son did start talking at some point, and the diagnosis was soon shown to be completely wrong.

When he started talking, he started talking in sentences. And he start- ed talking like a computer. Everyone used to call him Mr. Spock. But he always did well on tests. Always. Always in the ninety-ninth per- centile—English, reading, math.

They sent him to speech class, but it didn't change then. One day he just stopped talking like a computer. And he just started being himself.

He really loved mathematics, and when he was in the fourth grade, his teacher started telling me, "There's something with him with mathematical concepts. We're doing something and he'll explain some kind of concept that nobody's even told him about, and I don't know where it came from. Things we haven't even talked about." And he lost me in math in the third grade. When I was in school, I wouldn't have anything to do with mathematics, because I just didn't like it.

What was critical in this young man's development was his mother's strong belief in his ability to succeed and her continuing struggle to secure appropriate opportunities for him. This young man, once diag- nosed as mentally retarded, earned a near-perfect score on the math SAT and has subsequently completed a graduate degree in computer science.

Summary

Beginning in the preschool years, and continuing through the elemen- tary-school years, many parents carefully planned their sons' educa- tion, including education in math and science, to help ensure a good educational foundation for future development. The following summa- ry points are of special note.[7]

1. Many parents believed in helping their sons get a "head start" in school through extensive exposure at home to educational materials and toys, and direct teaching of basic skills. This strategy appeared suc- cessful for these sons.

2. Many of the parents believed that exposure to math and science materials would facilitate their children's interest in these areas. Equally important, when an early aptitude was shown in math or science areas, parents uniformly were encouraging and provided appropriate materials to contribute further to their sons' development.

3. The students attended a number of different types of schools. Although there may be advantages to certain kinds of programs and schools, no one sort of school or setting, in and of itself, appears essential. Parents were very active in ensuring an appropriate school setting.

4. Almost half the students early on demonstrated a special capacity in math or science. For many others, both capability and interest in science developed later, during the secondary-school years, to which we turn next.

MIDDLE SCHOOL AND HIGH SCHOOL

SUMMER PROGRAMS AND SPECIAL PROGRAMS

At the secondary-school level, many of the parents contributed to their sons' academic development by placing them in special summer programs in mathematics and science. As is clear from the first three parents quoted below, summer for some families was a high-priority time for their sons' continued academic involvement.

In the summer it was just an unspoken rule for our son that you either work or you go to school. And so we would look for summertime courses. And the Science Center in the county was very acceptable; it had great little mini-courses that he would take. And the park had a free science and nature center, and he often went there and explored that. Even though he didn't seem to have any particular leaning toward math and science, it was a summertime activity. And I think this is how we influenced him—"Take it, you will learn something."

We live in Columbia, Maryland, and there were a lot of programs during the summer—computer programs, math programs. Every summer we got him in a program. We took him to [North Carolina] A&T when he was in the ninth grade. They had an intensive science program at A&T. We took him to the University of Delaware for two years, tenth and eleventh grades—they had an intensive science program, six weeks. And there they had to study every night from seven to ten, Monday through Friday. This helped in his development, and he was always ahead of everyone else, so he always helped other kids.

Living in the Washington area is a very unique experience because there is so much free stuff available. We were resident associates at the Smithsonian, and they had many programs. Also, in the summer, when the kids were allowed to go to summer school, they went every summer. I mean summer was not free months of nothing. Because then it takes a month or two to get back into school again.

One parent described a set of science-based programs for urban youth developed at a local college, which began in elementary school and continued through high school. In talking about the high-school years, she reports:

In the summers, especially at the senior-high level, there were many different types of enrichment, special science project programs. They took them on many educational trips in science to gear them to take it in. They had a program where they brought these electronic chips and the children enjoyed making various little electronic projects. They spent a day doing that, and then of course they would have a day that they traveled. And I think this helped to teach them an interest in science.

For one family, enrichment experiences and programs were viewed as having a special urgency:

The problem that we had, my son was always big and they expected big, Black boys to be dumb jocks. So we had to create an atmosphere where he could do the science and do the math outside of school. We went to the museum in Baltimore, the science museum. He participated in programs with them. He participated in programs at the Smithsonian. He participated outside of the school system. . . . During middle school, we began to make sure that he knew about programs and made sure that he would go to those things.

Finally, several parents and sons emphasized the role of parent as advocate, helping to gain access to special programs, as indicated in the following excerpt from a son.

My mom helped me to get into a lot of math and science programs that I wanted to get into. There was one program called the Mathematics, Science, and Engineering program at the University of California at Berkeley. And my mom was so persistent, even when the program was over capacity, I was still able to get into the program. She told me the director called and said I couldn't come, but she took me down anyway, and I still got into the program.

PARENT AS TEACHER IN THE SECONDARY-SCHOOL YEARS

A number of parents served as a major academic resource for their sons in the secondary-school years, although fewer did so than in elementary school. For the most part, these parents had jobs or skills in a math or science area. The three sons quoted next, for example, had parents whose work directly involved math or science.

My mother is a math teacher, so whenever I had any question about math or calculus, I could go straight to her and she had old books that I could take as resources, and she would help me that way. I never had problems with math coming up through school because she was always there.

My mother is a nurse and she knows people doing biology. My father is an electrical technician, so he knows things like physics and some chemistry. They gave me an outlet where I can ask questions, and they introduced me to different situations, like books they might have in their libraries.

My father is a very technical person, and he really likes math. So all during school he was really into making sure that I got my math studies down.

In several other cases, the parent, usually the father, had jobs or interests that focused on the mechanical. In the two quotes below, we hear first from a father and then from a son.

I'm mechanically inclined, and I've worked electronics and all kinds of things myself, so there were always gadgets around. That had a lot to do with it. And I would help him with his science projects. I guess it was just a slow process, just doing certain things and seeing things when you help them—they took an interest and went on from there.

My father was a carpenter, and over the summer I would have to go to work with him sometimes. I use to hate it for a while because it would be hot outside and everything. But I would just work with him, and every now and then there would be a little problem as far as the work goes, and he would have to solve that problem. And you know, he might work a little more and then there would be another problem, and he would always have to fix it. And I saw, I actually saw math being used. And when I came home, I saw a different aspect. I saw that work didn't really end after his eight hours were up. And sometimes he would bring home little problems, like something that he encountered during the day, and he would tell me about it. And then he would ask, "Well, how would you do that?" And he had already figured it out, but then I would tell him and he would say, "Well, you know," or "No, but nice try." And he let me figure out even things like area stuff. When we first learned area in math class, I remember he was talking about digging a hole for concrete, and he gave me the dimensions and told me to figure out the volume and stuff like that. He asked me how much cement we would need. Just little things like that, which intrigued me and jogged my interest. And I always knew that I didn't want to be a carpenter because I didn't want to work out in the sun, but I wanted to do something like that. And then I found out that engineering was that field.

TUTORS

Several parents mentioned having arranged for tutors for their sons.

In seventh grade, he had problems with algebra. One of my neighbors was a professor at Morgan State, and I got him to do tutoring, and I also made my son go to coach class every day. We had a knock-down-drag-out battle about that. His grades were brought up and he started working to his potential.

When he went to the science and tech school, sometimes we couldn't help him with his homework. So we had a private tutor. When he would bring difficult homework home, he would go to the tutor for help.

PARENTAL ENCOURAGEMENT IN MATH AND SCIENCE

The vast majority of the mothers and fathers consistently and strongly encouraged their sons to study, and/or do well in mathematics and science. For example, four fifths of the students agreed with the questionnaire item "My mother has strongly encouraged me to do well in mathematics and science." A comparable percentage endorsed the equivalent item concerning their fathers. Similarly, more than four fifths of the students agreed with the statement "My father thinks that mathematics and science are some of the most important subjects I have studied." About three quarters of the sons responded similarly concerning their mothers. Finally, more than nine in ten of the sons agreed with the statement "My mother thinks I'm the kind of person who could do well in mathematics and science." The comparable percentage for fathers was more than eight in ten.

The interviews also revealed high levels of encouragement from parents regarding performance in math and science. For most parents, it was when they first noted that their sons had a special interest or capability in math and science that they began to support them to perform in this area. For others, this focus originated in their own interests or beliefs about the importance of math or science for their sons. In either case, the end result was that the students received consistently high levels of encouragement and support for their studies in math and science. Finally, some sons were influenced by extended family members, as indicated by the next quote.

I'd probably say my grandfather was more of an influence in guiding me toward science and mathematics than my mother and father. They always wanted me to do well in school, but they never really placed an emphasis on science like my grandfather did.

SCHOOLS AND TEACHERS

About 40 percent of the students attended special math and science programs or schools in middle or high school. An additional 15 percent attended a private middle school or high school. Thus, over half of the students likely benefited from enhanced course offerings, upper-level electives, high-quality teachers, and academically motivated peers—all potentially contributing to their academic success in general and their achievement in math and science disciplines in particular.

Course Offerings

Quality learning environments in math and science should encompass basic coursework and advanced elective subjects, challenging curricula, varied hands-on and laboratory experiences, and real-life applications.[8] References to these elements were made in various interviews. For instance, math in some middle school classes would involve ninety-minute rather than fifty-minute blocks. And, in some schools, there would be a special research-based science class:

There was a class in my school, science research, that I took for two years. You research a project for a couple of months or whatever, a year. And then you enter it in various science fairs. It's a pre-Ph.D. kind of scientist/research thing in high school.

Teachers

Students in special programs or schools were especially likely to emphasize that a key teacher was a primary influence on the development of their interest or aptitude in math or science.[9] Four representative quotes are presented below.

A major influence was my eighth-grade computer programming teacher. It was BASIC that year, and I was good at the subject, and I was interested in it. I would talk to my teacher about things, and he would give me extra things to do. I was like an unofficial teaching assistant in the class.

I was lucky in that in high school I had a lot of teachers in the sciences that were more interesting, and that made the subject matter more interesting than the other subjects. I don't think I had any initial love for them, though, more than any other subjects. I think it was just more that the professors I had made it, for me anyway, more fun and interesting and kept it fresher. And I think that's why I pursued math and science. One physics professor stood out. It's the first time I think my thought process changed, and I started thinking how you needed to think in order to be a scientist or an engineer. He really showed me that it's a way of thinking and a method of problem solving that a scientist or a mathematician has to have, that anyone in the math or sciences has to have in order to excel.

My high-school math teacher was instrumental in that he was a good teacher. An excellent teacher. I think the thing that he did that was most impressive is that if you were bright or smart he made sure you received a positive reaction from everybody.

For me it was my math teacher my senior year at high school, because math has always been a weak point of mine—the reinforcement that she gave by saying this isn't hard, you can do this, and from actually applying it and seeing it is possible. I'm a very analytical person, and I really don't see things unless I have proof, and she would give me applications in medicine and tell me I will need this later on. She made me see I should take this even if it is hard, why I should stick it out. So I think most of the support came from positive reinforcement.

Teacher Encouragement and Support

Independent of the special influence of outstanding teachers, the students as a group report being encouraged and positively influenced by their math and science teachers. Nine in ten of the students, for instance, agreed with the questionnaire item "Math and science teachers have made me feel I have the ability to go on in mathematics and science." Similarly, more than eight in ten of the students agreed with the statement "My math and science teachers encourage me to take all the math and science I can."

Clubs and Competitions

Almost half of the students participated in special school-based clubs in math or science.[10] Furthermore, science fairs were also important for some youth, as reflected in the following two excerpts from parents.

My son had made a B in his science class, but when they had a science fair he went all out on his project. The fair was at the state level, and it was a very good project. He was excited about the project and has been good at science ever since. Science was not his favorite subject, but winning that state fair kind of put him over the top. He was in middle school when he won the state fair.

I think he won a gold medal in middle school. His school went to compete against other schools. I think it was a math/science contest. And I think all those positive things helped to encourage him.

Guidance Counselors

Over half of the sons reported that guidance counselors were especially important in influencing their choice of math and science as an area to pursue. This influence is reflected in the following two excerpts.

Your guidance counselors and your peers and your parents are saying, "Well, what's more practical? To go with the sciences. And if you can excel in them, maybe you should concentrate on them."

I had a Black female guidance counselor, and she really helped me out a lot. She was helping me to figure out what I wanted to do, because I wasn't sure. I knew I liked science, but I wasn't sure which field. She really helped me out there.

STUDENT APTITUDE, LEVEL OF EFFORT, AND DEVELOPMENT OF INTEREST IN MATH AND SCIENCE CAREERS

The students we interviewed appear quite varied in their natural giftedness in math and science, the level of effort necessary for them to succeed in math and science, and why they developed an interest in math and science careers. A number of students (perhaps two fifths) appear to be highly, and in some cases extremely, gifted in math and science. Another one quarter to one third of the students were above average in math and science (as well as in other subject areas). Still another one quarter to one third of the students self-rated themselves as about the same as other people their age in terms of their ability in mathematics and science.[11]

It is difficult to discern the extent to which either nature (what one is born with) or nurture (that is, parenting and school experience) was primarily responsible for students' success in math and science. Some might argue that it is primarily nature, and that the parents' role was minimal. For our part, we would point out that the sample is somewhat diverse in terms of level of math/science and overall capability. We would also call attention to the sad fact that many African American students talented in mathematics and science do not succeed in school, and that parenting and school experience (nurture) are critical components of student success. Also, different pathways or sources of influence may be operative for students with higher levels of natural ability in math and science, compared to those with closer to average ability. For instance, supportive parents and highly challenging academic environments and programs may be critical in nurturing the development of students with unusually high levels of math or science giftedness. On the other hand, for students with average or somewhat above-average levels of math and science capability, a stimulating preschool environment (including, for example, educational toys and materials), high levels of parental pushing and academically supportive peers may be especially important.[12] Future research is necessary to examine these ideas more systematically.

In any case, it is clear that a fair amount of variation exists among these students in inherent math/science capability, in personality, and in level of effort. Some students, for instance, had to work very hard in order to do well in their math and science courses, whereas others did not. Some may fit the popular-culture image of the "nerd"—always studying, socially isolated, and lacking in the social graces. However, many others participated in a variety of activities including athletics, had close friends, and got along reasonably well with different subgroups of students. And another subset were extremely popular socially.

Most of the students initially developed an interest in math and science as a result of their own aptitude, enjoyment, and success in school in these areas. Others were less interested initially but were guided or directed toward math and science by their parents, teachers, and others.

For many of the naturally gifted students, their capability was manifest early on, as noted in the excerpts presented previously in the section on elementary school. For others, their special capability emerged in secondary school, as reflected in the following excerpt:

When Rubik's Cube came out, he was fascinated with turning and twisting and trying to get the colors just right. So we started to buy him things he could play with in the science and math fields. In the eighth grade, he also won a science fair. It was the inventions category. When someone wanted to buy his invention, that is when we realized that he really came up with something. On parenting, it didn't have a major effect, but it did remind us to keep encouraging him to do all he could do, and to give him all the support through it.

For a handful of the students, math and science were the only academic areas in which they excelled.

Really, math was the only class I ever did well in at school—math was one of the classes that I wouldn't fail. In high school my GPA just steadily went up because I took nothing but math and science classes.

Many of the students worked very hard in math and science courses. For some, this was because they did not have an unusual capability in this area, as reflected in the following excerpt from a parent.

I don't think my son is gifted in science and math. He works hard, but he is not gifted simply because when he was in middle school, he did a lot of science projects, and he didn't do that well. He didn't get good grades. When he got to science and tech, it was there that we told him that he has to do very well in all the subjects, especially if you want to get into the medical field. During those years, he found out he has to push hard in biology especially. He did extremely well in science and tech. This is about working hard. He can do very well in everything, but not high. He knew what he wanted to do—but he has to work very hard in the science field so he can go into medicine.

Other students did not appear to work as hard, which may be due in part to natural aptitude, but in nonmagnet schools this may also have been due to the lack of competition. For the following student, his lack of hard work is related to his high level of natural capability.

As far as my math and science classes, in high school I didn't have to try for those classes. Even in my math classes up here [in college] there is not really much effort put into it.

However, even the most gifted of these students learn that if they want to excel, there is no substitute for hard work as the coursework becomes more advanced. In general, the students are best characterized as extremely hardworking and extremely focused on succeeding.

Summary

A number of points about the secondary-school years are deserving of comment.[13]

1. Many parents continue to play an important role in the mathematics and science education of their sons, although the specific nature of the role varies across families. For some parents, ensuring their sons' access to special programs and emphasizing the importance of continued learning through the summer months constitute a major influence. For others, direct help with homework or science projects, or modeling based on their specialized skills or training in math, science, or technical areas, is important.[14]

2. The vast majority of sons report extremely high levels of encouragement and support from their parents in terms of succeeding in math and science courses. In some cases, parents encouraged their sons in this direction because of their own interests. In many others, the parents followed up on their sons' emerging interest and aptitude. In all cases, courses and careers in math and science are looked upon as valuable and important.

3. Many of the sons benefited from magnet programs or schools specializing in math or science, and in some cases from parochial or private schools. Advanced coursework, peers who were similarly motivated, and quality teaching were some of the important benefits of these schools and programs. Many parents continued to play close attention to the level of math and science courses in which their sons were placed by school officials, playing an advocacy role, when necessary, to ensure proper placement.[15]

4. Independent of the type of school or program, a majority of these sons found teachers who were encouraging and appreciative of their interest and capability in math and science. In many cases, guidance counselors were also important.

5. Some of the sons clearly had natural gifts in math and science, which contributed, along with parental and teacher encouragement, to their success in mathematics and science. Others who may have been less talented nonetheless succeeded as a result of sustained interest in a career in this area and intensive work, training, and effort.

What is necessary to help talented Black students succeed in math and science disciplines in college? And what can parents do to help? In the next section of this chapter, we turn to these questions.

Empowering Sons Through the College Years

> *My son came home from the Meyerhoff summer bridge session and said it was the greatest thing that ever happened. It was the first time in his life that he had been with a group of Black peers who thought like he did and wanted to achieve like he wanted. He's part of a group that he hadn't seen before.*

One might think that most African American students who do well in math and science in their precollege years, who achieve good grades in high school, and who have high SAT math scores and reasonable SAT verbal scores will go on to succeed in college in mathematics and science majors. Sadly, research indicates this is not the case nationally.[16] For instance, during the years prior to the creation of the Meyerhoff Program, students who entered UMBC with high school grade point averages and SAT scores comparable to those of the students in this book, and with initial interests in math and science majors, routinely got Cs (and sometimes worse) in their college math and science courses. About half did not even remain math or science majors, and others dropped out of college after disappointing performances.[17]

Nationwide, many African Americans enter college with the goal of majoring in the sciences, yet few succeed. One fifth to one third of

Black college students are interested in majoring in science, but more than half (and as many as two thirds) of these students do not persist in their science, math, or engineering majors.[18] Why is this? And what type of college environment should parents and sons look for to sustain the success that was achieved in the precollege years? Finally, what else can parents do to increase the odds that their sons will succeed in college, especially in difficult math and science majors? Throughout this discussion, we emphasize that simply bringing a student into a stimulating and challenging college environment will not necessarily result in continued success for that student. He likely will need help mastering the varied obstacles and challenges he finds therein.

OBSTACLES TO SUCCESS IN COLLEGE

Although many African American students who succeed in math and science in high school initially choose to major in these fields or engineering in college, more than half do not succeed in these disciplines, and fewer still continue on to graduate or professional programs in these areas. Indeed, as noted in chapter 1, only 764 African American males earned bachelor's degrees in the sciences in 1992, and only 121 African Americans received Ph.Ds in science.[19] A number of factors are critical for minority student success in science at the college level.[20] These include knowledge and skills, motivation and support, monitoring and advising, and academic and social integration. A brief discussion of these four sets of factors is presented below before we go on to discuss the experience of college students in a program that attempted to address these four areas of need.[21]

KNOWLEDGE AND SKILLS

Adequate academic preparation, especially in high-school mathematics and science courses, appears critical for success in college in science and engineering.[22] Basic intellectual ability and analytic and problem-solving skills also appear necessary for science mastery.[23] Furthermore, college students need strong study habits, time management skills, and the willingness to use available academic and support resources (such as advisors, faculty, talented peers, and tutors).[24]

MOTIVATION AND SUPPORT

Basic interest in a career in science is one precondition for student success and persistence in the physical science disciplines.[25] Because of difficult introductory and advanced science and mathematics courses, however, and the attractiveness of other majors, many students need additional sources of motivation to succeed in science. These include high expectations of student capability and success, continual challenges to do optimal work, research experience, involvement with faculty and staff role models, and support during times of stress and difficulty.[26]

Many external factors and sources influence a college student's level of motivation to persist and succeed in science. These include peers, faculty, administrative staff, family, and community. Each has the capability to be either a source of support, fostering African American student effort and enthusiasm, or a source of stress or distraction, diminishing student effort and enthusiasm. For a university-based program, the more sources of positive motivation generated and the more sources of support generated to buffer students from stress or distraction, the greater the likelihood of student success.[27]

MONITORING AND ADVISING

Many students, including large numbers of minority students, make unwise academic decisions in selecting undergraduate coursework and in positioning themselves for graduate study. Such choices can occur in math and science course selection (too many at once, starting at too advanced a level, not retaking key courses when necessary), time allotted to coursework (too little), not using academic resources (study groups, tutoring), choice of major, not getting involved with faculty or research, extracurricular or social involvement (too much or too little), and so on. Consistent monitoring ensures regular evaluation of students' academic and social situations and their choices each semester. Feedback and advising, and crisis intervention as appropriate, help students to find out about their strengths, weaknesses, options, preferred directions, and potential consequences of choices.[28]

ACADEMIC AND SOCIAL INTEGRATION

In addition to cognitive, motivational, and strategic factors, academic and social integration into the college environment are also important for college persistence.[29] Academic integration includes a sense of academic belonging, intellectual development, contact with faculty, and commitment to the school. For science majors, interaction with faculty and students in science will be especially relevant.[30] Social integration includes a sense of attachment to college social life, social contact with faculty and staff, positive peer interaction, and a general sense of belonging in the university. For African American students in predominantly White institutions, as for any group different from the majority of students on campus, achieving academic and social integration presents special challenges.[31]

A student's sense of academic and social integration will depend in large part on characteristics of both the particular student and the particular college environment. Programs that encourage positive and adaptive relationships with Black and non-Black peers, faculty and staff, and that provide an academically supportive environment would appear most likely to result in high degrees of student academic and social integration.

Summary

The obstacles described above have been potential impediments to the progress of the students we interviewed. By and large, however, these students have not succumbed to these problems and have continued to succeed at the highest levels in difficult math and science majors; most have gone on to graduate or professional school in science and other technical disciplines. How can we explain their success? We believe it can be attributed, at least in part, to the university environment that helped empower these students—a multiple-component program that built upon the strengths of students, and mobilized the peer, faculty, staff, family, and community resources necessary for sustaining success. Parents seeking a college environment that can empower their sons to achieve will do well to search the nation's campuses carefully for program components like those we now describe.

THE MEYERHOFF SCHOLARS PROGRAM

Many programs have been developed in the past fifteen years to help empower African American, and other minority students, to achieve in difficult science disciplines at the college level, and to go on to graduate or professional school.[32] For instance, the Calculus Workshop approach developed at the University of California at Berkeley in the 1980s was trailblazing in this regard, and the number of such programs is increasing.[33]

Building upon some of the components of the Calculus Workshop model and other successful programs, the Meyerhoff Scholars Program at UMBC consists of multiple components that, taken together, address students' key needs and related environmental factors emphasized in the literature. The program is based on a strengths model, which assumes that all students selected are capable of succeeding in science given the proper resources and opportunities.

The program consists of thirteen primary components:

1. *Recruitment*
   Outstanding math and science students are recruited during an on-campus selection weekend involving faculty, staff, and peers.
2. *Summer Bridge Program*
   The six-week summer program includes math, science, and humanities coursework, training in analytic problem solving, group study, and social and cultural events.
3. *Scholarship Support*
   Meyerhoff Scholars receive four-year comprehensive scholarships, and Meyerhoff finalists receive somewhat more limited support. Continued support is contingent on students maintaining a B average and a science or engineering major.
4. *Study Groups*
   Group studying is strongly and consistently encouraged by program staff.
5. *Program Values*
   Values consistently emphasized include striving for outstanding academic achievement, seeking help (tutoring, advising) from a variety of sources, supporting one's peers, and preparing for graduate or professional school.
6. *Program Community*
   The Meyerhoff Program represents a family-like, campus-based community for students. Staff hold group meetings with students regularly, and students live in the same residence halls during their freshman year.
7. *Personal Advising and Counseling*
   A full-time academic advisor, along with the program's executive director, director, and assistant director, regularly monitors and advises students.
8. *Tutoring*
   All Meyerhoff students are encouraged to take advantage of departmental and university tutoring resources in order to optimize course performance.

9. *Summer Research Internships*
   Program staff use an extensive network of contacts to arrange summer science and engineering internships.
10. *Faculty Involvement*
    Department chairs and faculty are involved in all aspects of the program, including recruitment, teaching, research mentorship, and special events and activities.
11. *Administrative Involvement and Public Support*
    The Meyerhoff Program receives high-level campus administrative support and high-level public support.
12. *Mentors*
    The program recruits an African American mentor for each student from among Baltimore- and Washington-area professionals in science, engineering, and health. In addition, students have faculty mentors in research labs both on and off campus, across the nation, and in other countries.
13. *Family Involvement*
    Parents are kept informed of student progress, are invited to special counseling sessions as problems emerge, are included in various special events, and have formed the Meyerhoff Family Association, a mutual-support resource.[34]

The Meyerhoff Program components, taken together, address each of the four primary areas of minority student need reviewed earlier. Most important, they do so by building upon each of five major sources of influence on students: peers, faculty, administrative staff, family, and community members.

STUDENT SUCCESS IN THE PROGRAM TO DATE

The postcollege destinations of Meyerhoff graduates to date reflect dramatic success. Specifically, 92.2 percent (71 of 77) of the first four graduating classes of Meyerhoff students are currently attending graduate or professional school. Fully 61 percent of those who have graduated (47 of 77) are in graduate programs in which they are headed toward a Ph.D. in science, engineering, and related areas; another 19.5 percent are in medical school (non-Ph.D.); and still another 11.7 percent are in master's degree programs in science, or in graduate programs not related to science.[35]

In research comparing Meyerhoff students to other groups of equally talented students, the Meyerhoff students are much more likely to maintain a science major (93 percent of students) and to maintain a grade point average in science courses of 3.0 or higher (with an overall GPA approaching 3.4). For instance, among students who were accepted into the program but declined the offer and attended another university instead, about one half of those who started off in science majors switched completely out of science into a nonscience major. Furthermore, comparably talented African American students in the past at UMBC achieved average science GPAs of 2.3, compared to between 2.8 and 3.0 for their comparably talented White and Asian counterparts. In dramatic contrast, the Meyerhoff students now achieve science GPAs comparable to, and even slightly better than, their equally talented White and Asian counterparts.[36]

The evidence to date thus indicates that the program is generally effective in its goal of helping students to achieve at the highest levels in science, to remain science majors, and to go on to graduate or professional school in science, mathematics, or engineering.

THE STUDENT PERSPECTIVE ON THE MEYERHOFF PROGRAM: SUSTAINING THE SUCCESS

We administered several questionnaire surveys in the past few years to the Meyerhoff students, focusing on their experience in both the program and the university. We also conducted interviews with a subset of thirty-seven male students in the Meyerhoff Program, from spring 1993 through spring 1995, asking about their experience in the program and the university. In the interviews, we asked students which aspects of the program had made the greatest difference in their lives. Five programmatic features were mentioned as especially critical to academic success. In order of decreasing frequency, they are peer support, Meyerhoff Program community, program staff, financial support, and the summer bridge program. After describing the student perspectives on these program components, we also discuss below a sixth important facet of the students' experience—their relationships with research mentors and classroom teachers.

Peer Support

The vast majority of students (84 percent) interviewed described support from their peers as instrumental in their success. This peer support was characterized as having both academic and social aspects. Academically, the most frequently mentioned form of support was study groups, which are strongly encouraged by the program staff. Questionnaire data indicate that students spend 11 hours per week, on average, in a study group (out of 25.7 hours of total study, excluding time in class and labs); only 6.9 percent of students report spending less than 1 hour per week in a study group.

Other forms of academic peer support mentioned in the interviews include having fellow Meyerhoff students in classes; obtaining notes from older Meyerhoff students; receiving praise from and engaging in friendly competition with fellow students; and giving academic assistance to, and receiving such assistance from, both older and younger Meyerhoff students. Below, we present three interview excerpts that illustrate the importance of academic peer support.

There is a group of Meyerhoff students that are biology students and biochem and so forth, that are taking classes with me right now, and we get together to study together and work. If somebody misses, we call each other up and ask, "Why didn't you come for the discussion last night?" That's very important to me because it is pretty much a spinoff of what the Meyerhoff staff are getting us to do, encouraging us to work together and get in study groups.

Without the Program initially it would be much more difficult, at least academically. I would be much more alone going to classes. You know that there is a sort of net under you in case you fall.

Number one in my book is the support. Having other smart, talented African Americans around you at all times is an asset. In high school I didn't have that. I could count on one hand the number of smart, intelligent Black people that I could come to and say, "I'm having problems in this class. What can you do? Maybe you can help me out, direct me to someone I can speak to."

Social and emotional aspects of peer support were also of great significance to the students interviewed. Generally, the students described having positive social interactions, supportive friendships, strong bonds, and a group of peers to rely on during times of stress.

I gained personally a lot of friends, very close friends who I would not have met otherwise. The program offered the unique opportunity to deal with Black men, intelligent, my age, interested in the sciences, which was something that was alien to me coming from a predominantly White high school.

There is a camaraderie within the Meyerhoff Program that a lot of other students don't get.

It would have taken me a while to become social with people. But in my first year of college, I knew about thirty people, so it was easy. I had friends. I didn't feel like an outcast. I would probably have been shy and been a loner for a while, but being in the Meyerhoff Program, I didn't have to go through that. In the program there were intelligent Black males and females who aren't nerds, who can have fun, who are down-to-earth. They are serious about their studies, but that's not their entire lives.

Meyerhoff Program Community

Nearly all of the students interviewed described the Meyerhoff Program community as a critical factor contributing to their success. As described earlier, the program strives to provide a family-like, community environment for the students. This close-knit environment is developed and maintained through a number of mechanisms, including (1) regular "family meetings" where students and staff meet to discuss individual and group academic progress, announce various opportunities and program events, and provide motivation and encouragement; (2) program-sponsored social and cultural events; and (3) an emphasis on each student's responsibility to do well because each represents the Meyerhoff "family," on helping their Meyerhoff "brothers and sisters," and on giving back to the larger African American community. This sense of being part of a larger, supportive community represents a continuation of the pattern of community support experienced in the precollege years, encompassing parents, siblings, friends, and church members.

Perhaps the best way to illustrate the significance of the Meyerhoff Program community to students is to listen to their voices as they describe how it played a key role in their success.

The Meyerhoff Program is like a family, and that adds a lot of support. There is a lot of help. You don't have to assume all the responsibility yourself at once.

We always have what they call "family meetings" where we all get together. Students who have done well are praised. They can raise their hands and say what grades they have gotten in their courses. So there is a chance for all students to be recognized in front of the group for doing well.

When you go out in public, you're not only representing yourself, but you are also representing the program. So you carry yourself with a little more pride, and a little more dignity.

I feel that it is my obligation to give something back, whether it be some test notes or class notes or solutions, things like that, to help out my little [Meyerhoff] brothers and sisters.

When I came into the program, I wasn't aware of a lot of Afrocentric ideas and things like that, so I've really learned a lot. And I think it's important to give back to the community as well, or to help to improve a lot of what is negative out there.

Meyerhoff Program Staff

More than nine tenths of the students interviewed cited the Meyerhoff Program staff as particularly important to their success. Staff members were generally characterized as supportive and encouraging. The students described the staff as individuals available to provide academic guidance and assistance, often in the form of connecting students with appropriate tutors, mentors, and summer research opportunities. The students are aware that the staff closely monitors their academic progress, and many feel that such monitoring helps motivate them to keep striving to do their best. In addition, staff members were seen as people with whom the students could discuss personal concerns. This involvement of staff continues a pattern of help received from teachers earlier in their academic carers. This in loco parentis role of staff and faculty is not unusual in college settings.

Below, a number of students explain the role the Meyerhoff Program staff have played in their academic success.

The Program staff will tell you if you're not doing well. They are really helpful in the sense that if you have a problem, they will listen to it. They'll push you to get good grades, and if you get good grades, you will be rewarded.[37]

I know that the staff are committed to me as a student because they always show interest, they are always keeping tabs on you. They seem to have a lot more confidence in what I can do than I do sometimes.

I think I wouldn't have been as aggressive academically if I didn't have their [the staff's] support. . . . If I went anywhere else [to college], if it wasn't for them pushing me, I probably wouldn't be focused as much on the future, not as focused on what I need to get done. I'd probably be a lot more laid back and not care as much.

The Meyerhoff staff really push you. You know that they believe in you, and that helps you even more.

My mom wanted me to come to the Meyerhoff Program because if I went to any other school, she didn't think I would do as well. And I have to admit the program was probably my best choice because I need someone—excuse my expression—but I need someone on my case to do well.

The staff just want you to do your best. If you are working hard, fine— doesn't matter what your grades are, just as long as you're doing your best. My parents are the same way, if you are doing your best.

Financial Support

Almost nine tenths of the students we interviewed indicated that financial support from the Meyerhoff Program was important for their overall success in college. The scholarships allowed them to attend college without placing a financial burden on themselves and on their parents. The financial support also allowed them more time to study because they did not need to work to cover educational and living expenses. Several students describe the impact of the financial support they received.

The financial support is a whole other aspect because you don't have to worry about a whole lot of things—having to get a job if you couldn't afford college, or putting that burden on your parents. So that's a large stress off your mind.

They have given me a lot of assistance. You don't have to worry about financial obligations. They take a lot off you so you can concentrate more on your studies.

The program really helps a great deal. They pay for your books. You don't have to worry about money, like a lot of other students who have to take a job to get through school. The Meyerhoff Program, you just do your work and everything is taken care of for you, so you can concentrate completely on academics.

Summer Bridge Program

Each class of Meyerhoff students participates in a summer bridge program prior to entering as freshmen in the fall. During this six-week program, the students take math, science, and humanities courses, receive training in analytic problem solving, study in groups, and participate in social and cultural events. It is during this intensive period that the students often form bonds within their Meyerhoff class and become particularly close to one another. Nearly all of the students interviewed specifically mentioned the summer bridge program as an important contributor to their success. Below are some representative excerpts.

It is a different type of bond that we have—we came into the Summer Bridge and we basically had the same start. It gives us an edge. It gets us acclimated to the college environment.

I think freshman year would have been a lot more hectic than it was, but because I had the summer bridge program, that helped me come in. I had thirty friends built in already, so I didn't have to worry about making a lot of friends. I could be more relaxed.

From the summer bridge program that we had, we kind of knew one another for the six weeks, and we formed friendships there, and most of them have lasted until now. Whereas if I wasn't in there, I might not have known these people, so I might not be where I am academically.

Research Mentors and Classroom Teachers

All the Meyerhoff students are exposed to research early on in order to gain hands-on experience and to develop a clearer understanding of what studying science entails.[38] We asked students about their research experiences, and, as indicated by the comments excerpted below, their reactions were generally positive.

The research experiences have been very valuable. I worked with Dr. Green my first year, and he set a basis for everything that I was gong to be using later one. Then Dr. Parkson—I presented at three different conferences on the research that I did with him about myoglobin. Then I worked with Dr. Simpson. He works in neuroscience, and his work was pretty interesting too. . . . [Most valuable has been] the thinking process, and how you go about trying to solve a problem, and all the different techniques you can use to get around problems. That, and the contacts.

Every summer I worked, I did research. My first year, I worked with Dr. Harvey; he is an African American, and one of the mentors for our program. We did basic stuff to help me along when I did my research next year, and it really did. The next year, I worked with Dr. Stein; he took an interest in me. He really kind of molded me along, and he guided me a lot. He actually helped me to apply to Harvard. Then Dr. Bronte this year—he's a real big name at Hopkins, so it was good working with him and with his graduate students.

I had the lab experience with Dr. Thompson. It was valuable to me because, number one, I met my first faculty person I could talk to, and I met a few graduate students just working in the lab who showed me some techniques. The lab was a microbiology lab, and they did a little bit of genetics work. I worked there the summer before I took genetics, so that helped me in my class.

I was lucky enough last year to get an internship in a Black professor's lab. I feel like I got to know him pretty well. We just talked sometimes, you know, just about the future and stuff like that, ways that I could do things in the future, different directions I could take.

The students also generally feel positive about their classroom teachers. Many indicated they agreed or strongly agreed with the questionnaire item "Most faculty members I have had contact with are genuinely interested in teaching." In terms of informal contact with faculty, half agreed or strongly agreed with the questionnaire item "I am satisfied with the opportunity to meet and interact informally with faculty members." In their interviews, the vast majority made positive comments about faculty. Many stressed the faculty's supportiveness, and a smaller number focused on important personal relationships they developed with individual faculty members. Many also commented on the faculty's high expectations of Meyerhoff students. These themes are reflected in the next set of excerpts.

I think most of the faculty present the students with challenges and hard work. They give you support and confidence so you can do the work. If you need a little bit of help, they will steer you on the right path. They say you can do it if you keep working.

The faculty that I have encountered are interested in teaching, and they are very interested in the students. If you go to speak to the professors and get to know them, and they get to know you, there is a little bit of bonding, a little bit more interest in your doing well.

In chemistry, when I first started having trouble, the professor was helpful and kept an eye on me. He would talk to me after every quiz, and the first time I talked to him he said, "You know you can do this, you just have to sit down and examine what you are and are not doing." He also asked if I was a Meyerhoff student and said, "Obviously you wouldn't be in the class if you couldn't do the work." He is very supportive of my effort in the class.

A number of the faculty have helped me, either one-on-one because I've had problems, or they've referred me to tutoring groups, or mentor groups, or whatever. And they pointed out students who are doing very well in the class and asked me to talk to them and see how they do it and study with them.

Most of the professors know if you're a Meyerhoff student. All the ones I've met have been very supportive. When you're the best in your class or among the best, it's just that much more advantageous. On the other hand, if you're doing poorly in your classes, a lot of time the word gets around. The professors know who you are, and they're looking at you, and Meyerhoffs are expected to perform better than average. I think at the beginning a lot of professors were skeptical, but our performance has proved that we can do what we need to do to be excellent.

After faculty figure out that you're a Meyerhoff, I guess there's this underlying assumption that you're going to do well. I try to push a little more in a professor's class after he knows I'm a Meyerhoff.

Once someone finds out you're a Meyerhoff student, they no longer question your abilities. They know that you're here because you're academically talented. They offer you special opportunities.

THE PARENTS' PERSPECTIVES

We did not explicitly ask parents about their sons' college experience. Nonetheless, in the course of the interviews, many parents commented on various aspects of their sons' experiences in the program to date. These comments are consistent with those of the sons presented above. The first five excerpts below are from fathers.

My son was skeptical about coming to UMBC, but he was really interested in the Meyerhoff Program and we encouraged him to go. He came home from the summer session and said it was the greatest thing that ever happened. It was the first time in his life that he had been with a group of Black peers who thought like he did and wanted to achieve like he wanted. Of all the Blacks in his high school, he was the only Black in his advanced classes. And some of those kids were smarter than he, I would bet, but they just didn't have the drive or didn't want to be bothered with the extra work. So being here in this environment was great for him because he saw Black kids aren't like all those other kids that he related to. He's part of a group that he hadn't seen before.

One of the things that I think has contributed considerably to my son's success thus far is the nurturing environment that the Meyerhoff Program brings. He has been able to communicate, live, associate with some very fine people, people who are interested in his welfare outside of academics as well. And that is so important. I think, where else—and I think about this all the time—where else can you actually pick up the phone and really walk in and make an appointment and talk to the president of the university?

The Meyerhoff Program brought that rootedness right home to us. The program director took us to church. And the whole structure of our son's support group was Black. That pleased us no end, because he didn't have any problems, you know, consciously, folding into that situation and loving it.

He was in a high school by himself, studying by himself, and surviving by himself. And just like Tom's son [see the first quote in this group], he came home up [feeling good] from the summer program. I think that was what convinced us that this was the place for him, because it provided more than just a place of learning.

He was enthused to be around so many Black kids who really were concerned about academics. Because, like I said, my big fear was that he would forget about his race and give up on it, but he didn't. And I was real pleased when he came here, and he was around a lot of Blacks, and did well in academics.

The next two excerpts are from mothers.

I think Dr. Hrabowski provides an excellent male role model for these boys. He talks to them. They listen to him. I was very happy when he invited them to church. . . . because I did not want my son to start thinking the only reason you go to church is because you are a woman.

My mother told me about the Meyerhoff Program when my son was in middle school. I took the information she gave me and I followed up. One of my coworkers was telling me about Dr. Hrabowski and said I should contact him. I told my son and he said no, that he would do it, and he did! After meeting with Dr. Hrabowski, he came home and told me how wonderful it was. My son really looked up to him.

PROGRAM LIMITATIONS AND WEAKNESSES

We do not want to suggest that the Meyerhoff Program is effective for all students, nor that the program does not have important limitations and weaknesses along with its strengths. In fact, not all students do well in the Meyerhoff Program, and even among those who do well, students regularly voice reservations about specific aspects of the program.

About 4 percent of male students accepted into the program have changed majors or transferred to another university, and another 4 percent have been dismissed from the program due to poor grades. (Three of the students we spoke with for this book fall into this latter category.) Among current male Meyerhoff students, about 8% have cumulative GPAs below 3.0.[39] (Another three of the students we spoke with for this book fall into this category.)

Among students who have not done as well as expected, five problem areas have been identified.[40] For some students, one area of difficulty is poor study habits, poor time management skills, or unwillingness to work in groups or to accept advice. A second problem area is overinvolvement in extracurricular activities, or pledging a fraternity. In addition, some students have personal problems involving family, relationships, and/or medical difficulties that negatively affect their coursework. A fourth problem area is unhappiness with their math and science majors. Finally, some students find the Meyerhoff

Program overly intrusive, and as a result, their relationships with program staff may not be as productive as is usually the case.

As part of our research on the Meyerhoff Program, we routinely carry out exit interviews with graduating students, and process interviews with students in their first three years in the program.[41] As part of these interviews, we ask students about program limitations and weaknesses. One area of concern (mentioned by 18.9 percent of those interviewed) focused on pressures students may feel as a result of their involvement in the program, as indicated in the following excerpts.

I think students feel a lot of pressure; they feel pressure to succeed because a lot is given to them, and a lot of people are looking at the program. So, in that respect, you might feel a lot of pressure to succeed or to do one's very best; I think that may be one of the negative aspects.

I think the fact that you're so highly scrutinized is a big negative aspect. Sometimes it seems like there's no room for error.

Sometimes teachers will expect more from you than other people, plus everyone in the program will know your course grades, test grades, and so forth. That's okay, that's part of the support system, but at times it can be real trying.

The staff, they want you to get to class on time, all the time.

I do kind of feel like I'm being watched, like they're looking to see how I do.

Another area of concern mentioned by students (24.3 percent of those interviewed) involves relationships with other students on campus.

Some of the students look at us and say, "Okay, well, you're a Meyerhoff. You are supposed to be special. Why are you getting this money and I'm not?" Things like that. It's kind of a jealousy, an envious attitude toward us.

I know as Meyerhoffs we are perceived as being maybe a clique. So I guess on campus maybe we have that problem. In many cases, though, that's over when people actually meet Meyerhoff students. But I think there is that perception first.

Finally, some students (13.5 percent of those interviewed) feel the program does not leave enough room for individual decision making and development.

All the checking up they do on us—at times I kind of resent it because I believe I can be doing as well on my own. But, like I was told, never turn down help. So I'm not, but at times I feel I can do it on my own.

Well, sometimes you do get labeled—you get a reputation of being Meyerhoffs. For me, I kind of shy away from being grouped. I want to do my own thing, be an individual.

The Program is like a family, and that adds a lot of support. You don't have to assume all the responsibility yourself at once. That's a plus, but, on the other hand, it's a fault too. When you get here, we're so focused on making an end product, reaching this Ph.D. degree, and far too much is outlined for you. I've seen people go through this process and realize that something's lost on the inside.

The students' comments about pressure and intrusiveness are similar in many regards to our earlier discussion about parents pushing children too much to succeed. We are aware that, both for parents and for programs, the tasks of balancing high expectations and challenge with support and nurturance, and of monitoring and shaping the behavior of young men without bringing about resentment or dependence are never easy. There clearly is no magic wand to child-rearing—or to running successful programs. Also, just as parents wonder if too much structure or nurturing in the home will cause problems for their sons when they move on to the realities of the college or work environment, so we wonder how these students will adjust to the realities of graduate or professional school life. Were the students well served by the program's four years of structure and monitoring, or will the challenges of adjusting to the unstructured graduate school environment be too great? Fortunately, anecdotal reports to date have been very positive.[42]

Summary

1. The Meyerhoff Program, for the vast majority of students, provides a continuation of the empowering and effective parenting the students received in their precollege years.[43] The program provides students with a guiding belief system or vision, opportunities to develop skills and knowledge, the chance to contribute to others, and sup portive resources, which together empower the students to beat the odds and achieve at the highest level in difficult science majors. Interestingly, 92 percent of the students agree with the questionnaire item that the program "helps you to feel special and good about yourself as an African American student."

As a surrogate parent, the Program continues to provide the firm structure, the motivational push, and the ongoing nurturance that these sons' parents and extended family provided when the students lived at home (and in many cases continue to provide). Over 90 percent of the students indicate that they "accepted and actualized" each of the following program values: to strive for outstanding academic achievement; to use all resources; and to support one's peers academically and emotionally.

2. The program challenges students to succeed. Students are fully aware that they are expected to achieve high As in all courses, if possible. A number of students do indicate that they wish there was less pressure. For the majority of students, though, the program is empowering—it helps facilitate a sense of self-directed mastery, capability, and success in achieving a primary life goal.

3. The program provides support to help students achieve. Perhaps the most important elements are peer support and the sense of being part of a larger community having an important vision and goal. For many of the students we interviewed, being around a critical mass of talented, capable, and motivated Black males is especially important in helping to stay motivated and directed. We have heard anecdotally from other Black students who attended top-notch universities in science scholarship programs but who did not stay in these programs, perhaps because there was no peer support system for them.

Additionally, the program staff, the scholarships, the university faculty, and the transition to college afforded by the summer bridge program are critical elements helping to sustain success. Over 75 percent of students report moderate to high levels of emotional and academic support from peers and from the program's student advisor. Ninety-two percent of students report that the Meyerhoff Program community (Meyerhoff peers and staff) contributes moderately to largely to their academic success.

4. The program provides meaningful opportunities for students to contribute to others, as well as to receive help from them.[44] In the study groups, in community service activities, as an older student in the program, and through many opportunities to represent the program to the public, students are asked to take on responsibilities that allow them to contribute to others. Most of the students develop a commitment to "give back" to others what they have received as a result of their involvement in the program. As described by one student in an exit interview, "We're told that 'to whom much is given, much is expected.' I feel it is my obligation to give something back—motivate the younger generation, let them see a positive role model."

5. Not all students succeed in the program, due to various factors. Our analysis of these factors suggests some concrete advice for parents who want to maximize the odds that their sons will succeed in college. Good study habits and good time management skills should be developed, ideally in the secondary-school years, with the active help and support of parents. As sons go on to college, communication with parents about the extent of involvement in extracurricular activities is essential. Although this involvement remains important in college, the large amount of time needed for academics (in contrast to high school) means that most students spend less time in extracurricular activity. Personal problems affect some students, and working hard to maintain open lines of communication between parent and son as the student moves to and through college, and into young adulthood, remains extremely important.

Unhappiness with a science major and perception of the program as overly intrusive may reflect the realities that science is not the appropriate major for all students and that any given program will not work well for all students. In this regard, parents and sons need to consider carefully the sons' particular strengths and weaknesses and to take these into account when searching for the most suitable college or university environment in which to pursue an undergraduate education.

PARENTING THROUGH THE COLLEGE YEARS

Although this section of the chapter has focused primarily on the influence of the college environment on students, we need to note that parents do not stop their close involvement with their sons when they go to college. Although supportive college environments and programs may be viewed as part of surrogate parenting in many respects, this analogy is limited. The continued influence and support of the parents are clearly important in helping the young males succeed in college.

During the interviews, a number of parents, and a number of sons, indicated some of the ways the parenting relationship continued to be very important during the college years. The next excerpt, from a father, is representative:

My son calls me on a weekly basis—not to report in, just to touch base. I tell him, "You call and talk to me, not just your mother. I want to know what's going on, what your plans are for the weekend." And I'm not dictating to him. He'll ask me anything about anything, including young ladies—how I feel about this, how I feel about that, and I will tell him to the best of my knowledge.

This final comment is typical of what we heard from sons.

Especially in college, my parents say to take the classes that you are supposed to take, and to make sure you are in the right major. They say that if it is too stressful, they would rather have me cut back. They don't want me to burn myself out. They are definitely looking out for my well-being. I'm grateful that they have kept parenting, because a lot of stuff they told me when I was younger—it took me until now to see it. And a lot of stuff they told me recently, I saw it almost immediately.

Summary

In the first section of the chapter, we discussed the early years through high school. In this second section we have described the components of the Meyerhoff Program, one program among many in the country designed to help college-age African Americans beat the odds, succeed in math and science majors, and go on to graduate or professional school. We hope that from reading this chapter, parents will become more fully aware of the challenges that their sons will face throughout their schooling. Parents should be prepared to help their sons meet the challenges that await them at each level of their schooling and to carefully help them select college and university environments that will empower them to succeed (see Appendix B).

In this chapter, as in the earlier chapters, we have heard a chorus of voices—voices differing in many details, but, when taken together, speaking clearly to us about challenges, support, love, and the fruits of commitment and hard work. We are now ready to bring together, in the final chapter, the major lessons we learned during this journey. Our hope is that parents, sons, educators, and policy makers will benefit from this discussion and that together we can help ensure in the future the emergence of an even larger chorus of voices of academically successful Black sons and their parents.

6

Parenting African American
Males for the Twenty-first Century:
What We Have Learned

> *I urge us to tell our sons every day, over dinner, in the bathroom, in school, on the basketball court, on the phone, during the commercial break, in Sunday school, before they go to bed, when they get up, when they head off to college, when they come home, when we visit them in jail, when we attend their weddings, when we mourn at the funerals of their friends, you have a choice, you are responsible for what you do, and your community will hold you accountable. Racism will never change that. Long after our eyes glaze over and our ears grow numb watching and listening to the TV roundtable discussions that seek to address our fate, we can still keep our sons awake and perhaps alive if we teach them that the first line of defense against racism is to mold themselves into disciplined, self-respecting refutations of its ability to destroy our souls or ourselves.*

> Marita Golden, *Saving Our Sons*

How do we understand the success of the sixty families represented here? What can we learn from studying these families that can help African American children (and children of other races) fulfill their potential? Before attempting to answer these questions, we provide a recapitulation of the previous chapters.

This book focuses on the voices of two groups we rarely hear from: high-achieving African American young males and their parents. We have talked with families from different backgrounds: those with two parents in the home, others with one, some with college education, and others who did not complete high school. What these families have in common are academically successful sons.

We want to emphasize that throughout our discussions with parents and sons, we found that the mother, more than any other member of the family—more than siblings, the father, and other relatives—is usually the central figure in the son's life.[1] However, the important role of fathers as well is evident in many of the families in our study. In addition, within the extended families of the parents, we found many family members who served as role models and worked to support the children.

Three Generations

It was important to us to look first at the backgrounds of parents and to gain a three-generational perspective. The parents' recollections of their own childhood experiences provided insights into what influenced their parenting styles. As we explored the parents' upbringing and how they raised their sons to be academically successful, we saw the strong influence of the parents' own mothers and fathers, who almost always worked in tandem. We likened it to a tapestry being intricately woven by each generation. Most of the parents in this study were raised in two-parent families, the norm during the 1940s and 1950s. Their parents' roles were often shared, and they were traditional in their values and their emphasis on work. Major lessons these parents learned included an emphasis on education and academic success coupled with a focus on hard work and overcoming adversity. Strict discipline and religion were also emphasized. Such practices were carried out by parents who maintained an active involvement in the lives of their children and worked together as a team, with clearly defined roles.

Mothers

We now turn to a review of the mothers' accounts. Although a significant number of the mothers were themselves raised in two-parent families, about 40 percent of them raised their sons without another parent in the home for at least some portion of the sons' lives. Based on the information gathered from the mothers, we found few differences between the parenting practices and concerns of single mothers and those of married mothers. In fact, it became very clear that these single mothers were able to provide their sons with the environment and support necessary to succeed academically. Whether the young males in this study had two parents in the home or one, however, several critical themes emerged from the interviews of the mothers. We heard consistently that these mothers focused on preparing their young boys for school, well before the age of six, by providing a variety of academic challenges. Further, a number of mothers (and fathers) served as their sons' chief academic advocates, employing a variety of strategies: (1) making sure students were placed in appropriate levels of classes (in a number of cases, the boys were initially placed in lower-level sections); (2) helping with homework; (3) strongly encouraging reading; (4) talking to teachers when problems arose; (5) supporting involvement in extracurricular activities; (6) moving their sons to different schools when necessary; and (7) insisting upon academic excellence. Many of these strategies are similar to those the mothers experienced when they were young.

Consistent with other research, we found that the mothers were more involved over the years than the fathers in preparing children for school (although as the boys became older, fathers became much more involved as advocates and tended to assume more responsibility for handling disciplinary problems and setting limits). We also found that while mothers were central in the development of their children, fathers in many cases contributed equally. The mothers also attached considerable importance to the role of extended-family members in supporting their sons.

Beyond academic issues, the mothers consistently expressed concern about the dangers their sons faced from the possible consequences of sexual activity, negative peer influence, and drugs. And both mothers and fathers consistently expressed concern about treatment of their sons by the police and the larger society, sometimes even by their own Black peers (that is, Black-on-Black crime). The mothers clearly were very knowledgeable about the lives of their sons, especially their strengths and weaknesses and the problems they faced. Nevertheless, as we found from interviewing the sons, the parents did not know all.

In preparing their sons to handle potential obstacles, the mothers focused on (1) creating an environment at home that encouraged discussion of appropriate values (what's right and wrong); (2) developing close relationships with their sons to encourage open discussion in a nonjudgmental way; (3) stressing the need to avoid dangerous situations involving drugs and fighting whenever possible; (4) talking about what it means to be a young Black male in America and the need to be aware of the impact of discrimination; (5) emphasizing the importance of family in African American culture, relying heavily upon family activities that become rituals and on the value of religious beliefs and prayer in handling life's problems; (6) setting high expectations regarding sons' behavior and future employment goals; and (7) drawing upon a variety of community resources to support their sons' success. In summary, the mothers were very connected to their sons and knew the importance of listening to them in order to understand them while, at the same time, demanding a great deal from them.

Fathers

Although we found the mothers to be central, we chose to discuss the fathers first in the body of the book because very little has been written about the role of fathers in African American families. We found that many fathers played a key role, and subsequent research needs to look more at the relationship between sons and fathers (those who live in the home and those who live outside it) and between young males and other older male role models in their lives. It is clear that other male role models—teachers, ministers, siblings, uncles, cousins—play a significant role in the lives of many young boys.

The fathers in our study saw their lives as exceptional within their own communities because of their unusually close involvement with their sons (for example, monitoring the time their sons spent with friends, as well as the time they spent watching television, playing video games, and doing homework). The majority of these fathers, in fact, believed they had been stricter with their sons than most people they knew. The fathers tended to be the disciplinarians, while the mothers tended to be the nurturers, though we found clear exceptions to this pattern. When only one parent was in the home, that individual assumed both roles. In cases involving stepfathers, the biological mother tended to play the dominant role.

Beyond academics, fathers felt that their primary responsibility was preparing their sons to handle challenges faced by African American males in society and that they, as males, could do this better than mothers. More specifically, the fathers' message to their sons was to know how to handle the possibility of mistreatment. In preparing their sons for these challenges, several messages to the sons emerged: (1) recognize that Black males are often placed in difficult situations, especially involving the need for avoiding violence and drugs, and that certain situations and locales should be avoided if at all possible; (2) learn the value of African American history and culture and have pride in one's heritage; (3) realize that life is not always fair and that it may be necessary to work even harder to achieve parity with others; (4) become highly educated in order to succeed and to help others in the race; (5) know how to handle fights (some fathers mentioned teaching their sons how to walk away from potentially violent situations, and others discussed the need for their sons to be able to defend themselves); and (6) learn to act responsibly, especially regarding sexual activity, and understand that respecting women is an important part of becoming a man.

These components of successful parenting are very apparent in the fathers' interaction with their sons. We observed, for example, fathers (1) constantly encouraging their sons to try hard, while also supporting them whenever they failed; (2) setting clear rules and expectations for academic work and personal behavior; (3) emphasizing ongoing conversation as a means of preparing their sons to handle problems; (4) emphasizing the need for taking pride in being an African American male; and (5) talking frequently about the important role of religion, the church, family, and friends in their lives. Regarding interaction with women, recall the father in chapter 2 who told us, "In terms of gender, I've taught my son that he should be very protective of women, the African American woman. Times when he was not treating a woman with respect, I talked to him about it." In some cases, fathers also felt the need to counter the mothers' tendency to overprotect their sons or to perform tasks for them that the young men should perform for themselves.

The vast majority of parents—both mothers and fathers—also have taken time to ensure that their sons understand the impact race may have on them in school and life. The parents have talked with their sons about the tendency of young Black males to underachieve in school; they see their sons as special and recognize that academic success has both its honors and its burdens. Although parents thought race might be an issue in a number of problems their sons encountered, they tended to convey a consistent message—that although their sons may be discriminated against because of race, their response must be more than that of a victim. Moreover, it is essential that they not become bitter and that they always believe they can overcome barriers. Even when parents talked about glaring cases of racism and prejudice, they were able to help their children move beyond those issues and deal with problems in ways other than simply getting angry or becoming paralyzed. In this way, parents both acknowledged that racism exists and empathized with their sons while also continuing to insist that racism not become a focal point.

Sons

The prevailing theme of this book is that we can find excellent examples of young, successful African American males from all types of socioeconomic backgrounds. The chief reasons for their success include effective parenting and the particular strengths of these young males and their families. Coming from a variety of economic and educational backgrounds, these young men have several common characteristics, including support from at least one primary adult who provides a stable, caring environment; involvement in the community through meaningful activities; strong belief in self; and considerable resilience.

We have placed the young men in our study into subgroups based on whether one or two parents were present in the home and on the educational level of their parents. We made these distinctions in order to explore similarities and differences among the students related to the wide variety of family backgrounds of young African American males in our society. In conversations with the young males we studied, as well as with the others in the Meyerhoff Program, several messages became clear. All the parents, regardless of the families' economic or living situation, expected their sons to succeed academically. It should not be surprising, though, that the higher the parents' level of education, the greater the tendency on the part of their sons to compare themselves to their parents, with the fear of failure serving as a significant motivating factor.

Sons and Single Parents

While many would consider the son of a single parent to be in the highest at-risk category, we observed many single parents who created very strong families in which high expectations were emphasized. In single-parent families headed by women, clearly there was a strong maternal influence, and the mothers' role as disciplinarian was central (though in four instances a single-parent family was headed by the father). We also found that common and enduring bonds between mothers and sons (and in many cases involving extended-family members, particularly grandmothers) were very important. Among this subgroup of students, we heard very little about male role models (with the exception of several supportive uncles or teachers), and although there was some mention of supportive peers, this group, more than any other, was most likely to indicate that their peers often looked down on them for doing well academically. Finally, these young men of single mothers tended to talk about parental "push" rather than parental support. It may be that this reference reflects the mothers' concern about major obstacles their sons would face. Most important, both single and married mothers and fathers knew the importance of serving as strong authority figures who expected respect from their sons, offered considerable praise for high achievement and support when they did not achieve, and established appropriate consequences for undesirable behavior.

Sons and Fathers

We found also that the higher the fathers' educational level, the more likely they were to serve as guides and mentors academically to their sons. The sons of college-educated parents were far more likely to view their parents as both authority figures and friends than were the students in other groups. Regardless of the fathers' level of education, however, the majority served as role models in helping their sons thrive in a predominantly White society. In fact, most were involved with their sons' teachers in middle school, and over half continued to be involved when their sons advanced to high school. Finally, although the sons were keenly aware of the negative expectations and stereotypes of young Black males, the vast majority benefited from being able to look to their own fathers, or to other role models in the community, as examples of academically successful Black males. These particular fathers were vital to the sons' success.

Key Factors Leading to Success

From our interviews and student questionnaires, we found a number of factors contributing to the success of these young men: (1) the importance of reading, beginning with parents (especially mothers) who read to their sons at a young age; (2) the parents' view that education is both necessary and valuable; (3) active encouragement on the part of parents toward academic success; (4) close interaction between the parents and their sons' teachers; (5) strong parental interest in homework; and (6) considerable verbal praise. Clearly, the sons are aware of the active and consistent attention given to them by their parents. We also found considerable agreement among sons and parents about the critical components of parenting, including the emphasis on love, with parents being there when needed.

What is significant about the success of these young men is that not only have they done well in general, but they have excelled in high school and college mathematics and science courses and performed well on standardized tests in mathematics. This success is especially noteworthy given the importance of math and science education as a foundation for careers in such areas as engineering, biotechnology, and medicine and the severe underrepresentation of African Americans in these fields. The question we have addressed is the extent to which the parents' role was important to their sons' success in math and science. What we found is that in the vast majority of the families, at least one of the parents was important in influencing the students' development of interests and skills in these disciplines. In a few cases parents served as actual teachers, while in other cases they served as resource people, encouraging and inspiring their sons even when they themselves knew very little about math and science.

Other Shared Experiences: Discipline, Educational Experiences, and Church Attendance

We also found that strong limit-setting and discipline played a significant role in the young men's development. Many parents knew how to set limits and to follow through with consistency. These parents did not apologize for being strict or demanding because they made it clear that they were motivated by love. Although in some cases their children did not like the discipline at the time, the sons came to understand later in their development that it was done in their interest. Not surprisingly, the perspectives of parents and their sons regarding discipline are quite different. The parents talked with pride about high expectations and limitations; the sons, on the other hand, talked about not liking parental discipline or structure while growing up, but appreciating it in hindsight. It is important, of course, to remember that the parents and sons are looking back, and their perspectives and interpretations are most probably influenced by the passage of time and opportunities for both groups to reflect on their experiences.

Regarding discipline, we are very sensitive to the question of whether parents should use corporal punishment, given the concerns in our society about parents being physically abusive of their children. We think it important, however, to report what we heard. In many cases, both the parents and their sons talked about corporal punishment as an effective way to control behavior. Although people who read about this approach will draw their own conclusions regarding what is appropriate and inappropriate, we should keep in mind that these parents are working in a context others may not fully understand. Specifically, the challenges regarding discipline are very special because the boys are strongly influenced by their peers. When thinking about parenting, the question is what parents can do to ensure that the children obey and have respect for authority. Of course, every child-parent relationship is different, and what works well for one child may not be effective for another (even in the same family). We are suggesting that parents need to be careful in determining the best approach for administering discipline. Some parents were very successful in having their children understand the consequences of their actions by grounding their children for extensive periods of time or even, in one instance, severing the cord to a video game. In some cases the punishment seemed harsh to us, although it was effective in these instances.

The majority of parents considered the first five years of their sons' lives critical to the boys' intellectual development. It was during this period that parents spent considerable time preparing their children for kindergarten, teaching them the alphabet, reading to them, and helping them recognize colors, numbers, and shapes. (In some cases, other family members, especially grandmothers, were particularly influential before kindergarten.) Parents often emphasized the importance of the mind and general problem-solving. One mother, for example, told us about using the food to teach basic lessons in arithmetic during mealtime, with her son playing a game that involved counting the beans on his plate before eating them. As their sons progressed through school, other parents used such exercises as dyeing Easter eggs, collecting insects, and reading maps on trips to teach science lessons. Many parents bought educational toys and materials, including Lego sets, electrical toys, chemistry sets, and multiplication-table boards, among others. A number of parents exposed their children to work that was more difficult than what they received in their classes. Parents also introduced their children to computers at an early age either at home, at their jobs, or in the library.

Community resources including, for example, the Maryland Science Center, the public library system, and the Lawrence Hall of Science in Berkeley, California, were also used. Some students talked about the important role that elementary-school teachers played in exciting them about science. In at least one instance, a teacher is remembered because she brought humor to math instruction, making math problems enjoyable. Many parents took special care in helping their sons choose not only appropriate classes but also appropriate schools when circumstances led to problems.

It is encouraging to see that the students varied widely in terms of when they first showed special ability in math and science. Some showed tremendous interest at a very early age and others only at a much later age, which suggests the need to continue encouraging students to become interested in math and science. The students came from a variety of schools, mostly public, ranging from comprehensive high schools to those with an emphasis on science. In the vast majority of cases, the students believed that their parents thought that math and science were very important and that their sons could do well in those subjects. Not surprisingly, some sons were naturally more gifted than others in math and science. It is interesting, though, that while some students took as many as three years of chemistry in high school, including a variety of advanced-placement science courses, others had only one basic course. Despite this wide gap in background, the overwhelming majority of students with less exposure have done equally well because of keen interest, hard work, and exceptional motivation.

We see that many families and their children are churchgoers and that church played an important role in the students' upbringing. In a number of the churches attended by the young men in our study, special Sundays are set aside to recognize high academic achievement with speakers, awards, and opportunities for the best students to play an active role in the service. Interesting practices during church services include citing the students with the highest grades and those on the honor roll, having students stand to be acknowledged and receive a round of applause (with members of the congregation giving praise and affection to these students after the service), giving youths opportunities to serve in leadership roles (such as reading the scripture, giving announcements, introducing speakers), and even inviting them to serve as main speakers. High academic achievers are seen as very prestigious children in these settings. Parents and sons also talk about the role of religion in helping to inculcate those values that lay the foundation for making the right decisions in life—distinguishing between right and wrong, resisting temptation, and striving to succeed.

The Meyerhoff Program

It is important to revisit the Meyerhoff Scholars Program, the university experience developed originally for high-achieving African American males in science and math. Special support for these students includes strong academic advising and personal counseling, emphasis on group study and peer support, appropriate tutoring and mentoring, involvement with faculty in research, and access to role models in science. Most important, students are expected to excel and are encouraged to seek not just As, but high As.

The Meyerhoff students benefit also from ongoing family involvement. It is significant that the role of parenting continues to be strong, even during the college years. We find that the young men and their parents talk regularly and rely on each other for emotional support and advice. Because of their knowledge of their sons' strengths and weaknesses, these parents are able to provide the program staff (who often serve as surrogate parents) with appropriate insights as the need arises, and these parents help each other in addressing problems from time to time. In fact, we observed that parents often have questions and anxieties about their sons' progress, state of mind, and future. Effective parenting sometimes calls for close involvement in the sons' lives even when the sons are in their early twenties.

Implications

We can now turn to the second question that began this chapter: What can we learn from studying these academically successful young men and their families that can be useful to other African American children (and children of other races) in fulfilling their potential? We offer a variety of suggestions for schools, policy makers, and parents. We recognize, of course, the difficulties of implementing all of these suggestions, but we see them as important components of larger systemic changes.

The tendency in some quarters is to blame the family and in others to blame the school system. Effective schools are the hub of the community and promote ongoing dialogue between parents and teachers. Parents of males of all ages need opportunities to talk with teachers and other parents, both with those who have already been through the experience of raising sons and with those who are going through the experience at the same time. Although we expected our sessions with parents to last roughly an hour, we found that they sometimes extended to three hours and could have gone on longer. Schools are excellent settings for such sessions involving parents. Churches can also provide such a setting. Parents of successful students who have graduated from middle school, high school, or college should be invited to address families and to form ongoing mentoring relationships with them. These successful students should be encouraged to become leaders in their neighborhoods and should be honored, just as they are honored by their churches.

The atmosphere of the school must be inviting. Some parents, including some we interviewed, are intimidated by their sons' teachers, division heads, principals, or heads of schools. This is particularly true for those parents who had negative experiences during their own education. Parent representatives, parent-teacher liaisons, faculty, and administrators must be sensitive to the parent who seems reluctant to meet to discuss a child or to the parent who does not appear to care. In some cases, though definitely not all, these parents care deeply but are unsure how to show it. There are also parents who question the school and appear angry and impatient with change. Interestingly, they may be a school's strongest allies because it is sometimes these parents who care the most about their children's education.

We know that many school officials are already reaching out to parents with self-doubts and are responsive to those with questions. Nevertheless, we still must address the issues of the underestimation of and underachievement by young Black males. It is important that teachers, school administrators, and parents work together to understand more about the challenges faced by young Black males.[2] We, as a society, must take the time to focus on young Black males because many of their problems are unique to their race and gender. We encourage schools to establish programs that will promote high academic achievement by providing incentives. One approach is to identify and engage those students already doing well (or almost doing well) so that they will continue to be interested and excel. In addition, several elements of the Meyerhoff Program can be used to focus attention on the students' level of performance. Several of these elements, in fact, are already being implemented by some school systems: (1) creating an environment that offers rewards for academic achievement; (2) providing opportunities for young males to come together to talk about their performance in school; (3) giving the parents of young males opportunities to gather to discuss issues of mutual interest, common problems, challenges, and proven solutions; (4) encouraging regular interaction between young Black males and role models; and (5) forming study groups, both composed of these young males and with others who are not necessarily African American.

We also encourage institutions of higher education to look at these initiatives and similar efforts by other universities including, for example, those institutions participating in the Alliance for Minority Participation (AMP) Program funded by the National Science Foundation. University-based AMP projects across the country are designed to increase the number of successful minority students in science and engineering, and they use similar approaches in working with university students.

We have heard stories time and again of children who were underestimated, presumably because of the color of their skin, because they were male, or both. Most schools have parent-teacher-administrator associations in place, or they have some forum where interested parties can discuss educational issues. This is the place where, on a school-by-school basis, and with keen appreciation of the neighborhood environment, expectations for minority children can be addressed. It is up to the schools, in partnership with parents, to take the lead in this area.

Schools need to be aware that students are not always in a position to know what decisions to make about their academic future.[3] Unless they are in contact with teachers or other students who can explain the value of advanced placement courses or of pursuing a rigorous science and math curriculum, they may simply follow the path of least resistance. Close relationships with teachers also can help bridge gaps and serve as a springboard for students. For these and other reasons, sound guidance programs in the middle and high schools that work with parents and encourage students to reach for excellence are critical.

While we encourage all churches and other community organizations, too, to emulate those churches and other groups that recognize academic achievement, the challenge is to encourage more African American families to participate in church activities that can reinforce appropriate values, support academic success, and provide opportunities for children to connect with other positive, successful adults. This strategy will not be easy to implement because weekly church attendance generally has been in decline.[4]

We strongly support systemic school reform of the sort currently sponsored by the National Science Foundation involving school systems and universities across the nation. Many of the students in our study referred to an elementary-school teacher who had a significant influence on their interest and performance in math and science. To increase the number of African Americans who succeed, especially in science, this nation will need to continue to strengthen the math and science backgrounds of teachers, particularly those at the K-8 level. Children, especially young males, need science instruction that emphasizes hands-on experiences and connections to real-life situations, as well as applications that draw upon the students' own experiences in the community.

Even as schools improve, communities will need to continue finding ways to ensure strong parental involvement in the educational process. We agree with Willie Pearson that "if Black participation and performance in science is to improve significantly, Black parents (especially those who are economically disadvantaged) will have to play a more active role in any such efforts. These parents must be made more aware of the economic opportunities available in scientific and technical fields."[5] In addition, school reform efforts should include programs designed to teach parents of young children how to teach science at home.

As we learned from a number of the parents we studied, home activities can be instrumental in stimulating a young child's interest in science. Even at the high-school level, parents who are not comfortable with math and science can be supportive of their sons. One mother, for example, talked about her son's difficulty in a calculus class in his senior year. Although the mother did not understand calculus, she knew the importance of asking her son daily to explain to her what he had learned in his mathematics course that day, and to watch him as he went through his notes during his explanation. When he was not satisfied with his explanation, she would suggest that he write down questions that he could ask his teacher the next day. The son eventually earned an A in the course.

When active parental involvement is unlikely, however, student-enrichment programs sponsored by churches and community organizations become even more important. Both local and nationally based mentoring programs have shown some promise to make a positive difference in the lives of at-risk youth. Project RAISE, for example, a Baltimore-based mentoring program, paired inner-city youth with mentors over a seven-year period. Findings on academic outcomes were especially encouraging for youths who developed positive relationships with mentors, and for youths whose mentors were recruited from local churches.[6] Furthermore, a recent randomized study of Big Brothers and Big Sisters has demonstrated positive outcomes for the youths who received mentors, in contrast to those who did not.[7] In fact, a number of community-based programs have been developed to support at-risk youth through substantive interaction with peers and positive adult role models. Many of the programs focus on the students' cultural heritage and on rites-of-passage training.[8]

We agree with Pearson also that "within the Black community, more can be done to utilize retired persons with training in mathematics and science. . . . Retirees could supplement the school system and develop intervention programs based in churches, recreation centers, and housing projects. . . . [Also,] predominantly Black fraternities, societies, and professional organizations can contribute substantially to scholarships and to intervention programs as volunteers."[9]

Keys to Effective Parenting and Academic Success of Young Black Males

Significantly, we find examples of successful parenting in many different types of family structures—families where there are two parents or one parent, families where the parents have completed college or graduate school, and those where the parents have only a high-school education. The critical ingredients appear to be active parental involvement in the child's life—loving, encouraging, challenging, and supporting the child as the number-one priority of the family. While this approach has been very effective with these young men, the same approach has not necessarily worked with others, even brothers in the same family.

In her book *Blacked Out*, Signithia Fordham found examples of educated families that provided a supportive, caring environment and tremendous opportunities for their children, but to no avail. In fact, in some cases, teachers thought the sons' parents had done too much to protect their children and had not expected enough of them. In contrast, what we learn from successful parents is that much is expected of these young men by their families, including cleaning their rooms, completing chores, maintaining order in the house, learning to follow rules, and understanding that there are consequences to their actions.

What we see today, however, are many examples in the African American community of families (both two-parent and one-parent homes) that do all they know how to do for their sons, and yet many of these males still fail to succeed academically. In some cases they fail because succeeding in school is simply not a priority for a variety of reasons, including wanting to be "cool" and not wanting to be different or a "nerd." It should be encouraging to parents, though, that some of the high-achieving students we spoke with have not always been successful. While there are no easy solutions to the dilemma of low academic achievement, we believe that listening to the voices of the parents and young males in this book can provide hope for others. And, even more important, constantly talking with other parents, teachers, and resource persons in the community can provide parents with clues to their own sons' success.

Every young male is different (even those in the same family), with varying levels of motivation, natural ability, and willingness to listen to advice or to open up to others. We found a number of examples of families in which another child, often another male, did not do as well in school as the students in our sample, even though they had the same parents and caring environment. No point in the book is more critical than the need for parents to listen carefully to each son and always to believe he can succeed.

More specifically, parents of young Black males need to know how important their actions on a daily basis are to their child's academic achievement, and that whether they are college-educated or not, there are many strategies they can use to be helpful, such as reading to their children at an early age, connecting numbers and word problems to real-life situations, encouraging the children to be curious and ask questions, and providing their sons with other role models and examples of successful African American men.

Many of the parents we studied regularly take the time to have conversations with their sons about the significance of being Black and male in American society. These parents talk to their sons in a way that does not leave the sons feeling bitter or as if they are helpless victims. Rather, the emphasis is on teaching them not only how to survive but also how to thrive in this society. It is an approach that focuses on empowering these young men to see the connection between hard work and success. We urge parents of all African American students to do the same and to strive to have calm, thoughtful conversations with their sons.

We recommend family discussions about the role of the family in supporting the education of children and in countering negative myths about possibilities for academic opportunities and success of African American males. The young men in this book (and the Meyerhoff Program in general) are a testament to the fact that great success is possible. Families should use the specific suggestions that parents offer in this book as guides to creating a successful learning environment in the home, one that emphasizes reading and studying and educational games rather than long hours of television watching or telephone conversations. Family discussions might include whomever the adults consider to be "family" and central to the children's achievements. The family needs to work as a team and take responsibility for what happens within the confines of the home. The school, in turn, must do its part and look specifically at its role in educating young Black males.

We know from family theory that children receive a more consistent upbringing and are less apt to be troubled in their home environment when parental figures agree on key parenting issues. The more consistent a mother and father (or a mother and grandmother, for example) are about the requirements of homework before play, bedtime, reading rather than watching television, involvement in extracurricular activities, and striving for excellence, the clearer the children will be about rules and expectations. It is when parental figures are at odds about such expectations, or when one parent is not consistent, that children most clearly sense that they will not be held accountable for their behavior.

Beyond the implications for parents and schools drawn above, larger-scale community and societal change are also needed to substantially enhance the numbers of academically successful African American males. In his book *Beyond the Classroom,* psychologist Laurence Steinberg emphasizes, among other things, the importance of establishing academic excellence as a national priority: "If we want our children and teenagers to value education and strive for achievement, adults must behave as if doing well in school . . . is . . . more important than any other activity in which young people are involved."[10] We fully support Steinberg's view that we need to focus attention beyond the classroom to effect educational change, and work to ensure that parents and the larger community place academic excellence as an overarching priority for the childhood and teenage years.

We also support many of the recommendations put forth in the recent report *Repairing the Breach.*[11] This report of a national task force on African American men and boys recommends, for instance, enhanced focus by the media on positive images of Black males, developing local community leadership and grassroots organizations to help rebuild a sense of civic community, and a national dialogue on race relationships. These efforts, as part of a larger social initiative to enhance the community fabric of life for African Americans and all citizens, represent examples of the broader network of activities necessary to ensure that larger numbers of Black youth have the societal support they need in order to beat the odds and achieve at the highest levels academically.

The Task Ahead

The road ahead is very challenging. We return to four key points from our research that inform the work that has to be done. First, these young men are caught between two worlds—the neighborhood, in its broadest sense, which requires one set of behaviors for success, and the school community, which sometimes requires different behaviors for success. These worlds must find more common ground if African American youth are going to be successful in the larger society. Second, even in the 1990s, and even for these most successful of young men, society continues to place obstacles in their path. When a young Black man feels he is a target, in his own neighborhood and in other communities, the prospects for success diminish greatly. Third, despite these obstacles, the sons we spoke with have succeeded, we believe, for three reasons: they have been supported by their families; they have been given the message that they must overcome whatever obstacles they find in their path; and they have worked hard to build upon their abilities. Fourth, education is highly valued in these families, as it has been traditionally for African Americans. Over and over, parents received the message, which they in turn passed on to their sons, that one's education and its benefits can never be taken away, no matter how hostile the environment.

To heighten the likelihood that young African American males will succeed, we have thought a great deal about the roles that the parents (and other key family members) have played in the lives of the sons we studied. It became clear that effective parents are primarily advocates, coaches, and experts.

Parents must be advocates for their children in school, in the community, and sometimes even within the family. It is the parents' role both to stand up for the child and to hold the child accountable. We urge judicious advocacy, not blind advocacy. If a parent is not holding a son accountable for his behavior, the parent is not teaching responsibility to the child or being responsive to the needs of the community. Communities need responsible citizens in order to maintain their vibrancy. Parenting becomes more effective when many people in the neighborhood share the same values about the importance of raising children responsibly and raising them to be responsible.

Parents also must coach their children through their development. An effective coach teaches concrete skills, pushes an individual to achieve his full potential, and is consistently supportive, win or lose. Effective parents become experts on their sons—they know their strengths and weaknesses better than anyone else. To become experts, these parents never stop studying their sons throughout their entire lives, spending time with them, listening to them, and learning about their schoolwork, friends, interests, and hobbies.[12]

Our hope is that every young African American male will be as fortunate as those we studied—fortunate to have loving and supportive parents and others who help them to succeed. And we hope that these young men will then become such parents to their own children, further weaving the tapestry across generations and expanding the numbers who beat the odds.

Appendix **A**
Overview of Study Procedure

Interview Samples

Letters were sent to the parents of current Meyerhoff Program males in good standing, along with parents of program graduates, inviting them to group interviews on the UMBC campus. Parents were informed that the interviews would form the basis of a book on parenting African American males, and would be videotaped and audiotaped, but that individuals would not be identified in publications. After the initial mailing, additional single parents and non-college-educated parents were further recruited via telephone, so as to have a large enough sample to gain insight into these important subgroups. In 1994 and 1995 five groups of mothers (N = 33) were interviewed by the African American female director of the Meyerhoff Scholars Program, and four groups of fathers (N = 24) by the African American male assistant director of the program. Prior to the start of each interview, parents completed a brief questionnaire. Additional parents were interviewed individually.

The subset of sons of the parents interviewed who were still in college, as well as all sons from single-parent families whose parents had not been interviewed, were invited to take part in the research by the African American male assistant director of the Meyerhoff Program. In 1995 and 1996, forty-seven interviews were conducted, encompassing seven groups of sons, and three individual interviews for those unable to attend the group interviews. Six of the group sessions, and all three individual interviews, were conducted by the African American male assistant director of the Program. One group session was conducted by a female staff member of the program.

In addition, tape-recorded, semistructured individual interviews, focusing on factors leading to success in school, were conducted with

Meyerhoff students attending the required six-week precollege summer bridge programs on the UMBC campus in the summers of 1991–1996. Fifty-two students in the sample were interviewed by trained Black female graduate students.

Trustworthiness of Data

Several steps were taken to enhance the credibility and trustworthiness of the qualitative data. The selection of Meyerhoff Program staff to conduct the parenting interviews ensured, in most cases, that the sons, fathers, and mothers interviewed had a positive, trusting relationship with the interviewer. The program has been extremely effective in empowering Black males to succeed in college and to go on to graduate or professional school, and many parents in particular seemed to welcome the opportunity to "give back" to the program leaders.

The decisions to interview multiple family members whenever possible, to carry out two types of interviews with sons at different points in time, and to use both qualitative and quantitative methods ensured multiple data sources and formats. This approach helped us to establish and support the veracity of our findings. A separate paper is in preparation which details findings from the quantitative portion of the research. Finally, a multiracial research team worked on the qualitative data analysis.

Interview Analysis

All parenting and school experience interviews were transcribed, resulting in over eight hundred single-spaced pages. Analysis proceeded on two related fronts. First, each transcript was reviewed by two or three faculty and graduate student research team members, who identified the primary contextual challenges and factors related to success. One or two research team members prepared a summary for each student, encompassing all available interviews (son, mother, father). The summaries identified and linked the various parenting and contextual factors related to the son's academic success.

A coding system was developed focused on the presence or absence of various factors that emerged from the thematic analysis as contributing to academic achievement (see Maton, Hrabowski, and Greif 1997). Four research assistants (one African American male, one African American female, and two White females) were trained to do the coding, each rating from eight to sixteen interviews. On a random sample of ten sets of interviews, an average interrater agreement of 77.1 percent was achieved (range = 74.5 percent to 87.5 percent, across six rater pairs).

Finally, two members of the research team compared the mother, father, and son interviews in order to evaluate consistency of responses across the data sources. A strikingly small number of discrepancies were found for most interview questions. The only research question in which substantive discrepancies occurred frequently focused on sons' problem behaviors. A sizable portion of sons reported behaviors (e.g., curfew violations, sexual behavior, alcohol, and in a few cases, gambling or theft) of which their parents apparently were not aware.

Additional details and findings related to the qualitative analyses can be found in Maton, Hrabowski, and Greif 1997.

Appendix **B**
National Science Foundation Minority
Student Development Programs

The National Science Foundation (NSF) is the major funding agency for science and mathematics education in the United States. The NSF also coordinates programs promoting science, math, and technology with other federal and state agencies. These programs focus on all levels of education, from preschool to graduate school and beyond. Many of the science and math programs the sons in this book participated in are, at least partially, funded by the NSF. The National Science Foundation annually documents the number of science and mathematics degrees awarded to minority students as part of their stated goal of increasing the numbers of minorities in science and mathematics.

NSF student development programs are grouped into three areas of focus: precollege, undergraduate, and graduate.

Precollege opportunities, aimed at elementary- and secondary-school students, are grouped under Career Access Opportunities in Science and Technology (CAO). The three programs supported under this initiative are Comprehensive Regional Centers for Minorities (CRCM), Summer Science Camps (SSC), and Partnerships for Minority Student Achievement (PMSA). All three programs aim to forge alliances between schools, institutions of higher education, community organizations, and private industry both to foster minority student interest in science, math, and technology and to increase minority performance in these fields.

Undergraduate programs provide outreach assistance and scholarships to increase the number of degrees awarded to minorities in science, math, and technology. The two programs supported under this initiative are the Alliance for Minority Participation (AMP) program and the Research Careers for Minority Scholars (RCMS) program. The

Alliance for Minority Participation program creates regional coopera-
tives of educational institutions to attract and retain minority students
in science and engineering undergraduate majors. Regional AMPs initiate and support such activities as summer internship programs, summer bridge programs, and student conferences and exhibits.

At the graduate-school level, the National Science Foundation focuses on supporting minority researchers through the Centers of Research
Excellence in Science and Technology and through minority graduate
fellowship programs.

To locate the programs in your area contact: Minority Programs,
Directorate for Education and Human Resources, National Science
Foundation, 4201 Wilson Boulevard, Arlington, Virginia 22230; (703)
306-1640.

The National Science Foundation also awards fellowships in math,
science, and engineering, at both the graduate and undergraduate levels. In addition, they provide a listing of research opportunities for
minority students. For more information, contact Minority Programs.

A list of publications (NSF 96-47, *Publications Catalog*) and information about NSF programs (NSF 95-138, *Guide to Programs*) are available
through the publications office at (703) 306-1130. For those with Internet
access, the publications list (and the actual publications) are found at
http://www.nsf.gov/od/lpo/news/publicat/nsf9647/start.htm.
A list of currently funded minority programs can be located at
http://www.ehr.nsf.gov/ehr/ehr/ipm/.

Notes

Preface

1. Stevenson, Chen, and Uttal 1990, p. 508.
2. Gibbons 1992, p. 1190
3. Gibbs 1988a, p. 238.

Chapter 1

1. Wilson 1996.
2. Majors, Billson, and Mancini 1992.
3. Steinberg, Dornbush, and Brown 1992.
4. Golden 1995, p. 7.
5. Carter and Wilson 1997.
6. Ibid.
7. Educational Testing Service 1995. The SAT scores are not recentered.
8. Ibid.
9. Miller 1995, p. 159.
10. See, for instance, Midgette and Glenn 1993.
11. Gates and West 1996, p. xv.
12. Majors, Billson, and Mancini 1992.
13. National Institutes of Health 1996.
14. Gibbs 1988a.
15. Gibbs 1988b.
16. Association of American Medical Colleges 1990.
17. Majors, Billson, and Mancini 1992.
18. Gibbs 1988a, p. 237.
19. National Center for Education Statistics 1995a; U. S. Department of Commerce 1995.
20. Smith and Johns 1995.
21. Majors, Billson, and Mancini 1992, p. 13.
22. Oakes 1985.
23. Ford and Harris 1991.
24. Maryland State Department of Education 1995.
25. National Center for Education Statistics 1995b; Murray, Herling, and Stabler 1973.
26. Weinstein et al. 1991.
27. Ibid.

28. Hare 1987; Reed 1988. Reed's analysis and discussion of this topic were of tremendous help.
29. Edelman 1995, p. 192.
30. Educational Testing Service 1995.
31. National Research Council 1995.
32. Billingsley 1992, p. 17.
33. Ibid., p. 28.
34. Ibid., p. 224.
35. Fordham 1996, p. 148.
36. Ibid., p. 171.
37. Spencer 1990.
38. Ibid.
39. Ibid.
40. Mfume 1996, 32.
41. Clark 1983.
42. Additional information about the methodology is detailed in Appendix A, and also in Maton, Hrabowski, and Greif 1997.
43. The questionnaire for the parents is available from the authors.
44. U.S. Bureau of the Census 1996.
45. See Maton, Hrabowski, and Greif 1997 for additional details about some of the questionnaires administered, and for findings that compare the male Meyerhoff students with lower-achieving Black males, high-achieving white males, and high-achieving Black female Meyerhoff students.
46. U.S. Department of Commerce 1995; U.S. Department of Commerce 1973; Maryland Department of Economic and Employment.
Development 1992.
47. Edelman 1995, p. 190.

Chapter 2

1. U.S. Bureau of the Census 1996.
2. Blankenhorn 1995.
3. U.S. Department of Commerce 1984.
4. U.S. Bureau of the Census 1994; U.S. Bureau of the Census 1995.
5. One father in this group is White and holds a bachelor's degree.
6. U.S. Bureau of the Census 1993.
7. Solid data do not exist on the percentage of African American single parents of children eighteen and over who were married at least once. For purposes of comparison, it is known that in 1993, 79.6 percent of African American men ages forty to forty-four and 85.6 percent of the men ages forty-four to fifty-four had been married at least once (U.S. Bureau of the Census 1994). Here, though, we are speaking about current marital status.
8. See, for example, Wade 1994.
9. Boyd-Franklin 1989.
10. Griswold 1993.
11. Wilensky and Lebeaux 1965.
12. Frazier 1948, p. 255.
13. McAdoo 1993.
14. Griswold 1993.
15. Bryan and Ajo 1992; Wade 1994.
16. Garfinkel and McClanahan 1986.

17. McAdoo 1993.

18. Willie 1988. Both Black fathers and mothers agree that men tend to spend less time on child care than Black women (Ahmeduzzaman and Roopnarine, 1992).

19. McAdoo 1993.

20. Zollar and Williams 1987. A recent study conducted by Bryan and Ajo (1992) of fifty African American fathers from two professional organizations and two homeless shelters attempted to learn more about father role perceptions. The role of father was conceptualized to include economic provider, advice giver, disciplinarian, companion to children in leisure activities, ensurer of children's safety, and child-care provider. It was hypothesized that the respondents' perception of the importance of fathering would increase with the fathers' educational level, work hours, income, and age. Half the fathers were living with their children. Higher income and employment did show a positive relationship with the fathers' perceptions of fathering. This reinforces the previous points concerning the significance of the provider role to a father's self-concept.

21. The literature on parenting has various definitions on what "authoritative" or "authoritarian" parenting means and how "autonomy" and "nurturing" are defined. Mosley and Thomson (1995), in reviewing some of the literature, make the following relevant points: Black parents were found in one study, when compared with White parents, to emphasize obedience over autonomy, and, in another study of middle-income Black parents, to be more involved and nurturing when compared with White parents. Mosley and Thomson's own findings supported earlier research findings that Black fathers were less actively involved than mothers and that fathers' involvement was beneficial for sons. These findings about the authoritarian and involved nature of parents, as well as about the different levels of involvement (fleshed out further in chapter 3) and the positive outcomes of that involvement, are consistent with our observations. We also are aware that the whole notion of what authoritarian parenting means may be culture-specific. For example, Chao (1994), in studying immigrant Chinese parents' apparently authoritarian parenting style and school outcomes among children, concludes that the concept of "training" is more culturally relevant and positively connotated. This is consistent with the classic work of Baumrind (1972) which concluded that when Black families were viewed by White standards, they appeared more authoritarian. Those Black families who were viewed as authoritarian also produced the most assertive and independent girls.

22. See Minuchin and Fishman 1981.

23. A few fathers stated they did not know they were "poor" until they grew up, left home and both saw how others lived in poverty and heard descriptions of it. This is also a point made by Henry Louis Gates Jr. about his own upbringing (Gates and West 1996).

24. The fathers were asked to describe the accuracy of a series of statements using a scale ranging from 1 to 5, where 1 indicated that the statement was not at all accurate, 3 that the statement was somewhat accurate, and 5 that the statement was completely accurate. The first statement was "In high school I monitored the amount of time my son spent studying." If a father gave a response equal to 3, 4, or 5, he was judged to be at least somewhat involved in monitoring his son's studying.

25. This is one of three biracial families in the book for which at least one member was interviewed.

26. See, for example, Imber-Black 1988.

27. By comparison, 17 percent of White children being raised by one parent are living with their father (U.S. Bureau of the Census 1994).

Chapter 3

1. Boyd-Franklin 1989, p. 70.
2. Herring and Wilson-Sadberry 1993.
3. U.S. Bureau of the Census 1995, 1996.
4. Taylor et al. 1990.
5. Rhodes, Ebert, and Fischer 1992; Parish, Hao, and Hogan 1991.
6. Jayakody, Chatters, and Taylor 1993.
7. Kitson and Morgan 1990.
8. Taylor et al. 1990.
9. Bank et al. 1993.
10. Entwisle and Alexander 1992, 1996.
11. Comparison data for mothers of children over eighteen is difficult to obtain. Eighty-eight percent of Black women ages forty-five to fifty-four have been married at least once (U.S. Bureau of the Census 1994). Here we are speaking about current marital status, however.
12. Data that looks at the percentage of children living with any parent in 1960 show that in this population, 75 percent were living with both parents. Yet this is somewhat misleading, as a significant percentage of children were living with other relatives or nonrelatives (U.S. Bureau of the Census 1991).
13. It is hard to calculate comparisons, as some data from that period provide figures on the percentage of those between eighteen and twenty-four who were in college during a certain period. For example, in 1960 the figure was 18.4 percent (U.S. Department of Commerce 1984). These mothers' parents could have been in college in the 1940s, when higher education was less common. We also know that some of these parents continued their education late in life. Despite this, we are comfortable in guessing that this level of education was above the norm.
14. Crosbie-Burnett and Lewis 1993.
15. Ibid.
16. Boyd-Franklin 1989.
17. Kelley, Sanchez-Hucles, and Walker 1993.
18. Ibid.
19. U.S. Department of Commerce 1984.
20. This would appear to be a somewhat higher level of involvement than that of the typical African-American parent, according to data taken from Zill and Nord 1994. Exact comparisons are difficult given the differences in the way the questions were asked in our data and in the U.S. Department of Education data that work cites.
21. This level of encouragement of involvement in extracurricular activities seems well above the national averages supplied by Zill and Nord 1994, though again the method of reporting is different.
22. Gary 1995.
23. Please see endnote 24 in chapter 2 for an explanation of the way questions were worded on the instrument. The questionnaire responses are on a five-point scale with "completely accurate" at 5 and "not at all accurate" at 1. If the score of 5 is used for comparison of these items, mothers were more involved.

Comparisons between mothers and fathers are difficult to make as they are not necessarily between mothers and fathers in the same family. Rather, they should be read as a group of fathers compared with a group of mothers.
24. Gill (1991), in providing suggestions for African American parents interested in improving their children's school performance, also encourages parents to see themselves as their children's primary teachers.

25. Wolin and Bennett 1984, p. 464.

26. Both are statistically significant at p>.05.

27. A recent study found that African Americans raised in interracial environments were less apt to maintain their closeness to other Blacks in adulthood (Harris 1995).

28. Del Carmen and Virgo 1993.

Chapter 4

1. See, for example, Taylor et al. 1990. Furthermore, most of the research has focused on lower income Black youths, with very little research focused on working-class or middle-class Black youth.

2. See, for example, McLaughlin and Heath 1993. More generally, as noted in an earlier chapter, many family researchers in recent years have argued for a strengths-based, rather than a deficits-based, approach to research on Black families (e.g., Hurd et al. 1995; McAdoo, 1988; Wilson 1995).

3. See, for example, Werner and Smith 1992.

4. Maton and Salem 1995. More generally, Luster and McAdoo (1994) argue for the importance of "understanding the processes (e.g., activities, roles, relationships) in the family, school, and community that contribute to success" among African American children (p. 1093).

5. A literature review by Taylor (1991) summarizes some of the differences in child socialization and parenting practices among African American parents based on socioeconomic status—including marital status of parents and parental education. More generally, Willie (1988) discusses various differences among affluent, working-class, and poor Black families.

6. Concerning the consequences of divorce, for instance, some studies have shown that Black youths whose parents have divorced report fewer adjustment difficulties than White youths whose parents have divorced (cf. Kitson and Morgan 1990). More generally, there is some evidence that children from single-parent families are good decision makers and that they have strengths and maturities associated with their experiences related to divorce (Hutchinson and Sprangler 1988). Many have argued that single-parent African American households can function quite effectively (e.g., Boyd-Franklin 1989; Jenkins 1989). Concerning socioeconomic status, the vast majority of Black males who go on to college are not from the higher-SES groups (e.g., Wilson-Sadberry, Winfield, and Royster 1991).

7. See, for instance, Hare 1987 and Staples and Johnson 1993, chapter 8. In addition to different challenges and stresses, the research literature suggests various other differences, relevant to the current focus, in single-parent versus two-parent Black homes. For instance, Prom-Jackson, Johnson, and Wallace (1987), in a sample of primarily Black, high-achieving youth from lower-income families, found different factors linked to higher GPA in single-parent and two-parent families. Specifically, for youth from single-parent families, the mothers' capability to communicate to them a sense of their identity as a male or female without stereotyping was linked to GPA, whereas for youths from two-parent households high levels of communication were linked to higher GPA. Concerning extended family support, Jayakody, Chatters, and Taylor (1993) found, in a representative sample of African-American mothers, that kin provided greater financial assistance to never-married than to married mothers. Thornton et al. (1990) found that never-married mothers and fathers were less likely to impart messages concerning racial socialization than

those who were married. Finally, in terms of general "family climate," Tolson and Wilson (1990) found differences on various family climate dimensions in single-parent versus two-parent Black families.

8. The importance of maternal education for educational attainment among Black young adults was found, for instance, in a widely cited study by Wilson and Allen (1987). Haertel and Wiley (1979) found that the effect of maternal education on educational achievement among Blacks was twice as great as the effect of poverty. Maternal education may affect specific child-rearing practices as well. For instance, Thornton et al. (1990) found that mothers with higher levels of education were more likely to impart messages and socialize their children concerning racial matters than those with lower levels of education; this was especially the case with older, highly educated mothers. Most recently, Luster and McAdoo (1996) found that the link between maternal education and longer-term educational attainment involved intervening impacts on both academic motivation and personal behavior of the young child. Finally, Maple and State (1991) found that maternal education level for Black males, but not for Black females or White males or females, was predictive of choice of a math or science major in college in a national sample of students.

9. As general support for this point, Cohen (1987) found that "white-collar" parents tend to influence the academic achievement of their children through expectations and modeling, while "blue-collar" parents did so through expectations only.

10. The general importance of economic resources, or socioeconomic status, for educational attainment was discussed in chapter 1. Many more specific links to academic preparedness or to parenting practices exist as well. For instance, in terms of academic preparedness, Entwisle and Alexander (1990) found that among Baltimore children, math reasoning skills at the start of first grade were related to economic resources in the home. Concerning child-rearing, Spencer (1990) found, in a sample of Black parents, that middle-income parents enlisted more community resources for help in child-rearing (e.g., literature, medical sources), were more likely to rate the role of the father as equally important in child-rearing, and were more likely to rate church attendance as "extremely important."

11. Steinberg, Dornbusch, and Brown (1992) in a large sample of high-school students, found that the absence of peer support for achievement was especially undermining of Academic achievement for Black youth. Luster and McAdoo (1996) summarizes some of the educational challenges and problems facing youth growing up in urban areas.

12. The numbers presented for the sons in each subset represent all sons in the research. However, different subsets of information drawn upon in this and the next chapter, were available for different sons. Forty-six of the sixty sons were interviewed especially for this book, but the other fourteen took part in other interviews, and completed questionnaires, as part of the larger research project, from which information is also drawn in these chapters.

13. See, for example, Banks (1984) and Hudson (1991) for discussions of the challenges of developing a positive racial identity for students growing up in varied neighborhood environments. Alvy (1997) has developed a parent training program which incorporates a focus on positive racial identity for all Black youth.

14. The names of the sons have been changed.

15. In family-theory terms, a "boundary" was drawn around the family, protecting the members from outside influences, while encouragement was given internally by a valued person.

16. In support of the importance of extended family, Thompson et al. (1992)

found that in a large sample of first-graders in Baltimore, children from single-parent families in which extended family were present in the home improved their conduct more over the first year of school than those from single-parent families in which an extended-family member was not present.

17. Baumrind (1996), among others, argues that physical discipline can be an effective form of discipline within a given cultural context, and is not necessarily related to tolerance of harsh discipline.

18. See Fordham and Ogbu (1986), for a discussion about coping with the "burden of acting white" for African American, academically oriented students in the urban high school context.

19. It may be that the stricter discipline is the result of having a father in the home and the lower educational attainment level of the parents.

20. Consistent with our interview findings, previous research has shown that physical punishment is prevalent among African-American parents of all socioeconomic levels, and more frequently used in disciplining boys than girls, Taylor, 1991. Boyd-Franklin (1989) reports that many Black parents take pride in upholding the "old school" of discipline (i.e., "spare the rod, spoil the child"), and view strict discipline as protecting children, and especially adolescents, from the severe consequences of acting-out behavior. Lassiter (1987) similarly notes that "The strong belief in the effectiveness and clear rewards of discipline, combined with the equally strong belief that a lack of discipline and parental authority can destroy a child, explains readily why . . . acts of discipline are perceived as expressions of parental love and caring" (p. 44).

21. Thornton, Chatters, Taylor and Allen (1990) examined the sociodemographic correlates of racial socialization, and find high levels in families from higher SES (socioeconomic status) subgroups.

22. See Steele and Aronson (1995) for research data that links "stereotype threat" to negative academic performance among African Americans.

23. In terms of African American family structure, Slaughter- Defoe et al. (1990) note that "though the greater risk and vulnerability associated with [single-parent] childhoods is well known, most researchers have continued to emphasize that family structure does not uniformly predict family functioning—and especially, achievement socialization" (p. 372). In terms of social class, Steinberg, Elmen and Mounts (1989) found the grade point averages of working-class and middle-class African American youths to be essentially the same (independent of family structure). In contrast, a relatively large difference between working-class and middle-class White youths was found on grade point average, which was especially pronounced when working-class and middle-class two-parent families are compared.

24. Research has shown a direct link between regular patterns of reading to children when they are young and subsequent literacy and school performance (e.g., Baker, Scher and Mackler 1997; Romotowski and Trepaneir 1977). In terms of television watching, Christenson, Rounds, and Gorney (1992), based on their review of available research, emphasize the importance of parents' limiting TV viewing to enable the child to participate in other, educationally related activities.

25. For these questionnaire items, students responded on a five-point scale ranging from "not at all accurate" (1) to "somewhat accurate" (3) to "very accurate" (5).

26. Previous research has shown that parents of successful African American students place a high value on education and the pursuit of high-status careers (e.g., Clark 1983; Ford 1993; Johnson 1992).

27. Research has indicated that most academically successful African Americans receive a great deal of encouragement from extended-family members, along with

one or both parents (Clark 1983; Lee 1985; Prom-Jackson, Johnson and Wallace 1987; Scott-Jones 1987; Wilson 1987). Much of this previous research has focused on lower-income African-American families.

28. Students were asked to respond either "true" (agree) or "false" (disagree).

29. Not surprisingly, research has indicated that reinforcement and feedback on homework produce higher student achievement (e.g., Keith 1987), and parental enforcement of consequences for completion or noncompletion may improve effectiveness (e.g., Harris 1983). In a study of lower income Black families, Clark (1983) found firm and consistent monitoring of home activities and study time.

30. For the high-school question, the four response categories were "none," "very little," "quite a bit," and "too much." The latter response category was not included in the elementary-school and middle-school items.

31. The high-school questionnaire item was, "In high school my parent(s) monitored the amount of time I spent studying." Students indicated the accuracy of the statement on a 5-point scale ranging from "not at all accurate" (1) to "somewhat accurate" (3) to "very accurate" (5). Responses of 3, 4, or 5 were considered indications of at least some parental monitoring.

32. The importance of parental involvement in education has been demonstrated in many studies. As summarized by Christenson, Rounds, and Borney (1992), "Parents participate in education both at school and at home. There is a substantial body of literature that documents the positive effects of parent involvement on student achievement. There is some evidence to show that the effects are most comprehensive when parents are involved both at home an school. Parent involvement in home learning activities that support school instruction is a strong, significant correlate of academic outcomes for students" (p. 192). This is echoed in previous research focused explicitly on African American families. Active parental involvement, particularly in the elementary-school years, has been related to high academic achievement for African American students (Clark 1983; Snodgrass 1991). In a study of low-income families, Clark (1983) found that the parents of high achievers had histories of frequent contact with the school, were involved in parent-teacher groups, and believed that their purpose was to work along with school efforts to strengthen their children's talents. Garibaldi (1992) found that parental nonattendance at parent-teacher conferences was associated with lower educational expectations and aspirations from teachers.

33. A number of researchers have emphasized that mutual respect and cooperation between families and schools contribute greatly to Black children's academic success (e.g., Comer 1980; Slaughter-Defoe et al. 1990). Taylor, Hintur, and Winston (1995) found that parent involvement predicted academic outcomes for 566 African American students, ages 5 to 18, in the National Survey of Family and Household data set. Connel, Spencer and Aber (1994) studied Black middle-schoolers, and depict a model leading from parent school involvement to self-system processes and student school engagement and ultimately to school adjustment and peformance. Christenson, Rounds, and Gorney (1992), based on their review of the literature, concluded that if what children learn in the home is supportive of what they learn in school, school achievement is considerably enhanced. In a recent longitudinal study, Luster and McAdoo (1996) found that maternal involvement in kindergarten was an important predictor of academic motivation and long-term educational achievement, through age twenty-seven.

34. Wilson-Sadberry, Winfield, and Royster (1991) found that among the 1,332 African American males in the High School and Beyond data base, 1,213 attended public high schools, 94 attended Catholic high schools, and 25 attended private high schools.

35. Based on their review of the research literature, Christenson, Rounds, & Gorney (1992) concluded that "A positive parent-child relationship is related to academic success. Parents who accept, nurture, encourage, and are emotionally responsive to their child's developmental needs tend to have children who are successful in school. This affective relationship is not associated with IQ, SES, or gender of the child" (p. 188). Additionally, shared responsibility between the adolescent and his parent has been found to be related to higher school grades (Dornbusch, Ritter, Mont-Reynaud, and Chen, 1990; Steinberg, Elmen, and Mounts, 1989).

More generally, a loving, nurturing family environment appears to be one of the pillars upon which successful childrearing is built. Clark (1983) found that compared to low achieving black children, high achieving black children had parents who were more active in their development and were more likely to engage in warm and nurturing interactions. Bradley, Rock, Caldwell, Harris and Hamrick (1987) in a study of Black elementary school children, found a positive relationship between academic achievement and parent responsiveness and the general emotional climate of the home. More recently, Luster and McAdoo (1994) found that a supportive home environment was one of the key elements differentiating high achieving from low achieving young African American children. Gonzales, Cauce, Friedman, and Mason (1996) found in a study of 120 African American junior high school students in the Seattle area, that maternal support was prospectively and positively related to adolescents' grades, independent of neighborhood risk.

36. Christenson, Rounds, and Gorney (1992), in their review of this literature, conclude that, "Parental discipline characterized by setting clear standards, enforcing rules, and encouraging discussion, negotiation, and independence is associated with positive academic outcomes. Over- and under-control are correlated negatively with student achievement" (p. 190). They also indicate that the evidence of a link between parenting style and academic outcome is stronger for White than African American families.

37. This item is from Moos' Family Environment Scale, and is answered either "True" or "False."

38. Many researchers have found a strong relationship between realistic, high parent expectations for children's school performance and positive academic performance (for a review, see Christenson, Rounds and Gorney (1992). Interestingly, the linkage between expectations and performance begins at a very young age. For instance, Entwisle and Alexander (1990) found that beginning school math competence was directly related among African American urban children, to high parent expectations for the child to do well (above and beyond influence of other factors such as ability or family socioeconomic level).

39. The nature, frequency, and some of the correlates of racial socialization by African American parents have been researched by Thornton et al. (1990), among others.

40. Bowman and Howard (1985) found that African American youth who had been socialized to be cognizant of racial barriers and cautioned about interracial protocol attained higher grade point averages than those who were taught nothing about race relations. Clark (1991) emphasizes the importance of a positive Black social identity as a critical protective mechanism contributing to Black youth's academic achievement. Ford (1995) explicitly links issues related to racial identity to underperformance among gifted African American students.

Overall, as a result of their upbringing the sons appear to have developed a positive racial identification, to have positive attitudes towards Whites, and to strive to relate to people as individuals rather than on the basis of the color of their skin. A recent dissertation (Greene 1995), indicated that the vast majority of sons were capable of negotiating the Black and White cultural worlds, and that the small subset who were unable to do so had greater levels of academic and personal difficulties.

41. Researchers have emphasized the importance for children's academic achievement of a positive link between the family and community cultural and social resources, both for youth in general (e.g., Bronfenbrenner 1986), and for African American youth in particular (e.g., Bowman and Howard 1985; Ogbu 1988; Slaughter-Defoe et al. 1990). The importance of non-parental sources of positive influence was a major finding in the interviews with academically successful African American and other minority students carried out by Bowser and Perkins (1991).

Hillary Clinton's 1996 recent best-selling book emphasizes the importance of community connectedness for families and youth. Thus, a larger influence network, including extended family, church, teachers, and peers, form the modern day counterpart of the African "village" which helps support parents and develop the students' character, skills, and positive academic focus. Indeed, as aptly stated by Andrew Billingsley (1992), "One of the most powerful truths about families is that they cannot be strong unless they are surrounded by a strong community" (p. 70).

42. Billingsley (1992) found a similar level of church involvement in his sample (p. 73).

43. Cauce (1986) and Patchen (1982) each found a direct relationship between having peers with strong academic values and African American youth's academic achievement. Clark (1991) emphasized the importance of a positive peer support network as a critical protective mechanism contributing to Black youth's academic achievement. Wilson-Sadberry, Winfield and Royster (1991) found a strong relationship between best friend's academic orientation and post-secondary educational experience among a large, nationally representative sample of African American males. Also, as noted in chapter 4, Steinberg, Dornbusch, and Brown (1992), in a large-scale study of academic achievement among high-school students, emphasized the special need for positive peer academic support for academics among African American youth.

The sample of academically successful working-class youth interviewed by Bowser and Perkins (1991) emphasized the critical influence of a positive, personal, mentoring relationship developed with at least one teacher in the school.

44. Interestingly, Paulson (1994) found that what best predicts achievement is an adolescent's perceptions of the parenting they received, not the actual behavior of the parents.

Chapter 5

1. The sons' average high-school grade point average was 3.49 (A-/B+), and their average SAT math score was 641.7 (89th percentile for all students). It should be noted that these students also generally performed at high levels in their nonmath/nonscience courses. A review of student grades in math/science and nonmath/nonscience courses during their junior or senior year reveals many students receiving mostly As in both types of courses, some students receiving more As than Bs in math/science courses and more Bs than As in nonmath/nonscience courses, and a slightly smaller number of students receiving more Bs than As in math/science courses and more As than Bs in nonmath/nonscience courses, or more Bs than

As in both math/science and nonmath/nonscience courses. The average SAT verbal score was 541.5 (84th percentile for all students).

2. Recent studies highlighting the importance of one or more of these factors, many focused explicitly on minority students, include Dick and Rallis 1991; Ellis 1993; Garcia 1988; Gibbons, 1992; Hill, Pettus, and Hedin, 1990; Naizer 1993; Oakes 1990; Reynolds 1991; Seymour and Hewitt 1997; Vetter, 1994.

3. That is, in fully 80 percent of the families, at least one family member we interviewed (father, mother, or son) singled out a parent as a primary influence in the son's math or science skill development, interest, or success.

4. In this chapter we focus on the positive contribution of schools to student success in math and science. We do not mean to imply that certain schools, curricula, or teachers do not also have a negative effect on African American males in general, and on their math/science learning in particular (see, for instance, Garza 1992; Vetter 1994). That is not our focus here.

5. Kokoski and Downing-Leffler 1995.

6. Vetter (1994) emphasizes the potential negative consequences of elementary school on students' natural scientific curiosity. "Although children enter kindergarten with a wonderful curiosity about the natural world, it appears to be squelched for many children . . . within the early years of school" (p. 9).

7. These summary points are generally consistent with previous research in the area (e.g., Vetter 1994).

8. See Fonken 1992. Maple and Stage (1991) found, among a national sample of Black males, that the number of math and science courses completed by the end of the sophomore year, along with positive attitudes to math and mother's level of education, was predictive of selection of a math/science major in college.

9. The special influence a math or science teacher can have on a secondary-school student is illustrated in the case of a recent Presidential Scholar in a *Washington Post* article (Verzemnieks 1996).

10. See Hofstein , Maoz, and Rishpon 1990 for research that indicates the positive influence of extracurricular involvements in science on student attitudes toward science.

11. These characterizations are based on multiple sources of information, including parent interviews, son interviews, responses to questionnaire items, high-school grades, and SAT scores. 18.3 percent of the sons achieved SAT math scores above 700, and an additional 26.7 percent received scores between 650 and 699. 15 percent achieved SAT math scores between 510 and 590. 16.7 percent of the sons earned a high school grade point average above 3.75, 36.6 percent between 3.50 and 3.74, 23.4 percent between 3.25 and 3.59, and 23.3 percent between 2.93 and 3.24.

12. Interestingly, in terms of the importance of natural aptitude, Vetter (1994) emphasizes that it is likely that most students can develop high levels of competency in math, independent of innate talents: "America tolerates underachievement in mathematics because of the common belief that mathematical ability is innate in certain people. . . . In many other industrialized countries, however, all students are expected to master a level of mathematical understanding equivalent to that attained by only our best students" (p. 7).

13. These summary points are generally consistent with previous research in this area. They are also consistent with some of the factors, especially the distinctive influence of parents, schools, and teachers, which Pearson (1985) found to characterize the backgrounds of a national sample of Black, in contrast to White, scientists.

14. Indeed, even after completing college, many of these young men continue to rely on their parents for emotional support while in medical or graduate school.

15. Useem (1992) researched parents' involvement in children's placement in middle-school math groups, emphasizing "the propensity of college-educated parents to be knowledgeable about their children's placement, to be integrated into school affairs and parental information networks, to intervene in educational decisions that school personnel make for their children and to exert an influence over their children's preferences for courses" (p. 263).

16. For example, see Hrabowski and Maton 1995.

17. See Hrabowski and Maton 1995.

18. Astin and Astin 1993; Elliot et al. 1995; Phillips 1991; White 1992.

19. Carter and Wilson 1994, table 17.

20. Many researchers and analysts have examined and reviewed various factors related to the low levels of persistence of African American (and other minority students) in math, science, and engineering majors (e.g., Culotta and Gibbons 1992; Elliot et al. 1995; Hilton et al. 1989; Pearson and Fechter, 1994; Seymour and Hewitt 1997).

21. The material presented below on these four factors is taken from Hrabowski and Maton 1995.

22. Garrison 1987; National Science Foundation 1990.

23. Atwater and Alick 1990; Hilton et al. 1989.

24. Blanc, DeBuhr, and Martin 1983.

25. Hilton et al. 1989.

26. Ibid; Fries-Britt 1997.

27. Steinberg, Dornbusch, and Brown 1992.

28. Glennan, Baxley, and Farren 1985; Penick and Morning 1983.

29. Loo and Rolison 1986; Tinto 1987.

30. Garrison and Brown 1985.

31. Nettles 1991; Sedlacek 1987; Tinto 1987.

32. See, for example, Bonsangue 1994; Carmichael et al. 1988; Gibbons 1992; Hume 1994; Matyas 1994.

33. See Clewell 1989; Fullilove and Treisman 1990; Treisman 1992. Such national agencies as the National Institutes of Health (NIH), the National Science Foundation (NSF), the National Aeronautics and Space Administration (NASA), and the U.S. Department of Education have all developed programs designed to increase the number of minorities in science. A number of colleges and universities have participated, for example, in the Minority Biomedical Research Support Program and the Minority Access to Research Careers Program, both funded by NIH. Other universities across the country participate in consortia under Alliances for Minority Participation sponsored by NSF. In addition, NSF has initiated a K-12 systemic reform movement involving both urban and rural school systems. These reform efforts have involved governors, state legislators, mayors, and other policy makers, school officials, business leaders, and parents. (Additional information on programs designed to increase minority participation in the sciences can be found in Malcolm, George, and Van Horne 1996.)

34. The importance of intervention programs engaging parents is discussed in Matyas 1994: "Parents play a key role in student enrollment and retention. Parental involvement in efforts targeted toward students is critical, even at the undergraduate and graduate levels. Programs should make efforts to help parents understand how and why students become scientists and engineers (including the training required and job opportunities available), how the program activities can assist stu-

dents in reaching their goals, and how parents can assist their children in this process" (p. 39).

35. These figures include the graduate destinations of the 1996 program graduates. Students who are in M.D./Ph.D. programs were counted for current purposes as in Ph.D. programs in science, and not as in medical school.

36. Maton and Hrabowski in preparation.

37. The very public messages and rewards for success in the Meyerhoff Program raise the interesting question of what happens to those students who do not do well. In our interviews a subset of students did note the stresses of the pressure to succeed and complained that too much pressure was placed upon students. There may also be a competitive element, though the program tries to emphasize success for all students and cooperation and camaraderie among the students.

38. The nature and importance of Meyerhoff student relationships with faculty was emphasized in a recent dissertation (Fries-Britt 1994).

39. As noted earlier, full scholarship support is contingent upon students' maintaining a GPA of 3.0 (B) or above. Most of these students had cumulative GPAs between 2.8 and 3.0.

40. The information that follows about problem areas was obtained from Meyerhoff Program staff and from student interviews.

41. These interviews are a part of the ongoing, grant-funded (NSF and Sloan) evaluation of the program, and are separate from the group interviews on parenting.

42. Future research is planned on the adjustment of the Meyerhoff students to their graduate- and professional-school environments.

43. An earlier publication described the key characteristics of the Meyerhoff Program that define it as an empowering setting. These characteristics are presented below (from Maton and Salem 1995).

1. *An empowering setting has a belief system that inspires growth, is strengths-based, and is focused beyond the self.* The Meyerhoff Program has an inspiring belief system that encourages members to strive for the highest levels of academic achievement and psychosocial growth. The goals are clear—to develop the skills necessary to achieve outstanding success academically and professionally in a primarily White work world. The means to achieve these goals are also clear—utilize all available resources including study groups, smart peers (regardless of ethnicity), tutoring services, summer internships, program staff, and research opportunities.

The belief system is strengths-based in that all students are viewed as having the capability to succeed in science, given the resources provided by the program and university. Students are also viewed as a valuable resource. Specifically, they are seen as having an important contribution to make toward helping others succeed in the program, establishing and maintaining the reputation of the program and the university, and enhancing the image of African American males and females in society. The belief system emphasizes the importance of focusing beyond oneself. Outstanding academic success is viewed as a way of "giving back" to the Black community by increasing the very small number of African American Ph.Ds. Furthermore, academic success is viewed equally as a group goal and as an individual one.

2. *An empowering setting has meaningful roles for members; these roles are pervasive, highly accessible, and multifaceted.* The Meyerhoff Scholars Program has a pervasive and highly accessible role opportunity structure. All students have access to and are encouraged by program staff to join study groups composed of their Meyerhoff peers. As recorded in field notes by a graduate-student research observer

assigned to live on a Meyerhoff residence floor: "The . . . study groups . . . are numerous (nightly). The groups . . . provide tremendous motivation to students that might otherwise deviate from their studies and succumb to social activities or to procrastination."

Additional roles emphasized by the program are internship and service roles. Students are strongly encouraged to take part in summer internships, which the program helps to arrange at leading academic and industry research sites. They are also encouraged to participate in community service outreach to at-risk African American children, to reach out to younger students in the program, and to take part in various opportunities to present the program to the public. The role opportunity structure is multifunctional, as it contains opportunities both for learning and for utilizing skills. Roles of student, counselee, advisee, and younger student represent key learning roles. Roles of veteran student and community outreach member represent responsible instrumental roles. Finally, summer intern and study group member represent roles in which learning/recipient roles and instrumental/provider roles are both present. More than 90 percent of students report moderate to high levels of involvement in the program.

3. *An empowering setting has a support system that is encompassing, is peer-based, and provides a sense of community.* As emphasized above, the Meyerhoff Program support system is encompassing in nature. Multiple domains of support are available, including emotional, academic, and financial. The support is available through multiple sources and channels, both formal (staff) and informal (roommates, friends). The support system is proactive as well as reactive, monitoring student progress and needs so that support is provided as problems emerge (e.g., a poor grade on a quiz; personal problems).

The peer-based component of support, in small group (e.g., study group) and dyadic (e.g., friendship) contexts, appears especially critical to the success of the support system. Shared academic aspirations, common academic challenges, and a shared ethnicity present ongoing opportunities for support from fellow Meyerhoff students. Positive peer support appears critical to counteract the influence of non-program peers who may view striving for academic success as "acting White." Positive peer models embody the possibility of success in difficult majors, and represent viable sources of academic and personal support.

Beyond support per se, students report a strong sense of familylike belonging. Shared goals, a common ethnicity, and program emphasis on group solidarity contribute to this sense of community. Students take many classes together, live together on campus, and populate their social networks largely with other Meyerhoff students. The Meyerhoff staff are viewed as parental figures, providing support, challenge, and guidance.

4. *An empowering setting has leadership which is inspiring, talented, shared, and committed to both setting and members.* The founding director of the Meyerhoff Scholars Program has a compelling vision of talented African Americans as achieving outstanding success at his university and in the larger society, and of helping to alter the negative view of Blacks in our society. This vision is repeatedly communicated to staff and students in one-on-one meetings, group sessions, and public talks.

Program leadership is shared among multiple individuals, and the number of leaders has expanded over time. Each leader is interpersonally talented—engaging, personally affirming of students, and able to relate effectively to diverse individuals. The program founder is organizationally talented, repeatedly demonstrating the capability to marshal needed resources and to deal with changing environments and circumstances.

The program leaders are committed to the students and to the program. As student needs are identified, resources are quickly mobilized to meet those needs and maximize the odds for student success. The leadership's commitment to and incessant hard work for the program and the students is well known both on and off the campus, helping to generate positive faculty, staff, student, and community response to the program.

44. Empirical support for the importance of involvement in meaningful activity for African American youth is presented in Maton 1990.

Chapter 6

1. Our analysis has been informed by sessions not only with parents and students in this study, but also with over two hundred of the families associated during the past seven years with the Meyerhoff Scholars Program.

2. Others have also argued similarly. For an excellent report, see Zill and Nord 1994.

3. Bowser and Perkins 1991.

4. While exact figures are difficult to obtain, one source reports that between 1980 and 1991, the percent of high school seniors who attend church declined from 43 percent to 31 percent for all races (National Center for Education Statistics 1993).

5. Pearson and Bechtel 1989, p. 140.

6. Maton et al. 1994.

7. Fierney and Grossman 1995.

8. Turner and McFate 1994.

9. Pearson and Bechtel 1989, p. 151.

10. Steinberg 1996, pp. 188–89.

11. Young and Austin 1996.

12. Comer and Poussaint (1992) provide specific, practical advice on parenting and schooling Black children, in response to nearly a thousand questions related to these issues.

References

Ahmeduzzaman, M. and J. L. Roopnarine. 1992. Sociodemographic factors, functioning style, social support, and fathers' involvement with preschoolers in
African-American families. *Journal of Marriage and the Family* 54, 699–707.

Alvy, K. 1997. *Effective black parenting: Parent's handbook.* Studio City, CA:
Center for the Improvement of Child Caring.

Association of American Medical Colleges. 1990. *Minority students in medical
education: Facts and figures IX.* Washington, D.C.: AAMC.

Astin, A. W., and H. S. Astin. 1993. *Undergraduate science education: The
impact of different college environments on the educational pipeline in the
sciences.* Los Angeles: Higher Education Research Institute, University of California, Los Angeles

Atwater, M. M., and B. Alick 1990. Coginitive development and problem solving
of Afro-American students in chemistry. *Journal of Research in Science Teaching* 27 157–72.

Baker, L., D. Scher, and K. Mackler, 1997. Home and family influences on motiva-
tions for literacy. *Educational Psychologist,* 32, 69–82.

Bank, L., M. S., Forgatch, G. R., Patterson, and R. A. Fetrow. 1993. Parenting practices of single mothers: Mediators of negative contextual factors. *Journal of
Marriage and the Family* 55, 371–84.

Banks, J. 1984. Black youths in predominantly white suburbs: An exploratory
study of the attitudes and self-concepts. *Journal of Negro Education* 53, 3–17.

Baumrind, D. 1972. An exploratory study of socialization effects on black children: Some black-white comparisons. *Child Development* 43, 261–67.

———. 1996. The discipline controversy revisited. *Family Relations,* 45, 405–13.

Billingsley, A. 1992. *Climbing Jacob's ladder: The enduring legacy of African-
American families.* New York: Simon and Schuster.

Blanc, R. A., L. E. DeBuhr, and D. C. Martin. 1983. Breaking the attrition cycle:
The effects of supplemental instruction on undergraduate performance and
attrition. *Journal of Higher Education* 54, 80–90.

Blankenhorn, D. 1995. *Fatherless America.* New York: Basic Books.

Bonsangue, M. V. 1994. An efficacy study of the calculus workshop model.
Research in College Mathematics Education 1, 1–19.

Bowman, P., and C. Howard. 1985. Race-related socialization, motivation, and
academic achievement: A study of black youth in three-generation families.
Journal of the American Academy of Child Psychiatry 24, 134–41.

Bowser, B. P., and H. Perkins. 1991. Success against the odds: Young black men
tell what it takes. In *Black male adolescents: Parenting and education in community context,* ed. B. P. Bowser, 183–200. Lanham, Md.: University Press of
America.

Boyd-Franklin, N. 1989. *Black families in therapy: A multi- systems approach.* New York: Guilford.

Bradley, R. H., S. L. Rock, B. M. Caldwell, P. T. Harris, and H. M. Hamrick. 1987. Home environment and school performance among black elementary school children. *Journal of Negro Education* 56, 499–509.

Bronfenbrenner, U. 1986. Ecology of the family as a context for human development: Research perspectives. *Developmental Psychology* 22, 723–42.

Bryan, D. L. and A. A. Ajo. 1992. The role perception of African American fathers. *Social Work Research and Abstracts* 28 3, 17–21.

Carmichael, M. W., J. T. Hunter, D. D. Labat, J. P. Sevenair, and S. J. Bauer. 1988. An educational pathway into biology- and chemistry-based careers for Black Americans. *Journal of College Science Teaching* 17, 370–74, 405.

Carter, D. J. and R. Wilson. 1997. *Minorities in higher education: Fifteenth annual status report.* Washington, D. C.: American Council on Education.

Cauce, A. 1986. Social networks and social competence: Exploring the effects of early adolescent friendships. *American Journal of Community Psychology* 14, 607–28.

Chao, R. 1994. Beyond parental control and authoritarian parenting style: Understanding Chinese parenting through the cultural notion of training. *Child Development* 65, 1111–19.

Christenson, S. L., T. Rounds, and D. Gorney. 1992. Family factors and student achievement. *School Psychology Quarterly* 7, 178–206.

Clark, M.L. 1991. Social identity, peer relations, and academic competence of African-American adolescents. *Education and Urban Society*, 24, 41–52.

Clark, R. 1983. *Family life and school achievement: Why poor black children succeed or fail.* Chicago: University of Chicago Press.

Clewell, B. C. 1989. Intervention programs: Three case studies. In *Blacks, science, and American education,* ed. W. Pearson Jr. and H. K. Bechtel, 105–22. New Brunswick: Rutgers University Press.

Clinton, H. 1996. *It takes a village: And other lessons children teach us.* New York: Simon and Schuster.

Cohen, J. 1987. Parents as educational models and definers. *Journal of Marriage and the Family* 49, 339–49.

Comer, J. P. 1980. *School power: Implications of an intervention project.* New York: Free Press.

Comer, J. P., and A. F. Poussaint. 1992. *Raising black children: Two leading psychiatrists confront the educational, social and emotional problems facing black children.* New York: Plume/Penguin.

Connell, J. P., M. B. Spencer, and J. L. Aber. 1994. Educational risk and resilience in African-American youth: Context, self, action, and outcomes in school. *Child Development* 65, 493–506.

Crosbie-Burnett, M. and E. A. Lewis, 1993. Use of African-American family structures and functioning to address the challenges of European-American postdivorce families. *Family Relations* 42, 243–48.

Culotta, E., and A. Gibbons, eds. 1992. Minorities in science: The pipeline problem. *Science* 258, 1175–235.

Del Carmen, R. and G. N. Virgo, 1993. Marital disruption and nonresidential parenting: A multicultural perspective. In *Nonresidential parenting: New vistas in family living,* C. E. Depner and J. H. Bray, eds., 13–36. Newbury Park, Calif: Sage.

Dick, T. P, and S. F. Rallis. 1991. Factors and influences on high school students' career choices. *Journal for Research in Mathematics Education* 22, 281–92.

Dornbusch, S. M., P. L. Ritter, R. Mont-Reynaud, and Z. Chen. 1990. Family decision-making and academic performance in a diverse high school population. *Journal of Adolescent Research* 5, 143–60.

Edelman, M. W. 1995. *Guide my feet: Prayers and meditations on loving and working for children.* Boston: Beacon Press.

Educational Testing Service. 1995. *College bound seniors: 1995 profile of SAT program test takers.* Princeton, N.J.: ETS.

Elliot, R., R. Adair, M. Matier, and J. Scott. 1995. *Non-Asian minority students in the science pipeline at highly selective institutions.* Final Report of NSF Grant RED 93 53 821.

Ellis, R. S. 1993. Impacting the science attitudes of minority high school youth. *School Science and Mathematics* 93, 400–7.

Entwisle, D. R. and K. L. Alexander. 1990. Beginning school math competence: Minority and majority comparisons. *Child Development* 61, 454–71.

———. 1992. Summer setback: Race, poverty, school composition, and mathematics achievement in the first two years of school. *American Sociological Review* 57, 72–84.

———. 1996. Family type and children's growth in reading and math over the primary grades. *Journal of Marriage and the Family* 58, 341–55.

Family income backgrounds continue to determine chances for baccalaureate degree in 1992. 1993. *Postsecondary Education Opportunity* 16, 1–5.

Fierney, J. P, and J. B. Grossman. 1995. *Making a difference: An impact study of big brothers/big sisters.* Philadelphia: Public/Private Ventures.

Fonken, E. 1992. Magnet schools: A quality alternative. In *Securing our future: The importance of quality education for minorities,* 115–26. Austin, TX: Lyndon B. Johnson School of Public Affairs Policy Research Project Report no. 96.

Ford, D. Y. 1993. Black students' achievement orientation as a function of perceived family achievement orientation and demographic variables. *Journal of Negro Education* 62, 47–66.

Ford, D. Y., and J. J. Harris. III. 1991. Meeting the socio-psychological needs of gifted Black students. *Journal of Counseling and Development* 69, 577–80.

Ford, D. Y., and J. J. Harris. 1995. Underachievement among gifted African American students: Implications for school counselors. *School Counselor* 42, 196-203.

Fordham, S. 1996. *Blacked out: Dilemmas of race, identification and success at Capitol High.* Chicago: University of Chicago Press.

Fordham, S., and J. U. Ogbu. 1986. Black students' school success: Coping with the "burden of 'acting white.'" *The Urban Review* 18, 176–206.

Frazier, E. F. 1948. *The Negro family in the United States.* New York: Dryden Press.

Fries-Britt, S. L. 1994. *A test of Tinto's retention theory on the Meyerhoff scholars: A case study analysis.* Ph.D. Dissertation, University of Maryland, College Park.

Fries-Britt, S. L. 1997, in press. Identifying and supporting gifted African American males. In *Enhancing the educational experiences of African American males,* M. Cuyjet ed. No. 80, New Directions for Student Services Series. San Francisco: Jossey Bass.

Fullilove, R. E., and P. U. Treisman. 1990. Mathematics achievement among African-American undergraduates at the University of California, Berkeley: An evaluation of the mathematics workshop program. *Journal of Negro Education* 59, 463–78.

Garcia, J. 1988. Minority participation in elementary science and mathematics. *Education and Society* 1, 21–23.

Garfinkel, I., and S. S. McClanahan. 1986. *Single mothers and their children: A new American dilemma.* Washington, D.C.: Urban Institute Press.

Garibaldi, A. M. 1992. Educating and motivating African American males to succeed. *Journal of Negro Education* 61, 4–11.

Garrison, H. H. 1987. Undergraduate science and engineering education for blacks and native Americans. In *Minorities: Their Underrepresentation and Career Differentials in Science and Engineering. Proceedings of a Workshop,* ed. L. S. Dix. Washington, D.C.: National Academy Press.

Garrison, H. H, and P. W. Brown. 1985. *Minority access to research careers: An evaluation of the honors undergraduate research training program.* NTIS Accession Number: PB86-161-270. Washington, D.C.: National Academy Press.

Gary, L. E. 1995. African American men's perceptions of racial discrimination: A sociocultural analysis. *Social Work Research* 19, 207–17.

Garza, D. T. 1992. Mathematics and science education: Reclaiming minorities at the elementary school level. In *Securing our future: The importance of quality education for minorities,* 85–104. Austin, TX: Lyndon B. Johnson School of Public Affairs Policy Research Project Report no. 96.

Gates, H. L. Jr., and C. West. 1996. *The future of the race.* New York: Alfred A. Knopf.

Gibbons, A. 1992. Minority programs that get high marks. *Science* 258, 1190–96.

Gibbs, J. T. 1988a. Health and mental health of young black males. In *Young black and male in America,* ed. J. T. Gibbs, 219–57. Dover, Mass.: Auburn House.

———. 1988b. Young black males in America: Endangered, embittered and embattled. In *Young, Black and Male in America,* ed. J. T. Gibbs, 1–36. Dover, Mass.: Auburn House.

Gill, W. 1991. *Issues in African American education.* Nashville: One Horn Press.

Glennan, R. E., D. M. Baxley, and P. J. Farren. 1985. Impact of intrusive advising on minority student retention. *College Student Journal* 19, 335–38.

Golden, M. 1995. *Saving our sons: Raising black children in a turbulent world.* New York: Doubleday.

Gonzales, N. A., A. M. Cauce, R. J. Friedman, and C. A. Mason. 1996. Family, peer, and neighborhood influences on academic achievement among African American adolescents: One-year prospective effects. *American Journal of Community Psychology* 24, 365–88.

Greene, M. 1996. *Sociocultural orientation among talented African-American college students in a race-specific program: Patterns, predictors and correlates.* Ph.D. dissertation, University of Maryland Baltimore County.

Griswold, R. L. 1993. *Fatherhood in America: A history.* New York: Basic Books.

Haertel, E., and D. Wiley. 1979. *Out-of-school determinants of elementary school achievement.* Paper presented at the annual meeting of the American Educational Research Association, San Francisco. ERIC Document Reproduction Service no. ED 170 067.

Hare, B. 1987. Structural inequality and the endangered status of black youth. *Journal of Negro Education* 56, 100–10.

Harris, D. 1995. Exploring the determinants of adult black identity: Context and process. *Social Forces* 74, 227–41.

Harris, J. R. 1983. Parent-aided homework: A working model for school personnel. *School Counselor* 31, 171–76.

Herring, C. and K. R. Wilson-Sadberry. 1993. Preference or necessity? Changing work roles of black and white women, 1973–1990. *Journal of Marriage and the Family* 55, 314–25.

High, M. L. and A. J. Udall. 1983. Teacher rating of students in relation to ethnicity of students and school ethnic balance. *Journal for the Education of the Gifted* 6, 154–66.

Hill, O. W., W. C. Pettus, and B. A. Hedin. 1990. Three studies of factors affecting the attitudes of blacks and females towards the pursuit of science and science related careers. *Journal of Research in Science Teaching* 27, 289–314.

Hilton, T. L., J. Jsia, D. G. Solorzano, and N. L. Benton. 1989. *Persistence in science of high-ability minority students*. Research Report no. RR-89-28. Princeton, N.J.: Educational Testing Service.

Hofstein, A., N. Maoz, and M. Rishpon. 1990. Attitudes towards school science: Comparison of participants and non-participants in extra-curricular science activities. *School Science and Mathematics* 90, 13–22.

Hrabowski, F. H. III., and K. I. Maton. 1995. Enhancing the success of African-American students in the sciences: Freshmen year outcomes. *School Science and Mathematics* 95, 18–27.

Hudson, R. J. 1991. Black male adolescent development deviating from the past: Challenges for the future. In *Black male adolescents: Parenting and education in community context*, ed. B. P. Bowser, 271–81. Lanham, Md.: University Press of America.

Hume, R. 1994. *The Challenge Program: A review of student retention and academic performance*. Atlanta: Georgia Institute of Technology Office of Minority Educational Development.

Hurd, E.P., C. Moore, and R. Rogers. 1995. Quiet success: Parenting strengths among African Americans. *Families in Society*, 76, 434–43.

Hutchinson, R. L., and S. L. Sprangler. 1988. Children of divorce and single-parent lifestyles: Facilitating well-being. *Journal of Divorce* 12, 5–24.

Imber-Black, E. 1988. *Families and larger systems: A family therapist's guide through the system*. New York: Guilford.

Jarrett, R. L. 1995. Growing up poor: The family experiences of socially mobile youth in low-income African American neighborhoods. *Journal of Adolescent Research* 10, 111–35.

Jayakody, R., L. M. Chatters., and R. J. Taylor. 1993. Family support to single and married African American mothers: The provision of financial, emotional, and child care assistance. *Journal of Marriage and the Family* 55, 261–76.

Jenkins, L. E. 1989. The black family and academic achievement. In *Black Students: Psychosocial issues and academic achievement*, ed. G. L. Berry and J.K. Asamen, 138–52. Newbury Park, Calif.: Sage.

Johnson, S. T. 1992. Extra-school factors in achievement, attainment and aspiration among junior and senior high–age African American youth. *Journal of Negro Education* 61, 99–119.

Keith, T. T. 1987. Homework. In *Children's needs: Psychological perspectives*, ed. A Thomas and J. Grimes, 275–82. Washington, D.C.: National Association of School Psychologists.

Kelley, M. L., J. Sanchez-Hucles, and R. R. Walker. 1993. Correlates of disciplinary practices in working- to middle- class African American mothers. *Merrill-Palmer Quarterly* 39, 252–64.

Kitson, G. C., and L. A. Morgan. 1990. The multiple consequences of divorce. *Journal of Marriage and the Family* 52, 913–24.

Kokoski, T. M., and N. Downing-Leffler. 1995. Boosting your science and math programs in early childhood education: Making the home-school connection. *Young Children* 50, 35–39.

Lassiter, R. 1987. Child rearing in black families: Child-abusing discipline? In *Violence in the black family*, ed. R. L. Hampton, 39–53. Lexington, Mass.: Lexington Books.

Lee, C. 1985. Successful rural black adolescents: A psychosocial profile. *Adolescence 20*, 129-142.

Loo, C. M., and G. Rolison. 1986. Alienation of Ethnic Minority Students at a Predominantly White University. Journal of *Higher Education* 57, 58–77.

Luster, T., and H. McAdoo. 1994. Factors related to the achievement and adjustment of young African American children. *Child Development* 65, 1080–94.

———. 1996. Family and child influences on educational attainment: A secondary analysis of the High/Scope Perry preschool data. *Child Development* 67, 26–39.

Majors, R., C. Billson, and J. Mancini. 1992. *Cool pose: The dilemmas of black manhood in America*. New York: Lexington Books.

Malcolm, S. M., Y. S. George, and V. V. Van Horne, eds. 1996. *The effect of the changing policy climate on science, mathematics, and engineering diversity*. Washington, D.C.: American Association for the Advancement of Science.

Maple, S. A., and F. K. Stage. 1991. Influences on the choice of math/science major by gender and ethnicity. *American Educational Research Journal* 28, 37–60.

Maryland Department of Economic and Employment Development. 1992. *1990–91 Maryland statistical abstract*. Baltimore: Maryland Department of Economic and Employment Development.

Maryland State Department of Education. 1995. *The fact book: A statistical handbook*. Baltimore, MD: Author.

Maton, K. I. 1990. Meaningful involvement in instrumental activity and well-being: Studies of older adolescents and at-risk inner-city teenagers. *American Journal of Community Psychology* 18, 297–320.

Maton, K. I., and F. A. Hrabowski III. In preparation. *Enhancing the success of African-American students in the sciences: Fourth year outcomes.*

Maton, K. I., F. A. Hrabowski III. and G. Greif. 1997. *Preparing the way: A qualitative study of high achieving African American males and the role of the family.* Manuscript.

Maton, K. I., F. A. Hrabowski III., B. A. Kojetin, M. L. Greene, and T. A. Collins. 1994. Educational empowerment of African-American youth: A tale of two programs. Paper presented at the 102nd annual meeting of the American Psychological Association, Los Angeles.

Maton, K. I., and D. A. Salem, 1995. Organizational characteristics of empowering community settings: A multiple case study approach. *American Journal of Community Psychology* 23, 631–56.

Matyas, M. L. 1994. Investing in human potential: Policies and programs in higher education. In *Who will do science? Educating the next generation*, ed. W. Pearson Jr. and A. Fechter, 20–42. Baltimore: Johns Hopkins University Press.

McAdoo, H. P. 1988. *Black families*. 2nd ed. Newbury Park, Calif.: Sage.

McAdoo, J. L. 1993. The roles of African American fathers: An ecological perspective. *Families in Society* 74, 28–35.

McLaughlin, M.W., and S. B. Heath, eds. 1993. *Identity and inner-city youth*. New York: Teachers College Press.

Mfume, Kweisi. 1996. *No free ride: From the mean streets to the mainstream.* New York: One World Ballantine Books.

Midgette, T. E., and E. Glenn. 1993. African-American male academies: A positive view. *Journal of Multicultural Counseling and Development* 21, 69–78.

Miller, L. S. 1995. *An American imperative: Accelerating minority educational advancement.* New Haven: Yale University Press.

Minuchin, S. and C. Fishman, 1981. *Family therapy techniques.* Cambridge: Harvard University Press.

Mosley, J. and E. Thomson, 1995. Fathering behavior and child outcomes: The role of race and poverty. In *Fatherhood: Contemporary theory, research and social policy*, ed. W. Marsiglio, 148–65. Thousand Oaks, Calif.: Sage.

Murray, H. B., G. B. Herling, and B. K. Staebler. 1973. The effects of locus of control and pattern of performance on teachers' evaluation of a student. *Psychology in the Schools* 10, 345–50.

Naizer, G. L. 1993. Science and engineering professors: Why did they choose science as a career? *School Science and Mathematics* 93, 321–24.

National Center for Education Statistics. 1993. *Digest of education statistics: 1993.* Washington, D.C.: U.S. Department of Education.

———. 1995a. *The condition of education: 1995.* Washington, D.C.: Government Printing Office.

———. 1995b. *Digest of education and statistics: 1995.* Washington, D.C.: Department of Education.

National Institutes of Health. 1996. *Director of the Office of Research on Minority Health: FY 1996 appropriations briefing.* Washington, D.C.: National Institutes of Health.

National Research Council. 1995. *The National Scholars Program: Excellence with diversity for the future.* Washington, D.C.: National Science Foundation.

Nettles, M. T. 1991. Racial similarities and differences in the predictors of college student achievement. In *College in Black and White*, ed. W. R. Allen, E. G. Epps, and N. Z. Haniff, 75–94. Albany: State University of New York Press.

Oakes, J. 1985. *Keeping track: How schools structure inequality.* New Haven. Yale University Press.

———. 1990. Opportunities, achievement, and choice: Women and minority students in science and mathematics. In *Review of Research in Education*, ed. D. B. Cazden, 153–222. Washington, D.C.: American Educational Research Association.

Ogbu, J. 1988. Cultural diversity and human development. In *Black children and poverty: A developmental perspective*, ed. D. Slaughter, 11–28. San Francisco: Jossey–Bass.

Parish, W. L., L. Hao, and D. P. Hogan. 1991. Family support networks, welfare, and work among young mothers. *Journal of Marriage and the Family* 53, 203–15.

Patchen, M. 1982. *Black-white contact in schools: Its social and academic effects.* West Lafayette, Ind.: Purdue University Press.

Paulson, S. E. 1994. Relations of parenting style and parental involvement with ninth-grade students achievement. *Journal of Early Adolescence* 14, 250–67.

Pearson, W. Jr. 1995. *Black scientists, white society, and colorless science: A study of universalism in American science.* Millwood, N.Y.: Associated Faculty Press.

Pearson, W. Jr., and H. K. Bechtel, ed. 1989. *Blacks, science, and American education.* New Brunswick: Rutgers University Press.

Pearson, W. Jr., and A. Fechter. 1994. *Who will do science? Educating the next generation.* Baltimore: The John Hopkins University Press.

Penick, B. E., and C. Morning. 1983. *Retention of minority engineering students:*

Report on the 1981–82 NACME Retention Research Program. New York: National Action Council for Minorities in Engineering.

Phillips, T. R. 1991. *ABET/EXXON Minority Engineering Student Achievement Profile.* New York: Accreditation Board for Engineering and Technology.

Prom-Jackson, S., S. T. Johnson, and M. B. Wallace. 1987. Home environment, talented minority youth, and school achievement. *Journal of Negro Education* 56, 111–21.

Reed, R. J. 1988. Education and achievement of young black males. In *Young Black and male in America: An endangered species*, ed. J. T. Gibbs, 37–90 Dover, Mass.: Auburn House.

Reynolds, A. J., 1991. The middle schooling process: Influences on science and mathematics achievement from the longitudinal study of American youth. *Adolescence* 26, 133–58.

Rhodes, J. E., L. Ebert, and K. Fischer. 1992. Natural mentors: An overlooked resource in the social networks of young, African American mothers. *American Journal of Community Psychology* 20, 445–61.

Romotowski, J. and M. Trepaneir. 1977. *Examining and influencing the home reading behaviors of young children.* ERIC Document Reproduction Service No. ED 195-938.

Scott-Jones, D. 1987. Mother-as-teacher in the families of high and low achieving low-income Black first graders. *Journal of Negro Education* 56, 21–34.

Sedlacek, W. E. 1987. Black students on white campuses: 20 years of research. *Journal of College Student Personnel* November, 484–95.

Seymour, E., and N. M. Hewitt. 1997. *Talking about leaving: Why undergraduates leave the sciences.* Boulder, CO: Westview Press.

Slaughter-Defoe, D. T., K. Nakagawa, R. Takanishi, and D.J. Takanishi. 1990. Toward cultural/ecological perspectives on schooling and achievement in African- and Asian-American children. *Child Development* 61, 363–83.

Smith, J. C., and R. L. Johns, eds. 1995. *Statistical record of black America.* Detroit, MI: Gale Research, Inc.

Snodgrass, D. M. 1991. The Parent connection. *Adolescence* 26, 83–87.

Spencer, M. B. 1990. Parental values transmission: Implications for the development of African American children. In *Black Families— Interdisciplinary perspectives*, H. E. Cheatham and J. B. Stewart eds. 111–130. New Brunswick, N.J.: Transaction Publishers.

Staples, R., and Johnson, L. B. 1993. *Black families at the crossroads: Challenges and prospects.* San Francisco: Jossey-Bass.

Steele, C. and J. Aronson. 1995. Stereotype threat and the intellectual test performance of African Americans. *Journal of Personality and Social Psychology* 69, 797–811.

Steinberg, L. 1996. *Beyond the classroom: Why school reform has failed and what parents need to do.* New York: Simon and Schuster.

Steinberg, L., S. M. Dornbusch, and B. B. Brown. 1992. Ethnic differences in academic achievement: An ecological perspective. *American Psychologist* 47, 923–29.

Steinberg, L., J. D. Elmen, and N. S. Mounts. 1989. Authoritative parenting, psychosocial maturity, and academic success among adolescents. *Child Development* 60, 1424–36.

Stevenson, H. W., C. Chen, and D. H. Uttal. 1990. Beliefs and achievement: A study of black, white and hispanic children. *Child Development,* 61, 508–23.

Taylor, C. T., I. D. Hinton, and M. N. Wilson. 1995. Parental influences on academic performance in African American students. *Journal of Child and Family Studies*, 4, 293–302.

Taylor, R. J. 1991. Childrearing in African-American families. In *Child welfare: An Afrocentric perspective*, eds. J. E. Everett, S. S. Chipungu, S. Leashore, and R. Bagart, 119–55. New Brunswick: Rutgers University Press.

Taylor, R. J., L. M. Chatters, M. B. Tucker, and E. Lewis. 1990. Developments in research on black families: A decade review. *Journal of Marriage and the Family* 52, 993–1014.

Thompson, B. S., D. R. Entwisle, K. L. Alexander, and M. J. Sundius. 1992. The influence of family composition on children's conformity to the student role. *American Educational Research Journal* 29, 405–24.

Thornton, M. C., L. M. Chatters, R. J. Taylor, and W. R. Allen. 1990. Sociodemographic and environmental correlates of racial socialization by black parents. *Child Development* 61, 401–9.

Tinto, V. 1987. *Leaving college: Rethinking the causes and cures of student attrition*. Chicago: University of Chicago Press.

Tolson, T. F. J., and M. N. Wilson. 1990. The impact of two- and three-generational black family structure on perceived family climate. *Child Development*, 61, 416–28.

Treisman, U. 1992. Studying students studying calculus: A look at the lives of minority mathematics students in college. *The College Mathematics Journal*, 23, 362–72.

Turner, T. A., and K. McFate. 1994. Community programs that serve young black males. Conference paper prepared for "Fulfilling the Promise: Community Programs for Young Black Males," Joint Center for Political and Economic Studies, Washington, D.C., June 6.

U. S. Bureau of the Census. 1991. *Marital status and living arrangements: 1990*. Series P-20, No. 450. Washington, D. C.: Government Printing Office.

———. 1993. *The black population in the United States: March 1992*. Series, P20 no. 471. Washington, DC: Government Printing Office.

———. 1993b. *School enrollment—Social and economic characteristics of students: October 1991*. Washington, D.C. U.S. Department of Commerce

———. 1995a. *Marital status and living arrangements: March 1994*. Current Population Reports. P20–483. Washington, D.C.: Government Printing Office.

———. 1995. *Household and family characteristics: March 1994*. Series P20, no. 483. Washington, D.C.: Government Printing Office.

———. 1996. *Marital status and living arrangements: March 1994*. Current Population Reports. P20- 484. Washington, D.C.: Government Printing Office.

U. S. Department of Commerce. 1973. *Statistical abstract of the United States 1973*. Washington, D.C.: Government Printing Office.

———. 1984. *Statistical abstract of the United States: 1985*. Washington, D.C.: Government Printing Office.

———. 1994. *Statistical abstract of the United States: 1994 (114th edition)*. Washington D.C.: Government Printing Office.

———. 1995. *Statistical abstract of the United States 1995*. Washington, D.C.: Government Printing Office.

Useem, E. L. 1992. Middle schools and math groups: Parents' involvement in children's placement. *Sociology of Education* 65, 263–79.

Verzemnieks, I. 1996. They're a calculated success: Behind a Presidential Scholar is a math teacher who figures prominently. *Washington Post*, June 20, B1–2.

Vetter, B. M. 1994. The next generation of scientists and engineers: Who's in the pipeline? In *Who will do science? Educating the next generation,* ed. W. Pearson Jr. and A. Fechter, 1–21. Baltimore: Johns Hopkins University Press.

Wade, J. C. 1994. African American fathers and sons: Social, historical, and psychological considerations. *Families in Society* 75, 561–70.

Weinstein, R. S., C. R. Soule, F. Collins, J. Cone, M. Mehlhorn, and K. Simontacchi. 1991. Expectations and high school change: Teacher-researcher collaboration to prevent school failure. *American Journal of Community Psychology* 19, 333–64.

Werner, E. E., and R. S. Smith. 1992. *Overcoming the odds: High risk children from birth to adulthood.* New York: Cornell University Press.

White, P. E. 1992. *Women and minorities in science and engineering: An update.* Washington, D.C.: National Science Foundation.

Wilensky, H. L., and C. N. LeBeaux. 1965. *Industrial society and social welfare.* New York: Free Press.

Willie, C. V. 1988. *A new look at black families.* Dix Hills, N.Y.: General Hall.

Wilson, K. R. 1987. Explaining the educational attainment of young black adults: Critical familial and extra-familial influences. *Journal of Negro Education* 56, 64–76.

Wilson, K. R., and W. R. Allen. 1987. Explaining the educational attainment of young black adults: Critical family and extra- familial influences. *Journal of Negro Education* 56, 64–76.

Wilson, M. N. ed. 1995. *African American family life: Its structural and ecological aspects.* No. 68 in New Directions for Child Development Series. San Francisco: Jossey-Bass.

Wilson, W. J. 1996. *When work disappears: The world of the new urban poor.* New York: Knopf.

Wilson-Sadberry, K. R., L. F. Winfield, and D. A. Royster. 1991. Resilience and persistence of African-American males in postsecondary enrollment. *Education and Urban Society* 24, 87–102.

Wolin, S. J., and Bennett, L. A. 1984. Family rituals. *Family Process* 23, 401–20.

Young, A. J., and B. W. Austin. 1996. *Repairing the breach: Key ways to support family life, reclaim our streets, and rebuild civic society in America's communities.* Dillon, Colo.: Alpine Guild.

Zill, N. and C. Nord. 1994. *Running in place: How American families are faring in a changing economy and in individualistic society.* Washington, D.C.: Child Trends.

Zollar, A. C. and J. S. Williams. 1987. The contribution of marriage to the life satisfaction of black adults. *Journal of Marriage and the Family* 49, 87–92.

Index

academic achievement
    Black fathers' recognition of, 39–41
    of Black males, ix, x, 7, 13, 19, 36–38
    Black mothers' role in, 73–77, 91, 93–94
    economic status and, 13
adversity, overcoming, by Black persons, 35
Africa
    Black extended families in, 30, 220(n41)
    Black fathers' role in, 26
African American. *See* Black(s)
African cultural heritage, Blacks' respect for,
    57–58, 60, 92, 96, 191, 201
AIDS, Black men and, 8, 24, 44
alcoholism, 87, 127
Alliance for Minority Participation (AMP),
    199, 209, 210, 222(n33)
ambition, of Black youth, x
aptitudes, of Black youth, 164–166
Asian Americans, higher education of, 7
attention deficit disorder, in Black son, 74
authoritarian parenting, in Black families,
    33, 132, 213(n21)

Baltimore, minority students in, 11, 18,
    85–86
BASIC computer program, 162
behavioral problems, of Black youth, 9
Beyond the Classroom (Steinberg), 204
Big Brothers and Big Sisters programs, 201
Billingsly, Andrew, 13–14
Billson, C., 8, 10
Blacks
    underrepresentation in gifted programs,
        10
    White attitudes toward, 82–83
Black children, education of, viii
Blacked Out (Fordham), 202
Black families
    child–rearing issues in, 41–51, 70
    definition of, 14
    economic status of, 13
    extended. *See* Extended families
    family rituals in, 50–51

gender roles in, 31–32, 67
involvement with Meyerhoff Scholars
    Program, 172
labor division in, 32
parenting components in, 34–35
role in sons' education, xi–xii, 3–22, 203
sibling role in, 32–35
two-parent households in, 25, 54–57, 63,
    103–104, 122–128
Black fathers
    discipline by, 45–47
    education of, 54–55
    parenting role of, 6–7, 14–15, 19, 35–36,
        126–128, 191–192, 194, 213(n20)
    recognition of sons' talent by, 39–41
    as single parents, 51–54
    sons raised by, 23–61, 103–104, 129–130
    views on Meyerhoff Scholars Program,
        180
Black females, Black fathers' attitude
    toward, 33
Black males
    academic and social integration of,
        169–170
    academic success of, keys for, 201–204
    disadvantages of, 8
    education of, 6, 10–13, 148–187
    health and mental health of, 9
    marriage of, 28
    mother relationships of, 62–100
    motivation and support of, 168–169
    rearing of, 14
    successful, 3–22, 61
Black mothers
    case studies on, 90–95
    education of, 65, 216(n8)
    parenting role of, 14–15, 19, 32, 95–96,
        189–191
    recognition of sons' talent by, 77–80
    relationships with sons, 62–100
    as single parents. *See* single mothers
    stereotypes of, 19
    as teachers, 159

237